ZULU ZULU GOLF

To Caleb

Enjoy.

ARN DURAND

Cape Town 7 - May 2012

ARN DURAND

ZULU ZULU GOLF

Life and Death with Koevoet

Published by Zebra Press
an imprint of Random House Struik (Pty) Ltd
Reg. No. 1966/003153/07
Wembley Square, First Floor, Solan Road, Gardens, Cape Town 8001
P.O. Box 1144, Cape Town 8000, South Africa

www.zebrapress.co.za

First published 2011
Reprinted in 2011

3 5 7 9 10 8 6 4 2

PUBLISHER: Marlene Fryer
MANAGING EDITOR: Robert Plummer
EDITORS: Anne-Marie Mischke and Beth Housdon
PROOFREADER: Rod Prodgers
COVER DESIGNER: Michiel Botha
TEXT DESIGNER: Monique Oberholzer
TYPESETTER: Monique van den Berg
PRODUCTION MANAGER: Valerie Kömmer

Set in 11.5 pt on 15.5 pt Adobe Garamond

Printed and bound by Interpak Books, Pietermaritzburg

ISBN 978 1 77022 148 2 (print)
ISBN 978 1 77022 203 8 (ePub)
ISBN 978 1 77022 204 5 (PDF)

To my father, who taught me to think with my head,
work with my hands and love with my heart

Contents

Author's note

I have written the story of my early experiences with Koevoet because it was stuck in my head and I needed to get it out. I owe the truth to many people, but most of all I owe it to myself. I can't change the past, but if I could I would go back and do it all again. I don't know why.

I fought for a reason that even I don't understand. I hope that I fought well and that I shall die one day with my honour, on my own. That is all I ask – and for a little stone cottage by the sea.

I would like to thank my mother, for crossing my 't's and dotting my 'i's.

Anne-Marie, for believing in me.

Everyone at Random House Struik, especially Marlene of Zebra Press, for that first email; Robert, for being Robert; and special thanks to Beth, who understands me. Thank you too to Kim and Rashieda.

I would like to thank Jim Hooper, author of the book *Koevoet!* He is a true friend who has stood by me and supported me. For further reading on Koevoet I highly recommend his book. True soldiers never fade away; they just shine more brightly.

I would also like to thank my enemies who are now my

friends. If SWAPO hadn't fought us, I wouldn't have this story to tell. I salute them; they were a worthy opponent.

ARN DURAND
CAPE TOWN
APRIL 2011

In humanity, as in nature, lies a deep and dark desire to kill and destroy in order to survive. We may deny its existence, but it is there, deep in our souls: we must destroy humanity so that humanity will survive, just as nature destroys nature so that nature may survive. Death has no mercy. This is how the blood on my hands became the food for my soul.

1

A licence to kill

It all started when the South African army came to Ovamboland and shot the holy bird of the Ovambo people. That is what the Ovambos believed.

Close your eyes, take a deep breath. Relax and feel your heart beating while you think of nothing. Don't be afraid; stay calm. You have no worries, no fear, no sorrow and no pain. You are calm and content.

Now open your eyes. You are standing on the white powdery sand somewhere in southern Angola. It's very hot and very quiet, apart from a few insects buzzing around.

It's okay, I'm with you. Trust me, you have nothing to fear.

With us is a captured SWAPO PLAN fighter. We tracked him for three days before we finally caught him. We've had him for four days now and we are finished with him. We tortured him with an arc welding machine and he showed us where he had buried an arms cache.

I look at you and calmly say, 'Okay, you can kill him now.'

You feel your heart beat as you tense up and pain rises through your stomach and up into your chest as you battle to breathe.

Yes, for the first time you are going to kill someone. You will do it.

Your hand trembles as I hand you the 9-mm Beretta, loaded and cocked.

'What? You can't kill someone? Sure you can, it's easy.'

Just put the barrel against his head, pull the trigger and blow his fucking brains out.

You've got 60 seconds to do it, any way you want to, or else I'm going to blow his brains out and then yours. If you want to live, do it now. Just kill him.

You are going to do it, so you had better start deciding how you are going to do it.

Do you want him to know that he is going to die or do you want to take him by surprise?

Do you want to give him one last chance to pray and to take one last breath of air?

Are you going to look him in the eyes and shoot him in the face? Or are you going to turn him around and shoot him in the back of the head so that you don't see his eyes?

It's up to you, because you *are* going to kill him. There is no way out for you; you will do it, so decide how you give a man his last moment. Decide now and do it. Just do it.

BANG! Your bullet goes through his brain at 1 200 feet per second, a sonic shock wave strikes his head and with a thud his body hits the sand at your feet.

You hear the glug, glug, glug of his gushing blood; the shot makes your ears ring.

You wonder what really happened in that moment when he died. Did you hear a rush in the split second when his soul left his body?

Don't worry, there is nothing anyone can do about it. This is Angola. Here we have a licence to kill.

We must make it look like a contact. Come boys, shoot his body. Fuck it up with your R5s, fully automatic. Empty your magazines and make it look real. If they find him with a single bullet hole in the back of the head, they will get suspicious and might ask questions. Make it look like it was a real contact.

It is in us; it is a part of us. We may deny its existence, but it is there. Very few of us would die instead of killing someone.

You did well. You killed him in cold blood, just like that. If it bothers you, just don't think about it. You will get used to it. You might even start enjoying it. Come, I'll buy you a dop in the pub at Eenhana tonight.

Let's fuck off. Just leave the gruesome scene of bright-red blood soaking into the white sand, snow-white bones broken and bent, dull yellow brains sprayed across the ground.

Come away with me to a time long past, to a place where I lost something 28 years ago and for which I am now looking. If I find it, it will finally set me free.

I hope it will still be lying there, that it will not be buried deep in that soft white sand in a remote desolate corner of a place we called Ovamboland.

A clever traveller will tell you of the places he visited; a wise traveller will tell you of the road he took to visit those places.

I am neither a clever nor a wise traveller; I am a just a traveller. I want to show you the road I travelled and the places I travelled to, but also the reason I travelled.

My little girl Caira-Lee was seven years old when she looked at me with her beautiful big eyes and asked me, 'Daddy, why do those men do what they do to make those people black and blue?'

She had found an old trunk in our garage in which I kept some souvenirs and photographs. She had seen the photos of countless dead bodies hanging over the spare wheels and bumpers of Casspirs like trophies on display. Piles of dead bodies on the ground, shot and killed and shot again and again and driven over. Broken bones, blood and brains. Gruesome scenes.

I wasn't a soldier. We called ourselves Koevoet. There were about 1 000 of us and in the end we had killed about 4 000 people who called themselves SWAPO PLAN fighters.

'Daddy, why do soldiers fight and do bad things to each other? Please tell me.'

I turned so that she wouldn't see the tears rolling down my cheeks. I couldn't speak; I just shook my head and walked away. I knew I had to destroy the contents of that trunk. The Makarov, my 21st birthday present from Frank. The Tokarev, the AK-47 bayonet, the Soviet water bottle, the Cuban and Soviet belt buckles ...

I even kept the R5 automatic assault rifle with three extra 35-round magazines, believing that one day I might have to point it at someone and pull the trigger again, spraying death into him and blowing his soul right out of his body.

It was time to get rid of it.

Now that my daughter is 25 years old, I can look into her beautiful eyes and tell her why I did what I did.

I was never in the army, but I killed some of those 4 000 SWAPO PLAN soldiers on the police unit Koevoet's scoreboard. It is impossible to tell you how many I killed, but I can tell you how I killed them and why I killed them.

You see, I didn't hate them. In fact, I had nothing against them. Most of them were Ovambos and the Ovambos are really lovely people. I didn't have to kill them; no one forced me to fight. I fought because I chose to. Some people tried to tell me that it was for God and country, but I said, 'Fuck you, fuck God and fuck my country.'

So I wasn't a soldier, I didn't have to fight and I wasn't fighting for God and country. What the fuck was I fighting for then?

I can't give you a simple answer, but if you listen to my story you might begin to understand why I did what I did.

I am sorry that all those people died. I'm not proud of what I did, but I am not ashamed either.

I don't know if it even was a war. What I know about war is that normally two countries declare war on each other and then they send their armies to fight until one side surrenders and the other side claims victory. That didn't happen in what is now known as Namibia and in Angola.

Perhaps it was right and perhaps it was wrong. I can't even tell you if we won or lost that fight, but none of that matters. What does matter is that a lot of people died because I killed them, and I lived. That is what I set out to do and that is what I accomplished.

So, to all those people I've killed, I am sorry you died, but fuck you all and damn the rest.

What I was looking for 28 years later in Ovamboland was the slug of a parabolic cone made of an alloy of copper and lead, two metals mined in the Soviet Union.

Some devil in the hellhole of a Soviet weapons factory smiled when he knew he had produced something unstoppable, a weapon of death and devastation. He would have smiled even more if he had seen just how well the new weapon served its purpose. With that weapon the human race would once more try to destroy itself.

Together with many other weapons of war and destruction, it was taken by a Soviet naval cargo ship to a base in Angola. There it found its way into the hands of a fighter, who carried it across the border into Namibia, where he was going to carry out a mission. He had been told that it would help to liberate his country from the evil and unlawful occupation of the racist running dogs of the Pretoria regime.

His mission was to lead 150 comrades into the white farming area of Tsumeb and to penetrate as far south as possible, where they had to blow up as many white farmers and carry out as many acts of terror as they could.

The commander and his comrades had one problem: we were right behind them and we were gaining on them, with one purpose in mind. We wanted to kill them, destroy them.

I had to respect this enemy. He and a few of his elite comrades decided to sacrifice themselves by ambushing us so that the rest of their group would have a better chance of achieving their objectives.

Knowing that he was going to die, he lay there waiting, like a serpent in the grass. It was suicidal. He and his comrades might as well have strapped explosives to their bodies and blown themselves up.

The commander takes a deep breath of hot dry air, breathes out and then half-fills his lungs with air. He relaxes his body and aims carefully. Gently but firmly he squeezes the trigger, just as he was trained by the Russian and Cuban instructors at his base deep in Angola.

The hammer falls on the firing pin, which strikes the primer and ignites the propellant. The rocket leaves the tube of the RPG with a bang at 117 metres per second and accelerates to 294 metres per second. Its tail fins pop out to stabilise it and start it spinning. With a deafening bang it hits its target 20 metres away.

This is a signal to his comrades to open fire. The ambush is set off.

Our best tracker has seen him. He rises in his seat to cock the light machine gun mounted in its turret above his head.

The rocket hits the side of the Koevoet Casspir, just above the right side window. On impact the nose of the rocket crushes against the armoured steel. The explosive charge detonates, the cone melts and the temperature at the apex of the parabola reaches 26 000 °C.

As it explodes and melts against the panzer steel, it melts the steel and blows a hole through it, flying through the Casspir with an ear-bursting bang. It sends a shock wave through the vehicle, rendering its occupants immobile. The white-hot molten metal slug from the RPG slices easily through the Casspir.

Shrapnel from the melted panzer steel and the RPG spray through the inside of the Casspir. The slug passes through the tracker's head, in through the right side of his skull, through his brain and out through the left side of his skull, blowing his blood, brains and bone all over the inside of the Casspir.

The slug passes out through the left side of the Casspir and soars through the air, leaves and trees, finally to fall and come to rest on the ground, where it cools down to remain for eternity on the white sand of that remote place in south-eastern Ovamboland.

Twelve Casspirs surge forward to battle a barrage of enemy automatic gunfire that bounces harmlessly off the armour-plated skins of the advancing beasts – 12 Casspirs with 12 LMGs, 120 Koevoet members with their rifles stuck out through the gun portholes of the Casspirs or standing up and firing over the top, every assault rifle and every light machine gun firing on automatic.

Some of the insurgents start to flee; they are no match for this kind of firepower. They have achieved their objective by delaying us; to stay and try to fight will mean certain death.

The Casspirs race forward, turn and circle and weave, cutting the enemy to pieces. They are shot over and over again, driven over, mangled and mashed by the nine-ton Casspirs.

In 60 seconds the contact is over.

But the good-looking young Ovambo who left UNITA a few years ago to join us is dead with his head blown off. He was one of our finest trackers and was always on the ground on the spoor during a follow-up, enthusiastically blowing his whistle and coordinating the follow-up, always inspiring his comrades to give more. I will never forget the way he just looked at us and smiled whenever we tried to speak to him. We often forgot that he couldn't speak a word of English or Afrikaans.

Later in the day we move off together, like one big, hurt, angry beast, to lick our wounds and to prepare for what is to come.

For the next 28 years I could see that slug in my mind. It was like a demon in my soul and in my dreams. Sometimes it would just be lying there on the sand in the open and the wind would blow and bury it, only to blow it open again. Sometimes I would see it lying there, hot and smouldering. Then the demons would creep up through my soul and into my head.

I had to find it and finally unlock that trunk of souvenirs, which I had locked after my daughter had discovered them years and years ago. I had to destroy its contents. Then I would finally be free.

The scoreboard in the ops room recorded how many kills and how many captures each of our groups had for the year. It didn't record how many civilians we shot. Nowhere was that record kept. If a civilian was killed in the crossfire, we could often claim it as a kill, provided there were enough enemy weapons to go around. Therefore it was a good idea to keep one or two spare unrecorded AKs or an SKS as proof, just in case you shot a civilian.

It's always the local population, the civilians, who suffer most during any war or conflict. That is inevitable. That is the price of war, but they are the ones that ultimately determine the outcome. In our arrogance we tend to forget that.

We sit in the International Guest House in Oshakati drinking whisky and eating steak. We get drunk and fight with the army or among ourselves. We live like kings, while the Ovambos, especially those in southern Angola, get fucked up by SWAPO and then by us, and then by us again and then by SWAPO again and then by UNITA and then by FAPLA.

They are very poor. Their clothes rot and fall off their bodies while they starve to death. They have almost nothing left and, when they have nothing, we take their lives. In the east, the Kwanyama, a subset of the Ovambo people, support us, so we fatten them with money, cars, gifts, luxuries and protection from the home guard, while SWAPO kills them, murders them, abducts their children for indoctrination and training and takes from them.

In the west, where the Ongandjera, the Kwambi and the Ombalantu support SWAPO, we fuck them up, we beat them, we torture them for information. We drive their fences and mahangu fields to hell, we catch them in the crossfire and we kill them. Fucking SWAPO supporters, they must die.

We blame SWAPO and SWAPO blames us. We dress up as

the enemy and kill their friends so that the enemy gets blamed. The enemy kills our friends so that we get blamed.

They plant landmines during the night so that we get blown up during the day, but more locals are blown up in the process.

We set up ambushes at night to shoot the enemy, but we shoot the locals who are late in getting home. It's all so fucked up, but it is the locals who pay the price of the war.

Here they say, 'Die PB [plaaslike bevolking] moet kak.' The local population must suffer.

'Contact, contact, contact! ... Zulu Sierra, contact.' We stop and listen because they don't want our help. They've made contact with SWAPO in the middle of a kraal complex. It's in the west so 'die PB moet kak'.

'Hey Piet, there's one hiding in that hut with the locals,' the radio crackles.

'Just throw a white phosphorous grenade into the hut and burn the lot of them.'

The gunship-helicopter arrives and the crew can't understand why a hut is moving around in circles. We listen to Zulu Sierra's explanation over the radio: the Casspir went through the hut and the roof is stuck on top of the vehicle as it drives around.

What happened to the locals who were hiding in that hut? The woman and the children? 'Die PB het gekak.'

There is movement ahead and Bennie's Casspir, Zulu Golf 3, races forward, spraying automatic gunfire as it charges.

'Contact, contact, contact!' someone calls over the radio.

We all charge forward, but it's a fuck up. It was some of the locals who ran for the safety of their kraal when they saw the Casspirs coming.

One of the guys signals to me to stop as he catches up from behind.

'They shot some of the locals back there by accident,' he tells me, looking pale and shaky. 'There were two children, a boy and a girl aged about five and eight. They were badly wounded. There was nothing I could do for them. I shot them with my 9-mm; I put them out of their misery.'

The Ovambo make up about one-third of Namibia's population and at the time were concentrated in the central north. The majority lived in a relatively small area in the middle of the operational area, which the army called the 'backbone' area. The army realised that the outcome of an election would be decided there, so they established a communications operation to win the hearts and minds of the people.

They even loaded an entire orchestra into some Buffels and drove from kraal to kraal to play music for the people, but we just fucked up everything they did.

'Elias, tell the others what the army taught you on the com-ops course.'

He shakes his head and laughs, and then he tries to be serious.

'They asked me what I would do if I came to my village and SWAPO was there, holding my mother and family at gunpoint.'

'I would fuckin' shoot the lot of them, my mother included,' Mbinga, our main hit man, snarls. He walks away, shaking his head as if to say, 'What a stupid question.'

She and her younger sister wore nothing except tattered short skirts. Her little breasts bobbed and her hips swung as she drove the pole up and down into the hollow tree stump, into the mahangu seed that had been harvested and threshed. They were making flour for a celebration of the goodness that nature had provided.

Good summer rains had made their cattle, goats and chickens fat. A good mahangu crop would provide bread and a special treat, mahangu beer, the local home brew made from millet, yeast and sugar.

Life didn't get any better than this. The hardships of surviving in this inhospitable place and living off the land had been eased by the rains. The little they knew of the outside world didn't matter, this was their world, this was their life and they were one happy family.

She was tiring, but didn't want to give up and disappoint her mother. She shifted her bare feet and changed her position slightly. She drove the pole down once more and the thick heavy stump on the top of the pole smashed down onto her head, leaving a deep wound.

'Sergeant Jimmy, can you help this girl?' the Ovambos pleaded later, when we arrived. 'She hurt herself.'

'No, fuck off, I'm not a doctor.'

I don't know how I had become our self-taught medic. Probably because no one else would do it. If anyone called me a medic I would have killed him. I was far better at killing.

'Come on, Jim, do your bit for com-ops,' someone joked.

'Okay,' I joked back, 'I'll put a bullet through her head.'

I could see fear and pain in her eyes. Something deep inside me made me give in.

'Bring the fucking medic bag,' I shout. 'Let me see what I can do. Don't be afraid, this good doctor is going to fix you. Here, suck this. It's good for you; it's vitamin C,' I say to her and hand her a sweet while Elias translates.

The wound looks bad. It's about three days old and it's starting to turn septic. It's a bit too old to put stitches in, but if

I don't it will never heal. There won't be anyone around to take the stitches out later so I use dissolvable ones.

'Okay, let's party,' I say as I open the medic bag and look inside.

'Elias, tell her she's going to have a lot of fun,' I say as I wipe her arm with an alcohol swab.

She pulls away as I try to insert the needle into a vein.

Okay, this isn't working; the little bitch won't hold still.

'Elias, tell her to open her mouth and lift her tongue.'

Twenty drops of volaron taste bitter so I give her another vitamin C sweet to suck. I then give her morphine.

Local anaesthetic, 22 stitches, antiseptic ointment, bandaged and topped off with a shot of penicillin. I admire my work while I hear the others calling me on the radio. They have found fresh spoor and need me.

I joke and tell her to come back to see the nice doctor in one week's time as I give her a ration pack. She doesn't understand and Elias doesn't translate; by now he has got to know my sense of humour.

Okay, let's go and join the follow-up and see if we can kill someone today. Hopefully I'll be rewarded for my good deed and will get to kill some motherfucker.

2

Primal instinct

Fill your head with Marxist communist ideologies. Pick up an RPG-7, an AK-47 and some landmines and hand grenades, put on a Cuban or Chinese camouflage uniform and march across the border of another country. Shoot and kill the locals who don't support your ideas. Abduct the schoolchildren at gunpoint, march them to your training bases to indoctrinate them and fill their heads with your bullshit to force them to do what you are doing.

You're looking for shit and you're bound to get your head blown off and those crap ideas spilt out all over the fine white sand.

Who the fuck were SWAPO and its military wing, PLAN, to do what they were doing? I was going to stop them, not because I was told to or forced to, but because I chose to fight and to show that the enemy could not be allowed to do what it was doing.

I was young, dumb and full of testosterone. Never mind what was right and what was wrong. No one had the right to do what they were doing and someone needed to stop the enemy. The world screamed, the world condemned, but fuck the world. If only the world knew the truth.

The great city of Constantinople fell to the Turkish invaders from the Ottoman Empire in 1453 and the Portuguese, among others, needed new trade routes. Thus began the age of the famous explorers. Bartholomew Diaz and Vasco da Gama explored the sea route around Africa, and during the following centuries Africa was colonised by the Portuguese, the Dutch, the British, the French, Belgians, Germans and Italians.

And then, in the mid-20th century, the time came for Africa to liberate itself from its colonial masters.

On 3 February 1960 the British prime minister, Harold Macmillan, addressed the South African Parliament in Cape Town. His country intended to grant independence to its colonies. In his front bench the South African prime minister, Hendrik Verwoerd, listened impassively. Or so it seemed.

'The wind of change is blowing through this continent,' Macmillan said, 'and whether we like it or not, this growth of national consciousness is a political fact.'

Did Britain suddenly have some moral dilemma as to what she had done in Africa? Bullshit. She was just shit-scared of what was happening on the continent. She didn't want to go to war to hold on to her colonies. The AK-47, a Soviet automatic assault rifle, had come to Africa, and with it a new way of thinking. Power comes from the barrel of a gun, the Africans thought.

And why were the Soviets interested in Africa? Did they want to liberate Africa from colonial oppression for moral reasons? Bullshit.

At the height of the Cold War between the superpowers of the time – the United States and the Soviet Union – mineral-rich Africa became in a sense a target as well as a theatre of war. In the nuclear-weapons race the Soviet Union had its eye on a specific scarce resource: uranium. The world's finest weapons-grade uranium was mined at Rossing in South West Africa (present-day Namibia).

Hendrik Verwoerd and his government listened to Harold Macmillan's speech and showed him the middle finger, so to speak. South Africa broke away from the Commonwealth of Nations and on 31 May 1961 became the Republic of South Africa.

On that day, at Chloorkop Primary School, the school near Kempton Park that my older brothers and sister attended, my mother was watching a little ceremony. The Union Jack was lowered and put away for ever. The orange, white and blue flag of the new Republic of South Africa, with miniatures of the Union Jack and the flags of the two former Boer republics in the middle, would from now on fly alone, as South Africa stood alone. My mother watched with pride, and in her womb she carried me. I was on my way.

War in Angola started in the mid-1950s. The Popular Movement for the Liberation of Angola (MPLA), backed by the Soviets, the National Front for the Liberation of Angola (FNLA) and the National Union for the Total Independence of Angola (UNITA) were getting ready to kick the Portuguese right across the Atlantic Ocean back to Portugal, as was the Front for the Liberation of Mozambique (FRELIMO) in Mozambique. It took them close to two decades to succeed.

In 1960 the South West African People's Organisation (SWAPO) was founded in then South West Africa, a South African protectorate. By 1966 SWAPO's military wing, the People's Liberation Army of Namibia (PLAN), was using guerrilla tactics to gain independence from South African rule.

Meanwhile, in what was still known as Rhodesia, Robert Mugabe's Zimbabwe African National Union (ZANU), and the

Zimbabwe African People's Union (ZAPU), led by Joshua Nkomo, formed a coalition, the Patriotic Front, after Ian Smith's unilateral declaration of independence from Britain in 1965. The ensuing civil war lasted 14 years.

In South Africa the African National Congress (ANC), which was founded in 1912, turned to armed struggle and in 1961 formed its military wing, Umkhonto we Sizwe (the Spear of the Nation), also referred to as MK. That was two years after Robert Sobukwe broke away from the ANC and founded the more radical and militant Pan Africanist Congress (PAC).

Soon after it was founded the PAC flexed its muscles. On 21 March 1960 it organised a protest march against the pass laws in Soweto, and another in Sharpeville near Vereeniging, the third-largest township in South Africa. At 10 a.m. between 6 000 and 7 000 people converged at the Sharpeville police station, asking to be arrested for not carrying passes. There were fewer than 20 policemen on duty at the station. The crowd quickly grew to an estimated 20 000 and 130 more policemen and four Saracen armoured cars were rushed in. Sabre jets and Harvard trainers flew low over the crowd.

A few stones were hurled, and by 1 p.m. a scuffle ensued when the police tried to arrest a protestor. As the angry crowd surged towards the fence, the first shot was fired. It was attributed to the nervousness of young inexperienced officers, but some degree of deliberation by senior policemen was also implicated.

Soon 69 protestors lay dead, many shot in the back, and 180 were injured.

Robert Sobukwe himself led a similar march in Soweto. He was arrested and jailed for three years for incitement. Afterwards he was interred on Robben Island and Parliament passed an Act which made annual renewal of his internment possible. When he was released in 1969, he was placed under house arrest in Kimberley. By then the PAC as well as the ANC had been banned and their exiled leaders were planning the armed struggle, with the support of countries in the Soviet bloc.

Of all this I was of course blissfully unaware.

In 1964, I was only three years old and I was still sleeping in a cot. We lived in a mine house at Glen Harmony, where my father worked in the uranium plant of the Harmony Gold Mine in the Orange Free State.

We had a big tabby cat called Tiger. One day my father brought me a kitten he had found on the mine premises. It was black with white paws and we called it Socks.

One morning at dawn, just as the light started seeping into the room, I woke with little Socks snuggled down next to me. I felt his heart beating in his warm little body.

Then something woke him. Perhaps he was hungry, perhaps it was the call of nature. He slipped through the bars of my cot. I watched as he darted down the passage towards the kitchen.

Suddenly Tiger pounced on him and went straight for the jugular. One bite and the life left Socks's little body. He was lying there on the cold passage floor, killed right in front of me.

'Don't let Arn see it,' someone shouted, but it was too late.

I lay motionless, without any feelings. In fact, it had been fascinating to watch and to see what death meant.

A few months later, in June 1964, I heard my father shout: 'They should have shot the bastard! They should have executed him on the steps of the Union Buildings!' The one o'clock news on Springbok Radio had just reported that Nelson Mandela had been spared the death penalty at the Rivonia Trial. He had been convicted of high treason and sentenced to life imprisonment. He was shipped off to Robben Island.

'What are you knitting?' someone asked my mother. She was always knitting. I guessed it was socks for me, but no. 'It is socks for the Portuguese Soldiers' Relief Fund,' my mother said. 'They're going through a tough time fighting in Angola and Mozambique. Some of the soldiers are so poor that they don't even own socks. See how we knit them, like a tube without a heel? When they wear out on one side the soldiers can turn them around and still wear them.'

Portugal, the poor nation of traders on the Iberian peninsula, was desperately trying to hold on to power in her two colonies in Africa where war was raging, Angola and Mozambique.

Portuguese nationals were being called up from all over the world to fight against the communist-backed uprising in Africa. Very soon the two colonies would be granted independence and most of the Portuguese living there would abandon their farms, businesses and homes and return to their homeland.

A few years later, at school, I would learn that of the total South African population at the time, only 9.7 per cent, or 4.5 million, were white. More than half of the white population, classified by the government as Europeans, were Afrikaans-speaking and the majority of the rest were English-speaking. There was a huge divide between the two language groups and it was against a youthful member of the Afrikaner community that I first learnt how to defend myself, at the tender age of five.

In 1966 we moved to a place called Canelands on the North Coast of the then Natal, where my dad had a new job at the Timberite factory, and we settled into a company house.

The house next door was vacant and I was told that we were getting new neighbours.

'Bloody Afrikaners, Dutchmen,' I heard my dad saying. 'We moved down here to Natal to get away from them and so that our children could get a proper education. Now we've got them moving in next door.'

Carpenters arrived before the neighbours moved in and built the most beautiful tree house in the back garden of the next-door house. I was forbidden to play in it, but boys will be boys. My fun stopped when the neighbours arrived and found out that someone had inaugurated their tree house before their arrival.

I was playing alone on the dirt road behind our house when I was confronted by the big fat boy from the next-door house. He was ranting and raving and his furious sweaty face came closer and closer to me. I didn't understand a word he was shouting and fear gripped me as I sensed an immediate threat.

He pushed me down to the ground next to a bougainvillea hedge. Right next to me I saw half a brick, and instinctively I picked it up, got back on my feet and faced my adversary.

Suddenly the tables were turned and the fat little Dutchman was running home in fear, screaming for the safety and comfort of his home and family.

Not quite understanding what had just happened, I looked down at the brick in my hand. Some primal instinct had made me defend myself. I had mixed feelings of disgust and victory.

In 1969, when I was eight years old, we moved to Red Hill next to Durban North, and this became a huge problem in my life. Red Hill was known for the notorious Red Hill Gang, although its members didn't actually come from Red Hill. It was in fact not a bad area at all, but if you said you lived in Red Hill, people treated you like scum.

My folks bought a dilapidated old house, which my dad decided to renovate. My brothers, sister and I were put to work to help rebuild the run-down place.

For the next few years I worked hard, really hard, and I was growing up to be big and strong. With adolescence approaching, I was about to change for the worse. Instead of being bullied, I was going to stand up and fight. I joined the Cardboard Gang and at the age of 14 I got on the wrong side of life and the law, keeping most of my life a secret from my family.

We never really saw ourselves as a gang as such – not in the sense of present-day gangs, with their culture of drugs and serious and violent crime. However, we did do some shoplifting and petty crime and our speciality was gatecrashing parties, which was a big problem for the community.

At that time, in 1973, my eldest brother, Martin, received his call-up papers from the army and marched off to do his military service. By then national service had become an integral part of every white South African male's life. By the age of 18 the army was on to you with a telegram explaining where and when you would have to report for duty. If you refused, the military police would come for you and you could end up in a military jail.

Rhodesia, under Prime Minister Ian Smith, had unilaterally declared Rhodesia independent from Great Britain, which had probably been glad to let go. The Soviets were quick to back Joshua Nkomo while China supported Robert Mugabe's Patriotic Front in the fight against Ian Smith's illegitimate government. War broke out in Rhodesia, and South African forces, including policemen, were sent to help the Rhodesians.

By 1979 Ian Smith's government came to the end of the road. Multiparty talks led to elections in 1980, which Robert Mugabe's ZANU won with a large majority. However, during the Rhodesian war South Africa had learnt many valuable lessons about modern guerrilla warfare in Africa and was able to prepare itself for the long and bitter fight that lay ahead. South Africa began developing its own weapons and great advances were made in the development of anti-landmine armoured vehicles.

Little wonder that military service by South African young men became quite an issue. By the time Martin was called up, the nine months' compulsory military service had been extended to a full year. After that my brother was called up time and again, always returning home, sworn to secrecy and unwilling to tell us anything. Even his letters home were heavily censored.

This was the time when various civil wars in southern Africa started.

In November 1975 Angola became independent. With the help of the Soviets, the MPLA, FNLA and UNITA had in effect kicked the Portuguese out of Angola. The MPLA took power with José Eduardo dos Santos as president, much to the disappointment of the FNLA in the north and UNITA in the south-east. South Africa and the US saw an opportunity to destabilise Angola. With their help, Dr Jonas Savimbi and UNITA developed a large guerrilla army and embarked on an extended war against the Soviet-backed Angolan government. The FNLA under Holden Roberto was stuck, landlocked in the north, so it disintegrated and disappeared. UNITA, supported by South Africa and the US, kept on fighting, but was unable to achieve its objectives. A state of instability and violence prevailed for more than two decades.

On South Africa's north-eastern border, Mozambique gained independence from Portugal in 1975, and FRELIMO, with Soviet backing, came to power and established a one-party socialist state. Its leader, Samora Machel, became president. In the same year a rebel movement, the Mozambican National Resistance (RENAMO) was formed, supported by South Africa and the US, and in 1977 Mozambique was plunged into civil war.

Meanwhile the situation in Angola was becoming a serious

threat to South Africa, more so after the ANC's military wing, Umkhonto we Sizwe, had established training bases in Angola. That in turn had implications for South Africa's involvement in South West Africa.

South West Africa was colonised by Germany in 1884, but after World War I South Africa received a mandate from the League of Nations to administer the territory, partly because South Africa, as member of the British Commonwealth, had helped to defeat Germany in World War I.

After World War II the League of Nations was replaced by the United Nations (UN), which instituted a system of trusteeship, requiring closer international monitoring of South West Africa's administration. South Africa objected and after 20 years of legal wrangling the UN ended South Africa's mandate in 1966. Nevertheless, the legal squabbling, and later the drawn-out international negotiations, went on for many years, while SWAPO's fight for independence continued.

Namibia is two-thirds the size of South Africa, with a total population now approaching 2 000 000, more language groups than South Africa and a history of strife between the indigenous peoples and white colonial powers.

During the 30 years of German rule, the Bondelswarts, a Khoi group, were the first to revolt. They were subjugated in 1894. From 1904 to 1908 the Hereros and Namas fought to preserve their system of communal landownership against private ownership imposed by the Germans. The Namas fought 295 battles against the Germans, the Hereros 88. In that war 2 000 Germans lost their lives, but in the end their superior weapons triumphed. Of the 100 000 Hereros only 20 000 remained and the Namas were reduced from 20 000 to 15 000. Later Ovambo Chief Nehale tried in vain to push the Germans back.

Enter South Africa, after World War I.

In 1916 and 1917, Kwanyama Chief Mandume fought the South African forces, and died in 1917 during an uprising against the South African control of his nation. He was the last Ovambo king.

In 1930 the Bondelswarts revolted against South Africa after they were forced to pay taxes they couldn't afford and the then prime minister, General Jan Smuts, sent in aeroplanes to bomb the 'rebels'. More than 100 Bondelswarts were killed, and their resistance was subdued.

Most of the Namibian population is concentrated in the north, where one also finds the Ovambo people. Their territory is known as Ovamboland and the Ovambo nation is divided by the border between Angola and Namibia.

The Ovambo are Namibia's largest and most militant group. It is therefore not surprising that it was largely the Ovambo who decided to fight for independence from South Africa, and it was easy for SWAPO, under the leadership of Sam Nujoma, and its military wing PLAN to establish military bases in Angola, where they could train and from where they could launch attacks into then South West Africa.

Back in Durban, in 1976, my brother Neil had found an alternative to national service in the army. Time served in the South African Police (SAP) counted as national service. My sister Jean had already joined the SAP in 1975, although national service was never compulsory for women.

At the time I was getting deeper and deeper into trouble, and news of the problem Cardboard Gang terrorising the residential suburb of Durban North finally reached Parliament.

Having a brother and sister in the local police force was not helping my criminal career and I was heading down a one-way street: I was going to end up dead or in some serious shit.

I masterminded the theft of a collection of records from a

neighbourhood house. We got busted, but the owner of the records said he would drop the matter if the records were returned. I kept one, though, and I've still got it – the soundtrack from the movie *Let the Good Times Roll.*

I had learnt to fight and I surely could do that well. I always carried a knife but, thank God, I never used it, though there was an incident where my friend Graham nearly sliced my right thumb off with my own knife while we were playing the fool.

In my dad's workshop behind our garage I forged a sword out of a piece of steel, using his oxyacetylene cutting torch, hammer and anvil.

Four of us from the Cardboard Gang were sitting in the Wimpy restaurant in Durban North one Saturday night. Our favourite trick was to have a meal and, as we left, to tell the cashier that the one behind us would pay. The last one out would either point to some strangers in the restaurant and say that they would pay, or just run like hell. Later we would sneak into the movies at the cinema nearby, again without paying.

On this occasion I had my sword hidden in my trouser leg. Alan, another member of our group, joined us. 'There are about 15 guys coming down the road, looking for us,' he says. 'They say they are going to fuck us up! Where is everyone? Where are Gavin, Lolly and Kim? Why aren't they here yet?' Alan is out of breath and quite stressed.

'Let's go and meet them, let's go and fuck them up,' I say as I get up from the table, the feeling of my sword against my leg giving me confidence.

As we leave the restaurant, a commotion breaks out behind us as once again we haven't paid the bill, but we're already heading down the road to meet our adversaries.

About 15 guys are coming down Broadway straight towards us, so out comes my sword as we charge towards them.

'There they are, let's kill them!' I shout, brandishing my sword.

In a sudden panic they turn and run and we give chase. We chase them for about a kilometre down the road until they find refuge in the house of one guy's parents.

'Come Graham, come Alan, let's get the fuck out of here!' I shout. 'They'll call the cops and they'll be here soon; let's go and hide in the cinema.'

We run, and about 100 metres from the cinema I look back and see the blue light of a police van coming.

Time to quickly get rid of the sword; I don't want to get bust with it. With great regret I toss it over the wall of a house into someone's garden. My sword is gone for ever.

'What's going on here?' I hear as the police van pulls up.

Oh fuck, it's my sister! She's on duty.

'Oh, nothing, Jean, we're just going to watch a movie. Some guys, about 15 of them, chased us, but we got away,' I say as innocently as possible.

'That's not the complaint we've received,' she says. 'They said something about the Cardboard Gang trying to kill them with a sword.'

'Look, Jean, there's just five of us. We don't have any weapons, we were on our way to the movies when they chased us, so we ran away and now we are here at the movies. I wouldn't lie to my sister, I promise.'

'Okay, just behave yourselves and be careful.'

Off drives Durban North's super-girl-cop and we're in the clear.

In 1976 my brother Martin was called up by the army once again. When he came back, some of the truth was starting to come out from him and other sources.

The South African Defence Force (SADF) had invaded Angola in an attempt to overthrow the MPLA government and to help put Jonas Savimbi's UNITA into power. The US backed the plan and the Central Intelligence Agency (CIA) was already giving support to UNITA.

The South African army launched its invasion from northern Namibia into southern Angola and rapidly drove north towards the capital city Luanda, annihilating all resistance.

South African armed forces reached the outskirts of Luanda and prepared to take the city and put UNITA into power, but the Angolan government was screaming blue murder to the United Nations, which then condemned the invasion as well as the US's support. The South African prime minister, John Vorster, had to decide: finish the job or pull out. It would have been a simple, quick and decisive victory for the South African armed forces, but South Africa was denying that its forces were in Angola, although they were ready to deliver the final blow. Vorster made the fatal mistake and ordered the South African armed forces to withdraw. His decision had dire consequences: the war would now continue for many years.

Angola cried for help and Fidel Castro responded to its call by sending 50 000 Cuban troops, mostly from his infamous Fifth Brigade, to help Angola against the South African threat.

'Please, Molly, won't you fight him,' I begged my friend Wayne Malloy. 'I'm only 14, you're 16 and he's 19,' I pleaded as I was marched by a prefect to a place behind the auditorium, where I was to fight some punk with whom I'd had an altercation the previous day. A fight had been arranged, supervised by the school prefects.

A lot of prefects and students had already gathered to watch the proceedings.

'So do you want to fight him?' a prefect asked me in front of an audience.

Not a fuck. How can I get out of this? I was desperate, but I couldn't avoid that one, not in front of the crowd. 'Yes,' I was forced to reply.

He came at me with his head down, not looking, punching wildly like a blind kangaroo. I didn't even bother to defend myself. Instead I hit him hard and fast, connecting with a very hard left punch to his nose. I felt his nose pop and I even heard the bone crack. Blood sprayed all over me, all over my shirt, and then he went down.

Someone shouted, 'Put a boot!'

I wasn't going to kick him while he was down, not in front of that audience.

A prefect helped him to his feet and the boy wanted to resume the fight, but he was totally defeated.

'No, take him away or I'll kill him,' I said, just as the bell rang. It was the end of break.

'What happened to you?' Mrs Heslop, our English teacher, wanted to know. I hadn't been able to wash all the blood out of my shirt and the buttons had all broken off.

'Touch rugby, ma'am.'

'No, ma'am,' Molly interrupted. 'He beat up this matric.'

Fuck, now I'm in the shit, I thought, as Molly told the story.

'Oh! I don't like that boy, he is horrible,' Mrs Heslop said.

I love you, Mrs Heslop. If only you knew how I perve over you in class. Those fantasies I've had about you since the time I sat in the front row and my knees stuck out under the desk and you stood in front of me, facing me, and you accidentally rubbed yourself against my knee; was that an accident or were you trying to tell me ...?

The end of my career in the Cardboard Gang finally came when my sister arrested me after some serious questions were asked in Parliament.

At a party at the Glenwood Club we beat up the son of the American consul. The newspapers were full of headlines such as 'Cardboard Gang Terrorises Durban North'. The MP for Durban North questioned the minister of police in Parliament about our activities, and the minister asked the district commandant at Durban North police station to compile a report about the Cardboard Gang. My name came up in a register that the police kept at the police station.

One Friday I was hauled out of class, taken to the Durban North police station and interrogated for two hours by a police colonel. As much as I lied, as much as I tried to convince him that the gang did not exist, I could not avoid the fact that my name appeared in the register labelled 'Cardboard Gang'.

I was under house arrest, indefinitely. End-of-year holidays came and I had the most boring holiday of my life, but slowly I began to reflect and to take a good look at my past. Eventually I decided that it was time to start a new life, although it would not be easy.

I resorted to building furniture for my family: bookshelves for my sister, then a hi-fi stand, display shelves for our lounge and a beautiful kitchen table. I covered the surface of the table with blue-and-white tiles and it became the centrepiece of our home. This was not only where we ate our meals, but where we enjoyed many evenings together, having fun.

When no one wanted any more furniture, I started leatherwork. I made belts and then I designed a handbag, and the leather handbags started rolling out – one for my mother, one for my sister and then for all their friends. They had to pay for the bags, of course. I'm not that charitable.

Then the cops arrived at our house. No, not to arrest me, not to question me. All my sister's cop friends came to visit, play cards and generally have fun around that big old kitchen table I had made. I was allowed to join them and so I heard every cop story ever told.

It was during this period that I learnt how passionate an Afrikaner can be about his sport.

One day my mother arrived home and there, on the back of our Toyota bakkie, was a table-tennis table. I am not sure what prompted her to buy it, but it turned out to be one of her better ideas.

We had not played the game before, but we soon got the hang of it and progressed from ping-pong to actual table tennis. Unbeknown to us, my mother had played league table tennis in her youth, so she enjoyed giving us a run for our money. Jean and Neil's cop friends who frequented our house got a lot of fun out of the game too.

There must have been some talk among the cops at the police station about this and one of them, who hadn't been to our house before, Abrie Vermeulen, bragged about what a champ table-tennis player he was. Every day he told tales about his prowess, until eventually he was invited to come around one evening for a game or two.

He arrived, wearing tennis shoes and white shorts and a white shirt, walking on the balls of his feet and flexing his muscles. One would have sworn he was about to take on Mohammed Ali.

We were very much the amateurs, playing for fun and enjoying it. So we didn't mind when he showed us his superior skills. He certainly was a good player.

Then someone suggested that my mother play against him, so she took off her apron and reached for a bat. Abrie had no idea what the old girl could do. As they played, the only sound was that of the bats hitting the ball. No one said a word.

Eventually the game was over and my mother had beaten Abrie. The score was something like 21–11. My mother was smiling, but the tears were running down Abrie's cheeks. I could hardly believe that a simple game of table tennis had roused so much emotion. He was clearly devastated and humiliated. Years later I remembered this every time I saw men cry when their favourite rugby team lost a game.

My brother Neil was back from the police college and after a few months he was off to Maloeskop for counter-insurgency training.

I went back to school, to Standard 9 (today's Grade 11), and for the first time in my life I focused on schoolwork. It paid off, because by the end of Standard 9 I was top of my class.

Neil came back from counter-insurgency training. He bought a .22 target pistol and took me to an old quarry for my first target practice. I was hooked; I became a gun addict. I read, studied and learnt everything about guns. My life became guns, guns, guns: muzzle velocity, trajectory, calibre, stopping power, revolver versus semi-automatic, you name it. I learnt everything there was to know about guns.

We had two Burmese cats, one blue, one brown. Smoky and Estalina were their names. Stray feral cats were coming into our garden and attacking and terrorising them. The stray cats became known as terrorists, and I couldn't believe it when my parents gave me their blessing to shoot the terrorists.

I was given the combination to the gun safe in Neil's bedroom. I couldn't wait until everyone was out of the house so that I could play with the guns. Soon all the feral cats had disappeared: It was, 'Here kitty, here kitty …' BANG, BANG, BANG!

I felt that by now I deserved another chance in life and that it was time to make new friends. I went to a good school, had a good family and I had paid for all the wrong that I had done. Just as I was contemplating this one afternoon when I was alone at home, the phone rang.

'Hello.'

'Hi, Arn, it's Dianne. I met you the other evening with my sister Vivienne at your house.'

'Yes, so what?' I remembered her, the dog. My mother had asked me if I thought she was beautiful. 'No comment,' I'd answered.

'What are you doing?' Typical female question, I thought.

'Shooting cats.'

'You aren't serious. I don't believe you!'

'Okay, listen here.'

BANG, BANG! I fired the gun down the passage, out the front door and into a flower bed.

'Do you believe me now?'

'I've got to go, just wondered how you were,' she replied feebly.

I put the phone down, thinking about her. What did she want? Maybe a relationship, maybe intimacy, maybe sex? No, fuck, I'd rather shoot some cats. I wouldn't know how to do that other stuff. I just wouldn't know what to do with a girl.

I had become a loner. I realised that I had no friends and it would be very difficult to make any, considering my past. I had tried a few times, but no one wanted anything to do with me. People shunned me, avoided me as though I carried the plague.

At the time Durban was changing, expanding northwards. Glen Ashley, La Lucia and Umhlanga Rocks were developing rapidly as its most upmarket exclusive suburbs, while Durban North was deteriorating. School zoning was brought in and these new upmarket areas became the feeder zone for Beachwood Boys High, which I attended. I now found myself mixing – or trying to mix – with the rich kids, and it just wasn't working.

I wondered what my old friends, Graham, Gavin, Kim, Lolly, Alan, Malcolm and the rest of the Cardboard Gang, were up to. All of them, except Wayne Malloy, went to other schools. Some lived in other suburbs. I was afraid and was lying low. School, rugby, home … and that was that. Walking home from school was nerve-wracking – I was afraid I might bump into them.

It dawned on me that one couldn't just leave the Cardboard Gang. How many guys had we fucked up in the past for doing just that? And now I'd left them without a word … I knew I was in serious shit. If ever I came across those guys, I was going to get killed or at least have the shit beaten out of me. I was stuck between the good and the bad. I was on my own.

I was deep in thought and oblivious to the phone ringing when my mother interrupted. 'Arn, it's for you.'

'What? For me?'

'Yes, it's a girl. She wants to speak to you.'

Fuck, how embarrassing.

I nervously took the phone, hoping that no one could hear the conversation, but I knew my whole family would be listening.

'Hello,' I said abruptly.

'Hi, Arn, my name is Mandy. I just want to invite you to a party I'm having at my house on Saturday night.'

'Do I know you?' I asked rudely, more for the benefit of my eavesdropping family than anything else.

'I don't know, but I know you, and all my friends know you

and we want you to come. We've heard that you've changed, so please come.'

'No, sorry, I can't.'

'Why not?'

'I just can't.' By now I was about to die of embarrassment.

'Well, here's my address, if you change your mind.'

'Who was that?' My mother was sticking her big nose into it.

'No one, just some stupid little girl,' I replied, totally mortified.

The little bitch called again the next evening, and again the next.

'Why don't you go to this girl's party, Arn? What's her name? Mandy? Come on, it's time you got out there and mixed with some nice people. Jean will take you and fetch you. She's off duty on Saturday night.' My mother was pushing me.

'Yes, come on, Arn. I'll take you and fetch you,' Jean chipped in.

Suddenly I was suspicious and very embarrassed. How the fuck does my mother know her name? Don't tell me Mandy phoned her. I'll kill the bitch.

'Come on, the Cardboard Gang won't be there,' Jean said.

Fuck, I don't need some cop escort there and back, I thought, but I didn't want to hurt Jean's feelings.

My mother and sister pushed me relentlessly and finally I gave in. Then Saturday night came.

'Drop me over here; that's where the party is,' I said, pointing.

Jean stopped her blue VW Beetle and I got out.

'I'll pick you up here at 12,' she said as she drove off, knowing that I didn't want to be seen being given a lift by my big super-cop sister.

There was a lot of noise and a lot of people were arriving as I walked towards the house.

Suddenly a police van pulled up.

'Come here.'

Oh, fuck, it was my brother Neil. He was on duty.

'We received a complaint that the Cardboard Gang is here, that they're going to gatecrash this party.'

'I was invited. Jean has just dropped me off,' I replied, 'and I haven't even gone inside yet.'

'Well, just be careful,' he said as he drove away.

I wanted to shout to him, 'Please wait! Give me a lift home. I'm in shit and I'm going to get killed.' But he was gone and I was too proud to cry for help anyway.

I was about to walk down the steps to the house when I heard from behind, 'Hey, Dodo, what you doing here?'

I recognised the voice. Kim Shultz, Cardboard Gang member. With nowhere to run to, I turned to meet my fate.

Yes, they're all here – Gavin, Graham, Lolly, Alan, Malcolm and Kim. Yes, the fucking little shit Kim, he'll start it. He will look for shit, taunt me, tease me until I retaliate, then the others will jump in to defend him. That's the way we always did it and that's the way it's going to be tonight. The wheel has turned and now it's on top of me.

My heart is pounding, the adrenalin is pumping, my hands are getting sweaty, clenching, making fists.

Don't do that, I say to myself. Don't let them see that you're getting ready for a fight.

They're forming a semi-circle around me; maybe I should strike first. I know I can take on each of them, one on one, but I've got no chance against all of them at once. If I hit fast and hard, maybe I can really hurt some of them and go down with the best fight ever.

I can't run; I can't get away. Stay calm, don't make fists, look at them non-threateningly.

'So where have you been, Dodo? Aren't we your friends any more; aren't we good enough for you?' Kim taunts me.

I don't think. The words just come out of my mouth. I say, 'I've changed my ways.'

There's a stunned silence and I can see that Kim is not amused.

Suddenly Alan bursts out laughing and he repeats, 'I've changed my ways.' Now they're all laughing, including Kim.

'Come, let's go party,' one of them says, and for now it seems that I have escaped my fate.

God, no, I didn't want to be seen arriving with the Cardboard Gang.

'Hey, guys, I'll be with you in a moment,' I said. They looked at me suspiciously.

'I just want to fetch my halfjack of vodka. It's hidden over there,' I lied in order to create a diversion.

I was tempted to make a break and simply walk home.

I was in a difficult situation. I didn't want to be seen associating with the Cardboard Gang and I didn't want them to realise that I was avoiding them. I also didn't know who this Mandy was and, after all, it was her party.

I sat on my own in a corner. As the music got louder I felt more and more uncomfortable.

Carol Frisbee came up to me. She had always been one of the Cardboard Gang's girls. She sat on my lap and started to kiss me. I had never been able to stand her and I remembered when Graham and Alan had made her drunk and taken turns with her.

She pushed a round boiled sweet that she had been sucking into my mouth with her tongue and I was revolted. I managed to get her off my lap, making the excuse that I needed the toilet.

Instead of going to the toilet I made my way out of the house and out of the front gate. I just kept on walking until I reached home about 10 kilometres away.

Jean was at home and her light was on. I knocked at her door.

'Don't worry about fetching me,' I said.

'How was the party?'

'Fine, quite fine,' I replied, and went to bed.

The next year, 1978, I was in matric, I made first-team rugby, I was a prefect and I was put in charge of school cadets. School cadets became compulsory and we could see that the government was just using it to try to indoctrinate the youth of South Africa.

Finally I was being accepted and I started making new friends. Soon I was quite a popular guy.

Garry Whitson was head boy and we became close friends. His family treated me as one of their own and often took me with them on their family holidays.

After the Rhodesian war was over and Robert Mugabe and his ZANU-PF came to power in Zimbabwe, we had an influx of Rhodesian families who wanted to start a new life in South Africa. We called them 'when-we's', because they began every story about the good old days in their fatherland with a 'When we were in Rhodesia …'

I heard a lot of heroic stories about the war in Rhodesia and became fascinated with those about the Selous Scouts. They were the elite of the Rhodesian armed forces. I often said that I was going to join the Selous Scouts after school.

I turned 17 in August 1978 and my army call-up papers arrived, but by now I knew how to dodge the army. Joining the South African Police meant six months of basic training at the police college in Pretoria, after which you were posted, with a bit of luck, to some place near your home. It also meant having to serve for three years in the SAP instead of two years in the defence force. However, the pay in the police was a lot better.

I chose to join the police, and so did a few of my friends, including Garry Whitson and Neil Callaway, but I enjoyed my final school year so much that I had to stay on for another year. I had failed mathematics. I had passed everything else, but the dreaded maths brought me down.

I was made a prefect again and again I played first-team rugby. My friends Garry and Neil had gone to the police college and soon I was friends with Garry's brother Mark. Oscar Dike, Brian Johnson and Wayne Malloy were also repeating their matric and our first rugby team was even better than before.

I started to party hard, until life became one big feast. I was also chasing girls, but unlike most of my friends I was unable to settle down in a relationship. I guess there was just too much variety, and I played the field.

Harold Becker threw the best parties at his house in La Lucia and it was at one of his famous parties that I had arranged to meet up with Nicky Westhof. Garry had introduced us previously at her parents' flat. She thought I was crazy and I thought she was really hot. For the first time I was interested in a girl for more than her looks. We were seriously attracted to each other, and when we lay on the couch during the party, kissed and held each other so close that we could feel each other's hearts beating, our souls danced. She whispered in my ear: 'I wish we could go somewhere private.'

I was falling in love for the first time.

Then I fucked it up. I lied to her when she asked me where I lived. She said nothing at the time, but that Monday at school Oscar Dike gave me the message that it was over. I was too proud to go back to her to try to make up. It hurt like hell but I wasn't prepared to do or say anything. I pushed all my feelings of love and sorrow deep down to the bottom of my heart and buried her there. I would think of her from time to time, wondering what had happened to her.

I became cynical and sceptical of love and romance. I became a hunter of girls. I was out to score as much as I could with them, without feeling for them. 'Love is something that you feel between your legs' became my favourite saying. It was the late 1970s, before the AIDS epidemic. It was the wild and wicked time of free love and sex and easy takings.

I finally just scraped through my final, final year of school. On 8 December 1979 I was sworn in as a student member of the South African Police at Durban North police station by my sister the super-cop, who had arrested me a few years earlier.

I had to work at the police station until 2 January 1980, when I would leave by train for training at the college in Pretoria.

As student constable I was posted as a station guard. This is crazy, I thought. It was 1 a.m. and I was lying on my back outside the Durban North police station, looking at the stars. They had given me an automatic assault rifle loaded with live ammunition to guard the station without showing me how to use it, although I had a good idea, given my interest in guns and my brother Neil's shooting lessons.

In the charge office was the register labelled 'Cardboard Gang' with my name in it. In five years I had gone from criminal to cool guy to cop.

It's a strange world.

3

The road to hell

It was 5 a.m. on a day late in August 1981 and we were lined up on the runway of Waterkloof airbase, Pretoria, to board a C-130 Hercules transporter plane that was going to take us to Ondangwa in northern South West Africa. Dressed in our camouflage uniforms, with the C-130 preparing for take-off, we looked pretty impressive.

I had bribed Sergeant 'Norch' Nortjé at headquarters (HQ) for this. He was the member at divisional HQ who had the power to decide who could go for counter-insurgency (COIN) training, and then for border duty. I had wanted to go for both, but Brigadier Mouton at the Durban police station had instructed that I could not go. Karools, as we called him behind his back, wanted me to play rugby for the police team. But I knew Sergeant Nortjé, and I knew why he had once fallen from the fifth floor of our barracks, so I gave him two bottles of whisky, which persuaded him to send me for COIN training. Another two bottles had bought me three months of COIN border duty somewhere between Angola and South West Africa. It was going to be the real deal and I was hoping to see some action. Three months from now I could be on my way home and able to say, 'Yes, I had a bit of action.'

'After take-off we'll climb to 30 000 feet to avoid detection, as we'll be flying over Botswana,' said Rob Mitchell, my brother Neil's friend. 'It's going to be a five-hour flight.' Rob had already done a couple of tours of duty and had become my mentor. Nothing counted more than experience in this game.

Rob was a few years older than me, shorter, broadly built, a bit overweight and had brush-cut blond hair.

The C-130 hurtled down the runway, gathered speed and was up in the air, faster than any 737 or 747 in which I had ever taken off.

We were sitting on nylon sling seats in rows parallel to the sides of the craft. The noise from the engines made it impossible to talk. We sat in darkness, without talking, in the belly of the beast.

Rob and Lorenzo Gianni sat next to me. We were the only three Durbanites and were bound to be given a tough time.

English-speakers were a very small minority in the armed forces, especially in the police. We were treated like shit, insulted and fucked around. They called us soutpiele, rooinekke and 'The English'. I felt their hatred towards me, the way a black person must have felt it too. Because we came from Durban, they believed we were hippies or dope-smoking surfing types. I was none of these.

There was the incident when we did a night shoot during my COIN training at Maloeskop, for instance.

'You will never be able to defend your country,' Sergeant Du Plessis, an instructor, screamed as he hit me with the butt of my rifle until I felt my ribs crack.

'You're a fucking useless soutpiel, and you shouldn't be here!' he shouted. 'Soutpiel', meaning 'salt cock', is a derogatory term describing English-speaking white male South Africans. It meant that you had one foot in South Africa and the other in England, with your cock becoming salty from the ocean between the countries. It implied that you were not a loyal or true South African.

When I had cleaned my rifle before the shoot, I had forgotten to close and set the gas plug. The sergeant lost his temper, lost control and got stuck into me. I was more embarrassed for the wives and children of the instructors who had come to watch our night shoot than I was worried about my own pain and embarrassment.

I came close to shooting the sergeant when he threw my rifle back at me. I too have a breaking point and that day I nearly reached it. I was tempted to stick the barrel in his face and pull the trigger. Only the fact that the women and children were watching stopped me.

This soutpiel and useless Englishman still made the 15-kilometre hike with full kit back to base that night. This soutpiel and useless Englishman refused to press criminal charges against Sergeant Du Plessis, although our commanding officer tried to get me to sign a sworn statement.

This useless Englishman and soutpiel, with three fractured ribs, tickbite fever and three days to go till the end of the course, refused to quit. I finished the course and stayed on for a mortar course.

After that I looked Sergeant Du Plessis in the eye and thought, one day you and I might meet again and it will be under different circumstances.

Now this useless Englishman and soutpiel was sitting in a C-130 on his way to the Border. Not that I wanted to fight for God and country – fuck all that. Some adventure and a bit of action was all I was looking for.

The pitch of the plane's engines changed slightly and brought me back to the present. We were making a gradual descent.

Suddenly the left wing of the C-130 dipped, and we started a fast downward spiral.

We're going to crash, I thought. What the fuck is going on? Is this the end?

I was being sucked down into my seat as we went down. I couldn't lift my hand up, and I could feel my cheeks being pulled down by the G-force.

Suddenly, at about 200 metres, the C-130 levelled out and landed in an instant.

Fuck, these pilots are damned good, I thought.

The plane had stopped and I heard the whine of an electric motor driving the hydraulics to open the rear cargo door. Bright white sunlight streamed in.

After five hours in the darkened plane, the intense sunlight was harsh on my eyes, but I could see two Alouette gunship-helicopters still circling. They were providing air cover for the C-130 to land at Ondangwa airbase.

We headed west in Casspirs down the tar road on our way to Kwambi for a week's refresher course. The countryside was like nothing I had ever seen. It was extremely dry. The place hadn't seen a drop of rain in years – it was in the grip of a severe drought. Ovamboland was completely flat. There was not a mountain in sight, nor even a hill. Military and civilian vehicles were racing up and down the road. The most popular Ovambo civilian vehicle was still the old Ford F-series, a four-wheel-drive pick-up and the most sold car model in the world.

The civilians travelled at about 60 kilometres per hour, their old and dilapidated trucks carrying up to 20 Ovambos on the back, plus goats and chickens and the occasional cow. The military vehicles travelled at full speed at about 90 to 120 kilometres per hour. There were no fences next to the road and cattle, goats, donkeys and pigs just strayed across it, often in front of oncoming traffic. This was the road to hell.

We passed kraal complexes with typical Ovambo homes made of tree branches, straw and other natural material; we passed shacks made of corrugated iron and many Cuca shops. Cuca was a brand of Portuguese–Angolan beer and 'Cuca shop' generally referred to any shop, pub, bar, spaza or shebeen. Some of them were brightly coloured and had elaborate names.

The scenes flashing by made me think that I was suddenly in some kind of Vietnam war movie. All we needed was some psychedelic rock music like Pink Floyd.

'So why did they send you here?' someone in the Casspir asked me.

'They didn't send me,' I replied. 'I wanted to come; it cost me two bottles of whisky to get here.'

'What the fuck would you want to come here for?' He was curious.

'So that I could travel to far-off interesting countries, meet the locals, learn their language and their culture … and kill them!' It was a line from some war movie I'd seen.

Rob and Lorenzo packed up laughing while the guy got pissed off with me.

'Fucking soutpiele. You Englishmen are all the same,' he muttered, and went into a sulk.

'Hey, Rob, are we gonna kill some gooks, man? I just wanna kill some gooks. I really have to kill a gook or I can't go back home.' Now I was pissing him off even more.

We turned off the main road through an army checkpoint and drove through the town of Oshakati, through the south gate and for another 20 kilometres on to Kwambi.

The sunset was so beautiful. As the sun went down, the sky filled with red and orange while the palm trees were silhouetted in black. It looked almost like a tropical beach scene, except the nearest beach was a long way away to the west.

I enjoyed the refresher course at Kwambi. I enjoyed the physical exertion, and the COIN instructors put everything they had into our training.

Sitting on benches under a steel roof, Sergeant Braam was going over the basic workings of a light machine gun (LMG) and some other weapons when suddenly he was interrupted by Lieutenant Nel, who had come to give us a political lecture about SWAPO.

The little I understood about SWAPO was that it was founded in 1960 by, among others, Herman Toivo ya Toivo, regarded as the father of the Namibian independence struggle, and Sam Nujoma, who was the first SWAPO president and who led the organisation while Toivo ya Toivo was in prison in South Africa after he had been convicted of terrorism. Toivo ya Toivo served 16 years, some of them on Robben Island with Nelson Mandela.

By 1962 SWAPO had become the dominant nationalist organisation of the South West African people. It used guerrilla tactics against the South African forces and the first major clash, on 26 April 1966, can be regarded as the beginning of the so-called bush war, though war as such was never declared in a conventional sense. In 1972 the UN General Assembly declared SWAPO the sole representative of the Namibian people, but that was not accepted by South Africa and the war was still going on while we were there in the early eighties.

SWAPO's military wing, PLAN, was established in 1966 and consisted of various detachments. Alpha, Bravo, Charlie and Delta were the ordinary foot soldiers. There were the special forces: air, navy, ground force and special, special forces, among them the unit specialising in deep penetration called Typhoon. There were political commissars, radio operators and medics. SWAPO was eventually supported militarily by the Soviet Union and Cuba, and received financial support from various European countries. A SWAPO group would have a commander, who usually carried a side arm, a Soviet Makarov or Tokarev, as well as some other weapon.

'We've infiltrated them,' Lieutenant Nel said. 'We've got people on the inside, even in SWAPO's high command.'

We were often told that the person who had addressed the United Nations as a spokesperson for SWAPO was a South African spy, Major Craig Williamson. Although the story sounded good at the time and made me feel proud, I now know better. I have learnt about those infiltrators and spies in SWAPO, the ANC and the PAC.

Ten years later I had the displeasure of meeting Major Craig Williamson. He and Captain Zach Edwards from the security branch in Port Elizabeth paid me a visit at my home in Plettenberg Bay and sat in my lounge. What they were trying to accomplish I never found out, because I promptly showed both of them to my front door.

On the internet you can clearly see what kind of a son of a bitch Major Williamson really was. His activities as a spy began in 1972 and he infiltrated various liberation movements until his cover was blown in 1980. His name was mentioned in connection with some assassinations, and at the Truth and Reconciliation Commission he got amnesty for the murders of

Ruth First in Mozambique and Katryn and Jeanette Schoon in Angola.

This is Major Williamson's famous quotation: 'I respect a person who is willing to die for his country, but I admire a person who is prepared to kill for his country.'

After our refresher course our company had to be split into three groups in order to relieve three bases, Ohangwena, Ongha and Okatopi. Rob, Lorenzo and I hoped that we would stay together.

'Right, divide yourselves into three groups,' the instructor shouted, and without much fuss Rob, Lorenzo and I were in the same group and on our way to relieve Ongha.

At Ondangwa (nearly every place name in Ovamboland starts with an 'O') we turned north onto a dirt road which, if we had followed it to the end, would have taken us to the Santa Clara border post and into Angola.

We had to drive through a hell of a dust cloud that the Casspirs ahead of us were throwing up. Everything was getting coated with dust, dirt and sand. Even breathing became difficult.

About 20 kilometres up the road we turned off to the west and into our base camp, Golf 7, at Ongha.

Rob, Lorenzo and I settled in to a three-man tent in the south-eastern corner of the base. We met the previous occupants, but they disappeared in such a flash that we didn't get a chance to get any information out of them. They were going home and they were in a hurry.

A meeting was called that first night and it started with prayers. That really pissed Rob and me off. Who the fuck were they to try to force their religion on us?

We soon learnt that our commanding officer, Captain Van der Merwe, was intent on avoiding action and was going to hide in his tent for the next three months. He did not once come on patrol with us. He was also going to try to make sure that we too wouldn't see any action.

One of our duties was to guard Echo Tower. It was a water tower and reservoir on the water pipeline that ran past our base from Ondangwa to Alpha Tower in the north. We took turns to guard it in groups, made up of two white and 10 black base members for a week at a time.

Rob and I soon volunteered to guard the tower, just to get away from the base and all its politics. We were dropped off one morning by some of our base colleagues and the first thing we did was to climb up the tower and look out over the terrain. It was flat as far as we could see, with dry, dead vegetation. The sand was brilliantly white, soft and powdery.

From up there we could see the convoys coming out of Angola and travelling down the road towards Ondangwa. Day and night the convoys drove past. Soviet trucks full of Soviet military hardware, Cuban trucks laden with Soviet hardware. Soviet tanks, Cuban equipment, Soviet equipment, guns, cannon – all the hardware of war was moving past in a huge cloud of dust.

Something was happening in Angola. There must be fighting and we must be fucking them up, we thought, judging by the amount of equipment that had been captured.

In fact, Operation Protea in Angola was drawing to a close. About 5 000 South African soldiers were deployed in Angola during the operation, which lasted from 23 August to 4 September 1981, and its purpose was to fuck up the SWAPO command and training centre at Xangongo and its bases at Xangongo and Ongiva.

The destruction of the two bases would ruin SWAPO's ability

to perform operations on the north-western front and make them realise that they were no longer safe in southern Angola. Operation Protea also proved that the Soviets were involved with SWAPO and enabled the South African forces to seize thousands of tons of military hardware worth over 200 million US dollars, as well as vast quantities of small arms and ammunition. This included tanks, anti-aircraft guns, armoured vehicles, trucks and other logistical vehicles. No less than 1 000 members of SWAPO and FAPLA, the People's Armed Forces for the Liberation of Angola, were killed during the operation, while 38 prisoners were captured, including 10 SWAPO members. South Africa lost only 10 men.

The fact that SWAPO had acquired tanks and armoured personnel carriers indicated that the organisation was going to try to change its tactics from guerrilla to conventional warfare in South West Africa.

Operation Protea, which caused major setbacks for SWAPO, was quickly followed by Operation Daisy.

'Hey, Rob! What if we get attacked here, I mean, what if SWAPO comes?' I asked. 'We're sleeping here in the pump house while the Ovambos are sleeping up on top of the reservoir. Anyone could walk through the gate. Shouldn't we be sleeping up there with the Ovambos?'

'Yes, we're taking a chance sleeping here like this,' he replied, 'but I'm not sleeping up there with the Ovambos.'

I thought it wise not to ask why not.

Rob changed the subject. 'Sapper Van der Mescht was captured from one of these towers.'

'Wasn't he branded a traitor after he was captured? Didn't he cooperate with them and even work in an ops room in Lubanga and didn't he even take an Angolan wife?'

But Rob didn't seem interested in the unproven gossip about Johan van der Mescht, who had been captured by SWAPO three and a half years previously and at the time was still being held prisoner.

'Fuck, if I was captured, I'd cooperate. I would tell them everything,' I said.

'They would probably let you go because you would talk them to death. Now let me go to sleep.' Rob was being nasty.

Our week guarding the water tower turned out to be uneventful, apart from observing the steady stream of military hardware flowing out of Angola and past us.

After a week of boredom, we were relieved. Back at the base, life went on with us doing the occasional patrol and one or two follow-ups of suspected enemy tracks, but nothing came of those.

We were not allowed to overnight in the bush. This was a strict order from the top, from my namesake, Colonel Du Rand. So no matter what, we had to return to base every day. This order defied any logic.

One night Lorenzo and I were fast asleep and Rob was on guard duty at the bunker at the entrance to our base when an explosion followed by a burst of machine gunfire woke me. It was 1 a.m.

I heard the captain running through the base shouting, 'Contact, contact, contact!' while our radio operator – our pronto – was shouting, 'I'm coming, Captain, I'm coming!'

Now what did Rob say? 'If the bullets start flying, if our base gets attacked, hit the deck below the level of the sandbags around our tent.' But the bullets weren't flying and I was the mortar man. I needed to get to the mortar pit.

Lorenzo was beside me and handed me the first mortar bomb.

I was preparing to drop it down the tube and let rip into the night, but I hesitated because nothing was happening.

The captain came running. He shouted, 'Fire! Fire the mortars!' He was stressed and panicking.

'Yes,' I said, 'let me flatten the local kraals.'

'No, hold your fire,' he stammered. 'We don't want to kill civilians.'

No one knew what the fuck was going on.

Then the captain said, 'Boys, we need to sleep in the bunkers tonight; we could be revved at any moment.'

The next morning all was revealed. Sergeant De Villiers, our base's buddy master – the member in charge of the Ovambo special constables – had assaulted one of the special constables, who got totally pissed off and decided to fire a rifle grenade at the base in the middle of the night. Rob had retaliated with a burst of machine gunfire.

The special constable was arrested and shipped off to the training base at Ondangwa to be dealt with.

Never get physical with an Ovambo. They take it very personally and they never forgive or forget. That was the lesson I learnt.

The joke for the duration of our camp was that every time the pronto walked past, one of us would shout, 'I'm coming, Captain, I'm coming.'

One evening I made my way to the ops room in the middle of our base to do the midnight shift.

It was very quiet, apart from the radio hissing and crackling away. There wasn't much to do on the midnight shift, except to try to stay awake. I was paging through the occurrence book when a pretty little grey cat padded into the room. She was mewing and seemed in distress. I thought she was hungry, but she refused the bully beef and milk I offered her on a plate.

It seemed as if she were trying to tell me something. I noticed that her stomach was very swollen and realised that she was about to give birth and was asking for help.

Now I had something to do until sunrise. I found an old empty box. It was warm, so I took my jersey off and lined the bottom of the box with it. I put the box in a dark corner and placed the cat in it. She settled down immediately and I was tempted to watch and help, but decided to give her space and let nature take its course.

By 2 a.m. the first faint mewing came from the box and two hours later I went to have a look at the mother cleaning and suckling her new babies. I felt like a proud new father.

A few days later, when we returned from a patrol, I was eager to check on my kittens and their mother. I rushed to the ops room, but they weren't there.

'Where are they?' I asked the pronto, but he didn't answer.

Then someone told me with a smile: 'We drowned them in a bucket of water. There are too many cats on this base, so we decided to get rid of them.'

I was upset, sad and angry, but said nothing – they might have seen my feelings as a sign of weakness.

By this stage I was running out of money and didn't want to borrow from Rob or Lorenzo, so my next trick was to teach the Dutchmen how to gamble. Blackjack and poker games made me enough money for the rest of our stay at Ongha, but some of the guys refused to join in for religious reasons.

Food became a problem. Members were complaining about our Ovambo cook and the food he was preparing. At a meeting it was decided to fire him and to take turns to do the cooking ourselves.

'You soutpiele from Durban, you should know how to make curry,' some of the members said.

Yippee, I thought, now I'll teach them a lesson.

Rob was going to Ondangwa and Oshakati the following day to fetch supplies, so he could get some of the ingredients I needed: hot curry powder, chillies, peri-peri powder and any other hot spices he could find.

Rob came back with some news: Operation Protea was over and Operation Daisy was under way. He had been at Ondangwa airbase and had witnessed a campaign-opening ceremony. One of our Mirage fighter planes, flown by Captain Johan Rankin, had shot down an enemy MiG fighter plane over Angola. Rob had been there when the captain had told his story.

Rob also had a present for me: hot curry powder and chilli powder. That night I made a good Durban lamb curry for the entire base. That was the last time I was asked to cook, and soon our Ovambo cook was rehired.

A pair of cocky Dutchmen from Ohangwena Golf 6 up the road from us waltzed in on their way home, just looking for shit.

'Frans Conradie says you guys are useless,' one of them said. 'He's been shooting terrs right here near your base. Captain Malherbe wants to go on a joint ops, your base and ours, but we don't think you guys are up to it.'

'How many kills have you guys got?' I asked. 'How many contacts have you had?'

'Well, none, actually.'

I left it at that. I had made my point.

Captain Malherbe was self-centred and arrogant, with an

ego the size of Ovamboland. He was the commanding officer of Ohangwena Golf 6. During our refresher course at Kwambi he had had a fight with the COIN instructors because there had been no hot water – the geyser had broken. He had tried to fix it himself but he'd hurt his back, then lain on his bed for the rest of the course, sulking. Now we were going to team up with him and his guys for a joint ops.

We drove out of our base under cover of darkness. Driving onto the road that connected our base to the main road was always a tense moment. It was the ideal place for the enemy to plant a landmine but we had been assured that in the event of a Casspir detonating a landmine the occupants would normally survive unhurt. The Casspir could handle it.

We passed the place where a guy had been blown up the previous year.

I had seen the 'before and after' photographs during training at Maloeskop. SWAPO had rigged and booby-trapped an 82-mm Soviet mortar bomb and then left it just outside the base.

Two of the guys from the base found it. One of them picked it up and posed while the other took a picture. The guy holding the bomb noticed that the nose cone was skew. As he straightened it for the next photograph, it detonated in his hands. The photographs taken of him posing with the bomb and then after it had blown up became valuable training tools.

The sun wasn't up when we arrived at Ohangwena, and they weren't ready. Eventually we were called for a briefing in their ops room.

'We'll deploy as one group here to the south-east and then we'll split up,' Captain Malherbe explained. 'If either of us pick up spoor, we'll join up and together carry on with a follow-up.

Intelligence reports indicate that this area is a hot spot and a main infiltration route for SWAPO.'

Intelligence, what intelligence? He's just after glory, I thought. He just needs to prove a point.

The area to which we deployed was full of dense forest that was almost impenetrable. Moving through the vegetation became a nightmare and soon our Casspirs were overheating and breaking down.

At 1 p.m. we stopped for a break, parking in the shade of a big tree. It was hot, about 45 °C. Millions of tiny gnats were flying around, getting into everything – our ears, eyes, hair and food. I was trying to eat a tin of sweetcorn and a tin of bully beef, but I had to throw them away as they quickly became full of insects. My eyes wandered across to the waiting Casspirs. The scene was impressive: the Casspirs with the mounted machine guns, the men in their camouflage uniforms and all the military equipment.

I picked up a rifle grenade. 'Hey, Rob, Lorenzo, I wish I had some margarine.'

'What for?' they asked.

'I could make a brilliant advert. We're sitting here like this and I smear some margarine on this rifle grenade and take a bite out of it. Then I say, "This margarine makes anything taste really good."'

'You're mad,' Rob said.

'They've found spoor!' someone shouted from another Casspir. 'Come, let's join them.'

The follow-up was going fast. The Ovambos were tracking at great speed and there was talk of calling in some gunships for air support.

I had been on the ground running with the trackers. I didn't know anything about tracking, but being with them on the ground gave them a lot of moral support and showed them that we were not scared to be out in the open with them.

'Fuck, it's hot in here!' Lorenzo exclaimed when he got out of the gunner's seat to replace me on the ground. I jumped into the gunner's seat. I grabbed the two handles coming down from the turret mounted above me and swung the turret left and right, up and down, just to check it.

'Do you know how to operate that?' Sergeant Diff asked while he drove through the dense bush.

'Yes, is it loaded?' I asked.

Before he could reply, a thick branch caught the turret on the outside and with the Casspir moving forward, it spun around. The left handle flew back into my shoulder, pinning me back against my seat. The blow was so hard that I was temporarily paralysed.

Eventually I was able to get the hell out of the gunner's seat and into the back of the Casspir to try to recover.

The group of five now knew that we were chasing them. They scattered in different directions – or bombshelled, as we used to say – and we were left with one set of spoor, or tracks, which started to anti-track. The enemy used various anti-tracking techniques. They would cut the tread off their boots so that the sole was smooth and flat. They would wear civilian shoes, go barefoot, use branches with leaves to dust their tracks behind them or carefully select harder and better terrain to walk on.

Eventually we developed techniques to anti-anti-track, and this became one of my specialities.

After a while the Ovambos lost the spoor and it was over. We had lost this one. It was late and it was time to return to base.

'Hey, Rob, who is Koevoet?' I asked one night as we were going to sleep. 'Everyone says they kill more of the enemy than anyone else.'

'They are the best, mostly policemen like us, but they also come from other walks of life,' Rob explained. 'Some of them are from COIN, others are former members of UNITA, SWAPO, the FNLA, the Selous Scouts and the army. They're based in Oshakati and have a base at Opuwo and another at Rundu.'

'So can anyone join them?'

'No. You have to be good and they are very selective.'

Suddenly I had an idea. 'Why don't we try and join them? I've got one year left before the end of my national service, so let's join Koevoet for a year and then go back home.'

'Yes,' Rob replied, 'and after a year we can get a vehicle and drive back to Durban.' He said Durban was about 3 000 kilometres away.

'What about you, Lorenzo? Are you going to join Koevoet with Rob and me?'

'No, I want to get back to my girlfriend.'

Then Rob got grumpy. 'Now will you guys shut up and go to sleep?'

A few days later we took our Casspirs to the police garage at Ondangwa for repairs and servicing. At the garage I met some guys from Koevoet.

'Are you guys from Koevoet?' I nervously asked one of them in Afrikaans.

He said something in English to his friend and then turned to me.

'Yes, why?' he asked me in Afrikaans.

'You are English-speaking, aren't you?' I asked in English.

'Yes, so what? There are lots of English-speaking guys in Koevoet.'

I wanted to know how one could join Koevoet.

'Just go to the office in Oshakati and see Captain Botha and the brigadier,' he replied before he left with his colleagues.

One of our Casspirs could not be fixed and had to be left at the garage for a few days. When some of our guys went back to fetch it, it had gone missing. A few days later it was found in Oshakati. It was presumed that Koevoet had stolen and then abandoned it.

We went to see our captain and I didn't beat around the bush. 'Captain, Rob and I want to go with the guys who are going to fetch our Casspir from Oshakati, because we want to join Koevoet.'

He almost exploded. 'You guys are mad! They are a bunch of barbarians. Savages and criminals. They stole our Casspir and now you want to join them!' He calmed down a bit and then said, 'Look, I can't stop you, but I strongly advise you against it.'

So Rob and I went along to Oshakati. We were dropped at the house that served as the Koevoet headquarters and were told that we would be fetched later. Nervously we entered and were met by Captain Potgieter. I built up some courage, cleared my throat and blurted out, 'Captain, we would like to join Koevoet.'

He just looked at us for a moment, and then said, 'Go and see Captain Botha in the office at the back of the house.'

'May we enter?' Rob asked when we reached Captain Botha's office.

'Yes, come inside.'

Rob and I came to attention and gave the captain the smartest salute possible.

He looked up and said, 'No, don't do that. Here we don't have time for formalities. Take a seat.'

Captain Botha was short, round and plump, with a nose like an eagle. He was friendly and relaxed – hardly my idea of a ruthless bush fighter. He was in fact the admin man, but I soon learnt that he was very intelligent. I got straight to the point. 'We want to join Koevoet.'

'Well, we sure need more good men, but there's a heap of paperwork to get through.' He shuffled some papers on his desk, then said, 'You'll be joining the security branch, so they'll do a comprehensive security check on you. The whole process could take up to three months. Remember that you are applying for a transfer to security branch headquarters in Pretoria.'

I wondered about Koevoet, but he answered my question before I could ask.

'Koevoet does not exist – not officially, anyway – so that's why everything we say and do is top secret.'

He hauled out two folders that were almost as thick as Bibles. 'Arn, you will be number 0034 and you, Rob, 0035. The 34th and 35th permanent members of Special Ops (K) Koevoet.'

I didn't question it, but I found it hard to believe that I was only the 35th member. After all, Koevoet had about 20 teams with three or four white members each, some permanent, some temporary. There were many more Ovambo members.

About two and a half hours later we had worked through all the paperwork. Captain Botha now knew everything that he thought he needed to know about us. We were sworn to secrecy. I nevertheless phoned my parents later and told them that I was becoming secret agent 0034. I didn't tell them about Koevoet, though.

It was time to be interviewed by Brigadier Hannes Dreyer, commanding officer of Special Ops (K) Koevoet, and I was nervous.

Passing through the ops room we bumped into Captain Potgieter.

'Just tell him you want to kill kaffirs,' he grinned. Now I was even more nervous.

The brigadier was a tall slender man and I guessed him to be about 50 years old. He had hawk-like features and a deep soothing voice.

Our interview lasted roughly 10 minutes, with questions mostly about where we came from and what our parents did. Luckily I had a brother and sister in the SAP. The fact that my sister was posted at security headquarters in Durban would later prove to be a great help.

With our interview over, we were back in the hands of Captain Botha, who told us that we were finished, we must go back to base and when our camp at Ongha was over, we were to return to Durban and wait for our transfers to be approved.

Outside, the guys from Ongha were waiting with our Casspir and we returned to the base.

Late one afternoon we received a desperate call from Ohangwena Golf 6 for assistance. They had been in a contact with SWAPO, had shot three enemy fighters and needed help.

By the time we arrived at Ohangwena, they had already made it back to base. I was disappointed, angry and envious that they had finally achieved success and we had not, but soon my feelings changed to utter disgust.

A scene of gory jubilation met my eyes. Two of their Casspirs were parked outside the base. The dead bodies of the enemy were tied to the spare wheels on the sides of their Casspirs. The mangled, mutilated bodies had been shot to shit, and those guys were celebrating.

The beer was flowing and some of their guys were over-keen to relate the events of the contact.

'The last one was hiding behind an anthill during the contact,' one told us. 'Every now and then he jumped out and put his hands in the air to surrender, but as we shot at him he would jump back behind the anthill to hide. Finally Koos drove over him, smashing him and the anthill at the same time. Fuck, it was amazing.'

When we drove off, my stomach churned as I thought about what I had just witnessed. This was disgusting behaviour. Didn't those wankers have any respect for the dead? They killed them, sure, and that's right, that's war, or whatever it is that we were supposed to be doing. But I was shocked that they were so proud of killing an enemy who was trying to surrender.

Soon after that, with just two weeks to go, I got one last chance to see some action.

The security police from Oshakati requested some assistance with investigating SWAPO activities in the far east of Ovamboland. They had only one Casspir at their disposal and requested one of ours. At the same time they invited some of us to come along for the ride.

Captain Van der Merwe was only too happy to get rid of one of our Casspirs and some of us – as long as the base did not have Casspirs, there was no way of doing any patrols. By this stage we were openly ridiculing the captain and calling him a coward.

Lorenzo and I volunteered to assist the security police immediately, expecting Rob to do so as well.

'No, you guys go ahead. I'm tired and I don't feel like it,' he said.

I was a little disappointed, but soon Lorenzo and I had joined the Oshakati security branch on a fact-finding and information-gathering mission to the east. I was about to learn what SWAPO was really all about.

We drove up the road past Etale army base and, before reaching Ohangwena, we turned right onto Oom Willie se Pad, heading east.

The first night we spent at Eenhana army base and the next morning we set out further east along Chandelier Road. Eventually we turned south off the road and came to a kraal, where our first investigation was to take place.

Lieutenant Smith was in charge. After a lengthy formal introduction to the headman, he and an Ovambo, Warrant Officer David Lomba, sat down in the shade of a big tree. They talked and talked with the headman while Lieutenant Smith was writing away. An hour passed, two hours passed, three hours passed.

What the fuck were they doing? Talking and writing all day while we sat doing nothing. Boredom was setting in and I was getting frustrated.

Eventually we were finished and on our way. Warrant Officer Lomba was sitting opposite me in the Casspir. I found it easy to make friends with the Ovambo people. If I showed a little interest in them and treated them with respect, they responded well.

'What was that all about?' I asked the warrant officer.

He gave me a full summary of what had happened at the kraal three months before. Six SWAPO PLAN fighters had come to the kraal, preaching the word of liberation, communism, final victory and all the propaganda that they had been taught during their training in the SWAPO bases in Angola, as well as demanding help and cooperation from the chief. The chief had refused and had then promptly been executed by the six, in front of the entire village.

Our journey of investigation continued. Now that I knew what was going on I was taking an interest. I learnt that here, among the Kwanyama people of the far east, there was little sympathy for SWAPO, which did not get all the support from the locals it expected. As a result SWAPO met any resistance by systematically executing anyone with whom it was not happy.

For the next week we travelled from kraal to kraal, taking eyewitness statements from countless people who had witnessed SWAPO murders, executions and abductions.

The most difficult statements to obtain were from the teachers at schools, where SWAPO had abducted young boys between the ages of 14 and 18 at gunpoint and marched them to the training bases deep in Angola. The parents of these boys were also unwilling to talk for fear of what might happen to their children if they did.

Every young Ovambo had a dream of receiving an education. One of SWAPO's tricks was to make big promises of education to those who would accompany them. Once they had arrived at the bases in Angola, the boys were told another story: first the liberation of Namibia and then education. Trapped in the training bases, the children would be isolated from the outside world and would go through intensive indoctrination and military training, after which they would be sent back to fight.

Lieutenant Smith had given us strict instructions: this was a fact-finding mission; we were not on this mission to fight. Even if we found enemy spoor, we were to leave it and continue with the job we were meant to do. If we were to bump into the enemy by chance, that would be another story.

Finally we reached Okongo, which was the easternmost point

of the Ovambo area. Lieutenant Smith was happy with the mission. He was satisfied that he had obtained enough evidence to report back to head office and that it could be used as ammunition in the UN debates on the Namibian situation.

Although the week had been quite boring for me, it had also been an eye-opener. I knew now what SWAPO got up to and I was beginning to understand some of the complexities of this conflict.

'Whoa!'

We had come to a sudden halt in the middle of thick vegetation. We were about 20 kilometres west of Okongo and 20 kilometres south of the Angolan border.

There were six sets of spoor, definitely SWAPO enemy spoor, heading north. We had two Casspirs, twenty men and we were going to give chase.

Some of our trackers were on the ground and were flanked by our two Casspirs. The spoor was easy and we moved at great speed.

They heard us coming and they knew we were chasing them. From reading the spoor our trackers could tell what their plan was. They bombshelled, splitting up into three groups of two men each, and decided to give it all they had. They knew they would be safe once they reached the border – they knew that we were under strict instructions not to cross the Angolan border under any circumstances. They were going to run like hell for it.

Our trackers chose a pair of them to chase and we followed their spoor. Would we be able catch up with them before they reached the border, or would they make it?

Gunship-helicopters joined us from Eenhana to give us air support and possibly get a visual on the enemy while they circled ahead of us.

One of our trackers scrambled into the back of our Casspir to be relieved by another. He was totally out of breath and exhausted. 'Any moment now!' he gasped. 'We are right behind them; we've got them – they won't make the border.'

The tension and excitement mounted. I stood up, looking ahead out of the Casspir with my R1 rifle ready.

At any minute the first shot would ring out and finally I would have my first contact. A gunship passed overhead and the duk-a-duk-a-duk of the rotors boosted my confidence.

The border was about four kilometres away, but the enemy wouldn't have the stamina to keep it up. We only had about one hour of sunlight left, but that was all we needed.

The Casspir rocked, rolled and roared as it raced forward. The trackers were running at full speed, putting everything into it, and we were ready for the kill.

Fuck, what now? We stopped. Syringes. Two used syringes had been discarded next to the spoor. Adrenalin. They had injected themselves with adrenalin!

We had lost and they lived.

The gunships withdrew, flying off east into a beautiful sunset, back to Eenhana.

We stopped at the border. So that's Angola. On the other side of this simple dirt track and an almost non-existent barbed-wire fence was another country.

It was over. Disappointed, I looked at Lorenzo and I saw that he too was disappointed.

'We should have brought our passports, then we could have gone after them,' I said, and managed to get a laugh out of everyone.

Okongo was a 30-kilometre drive away and it was getting dark. We headed for Okongo and were lucky to find a dirt road, which we followed down to the army base. The lieutenant had cleared it with the army to let us slip in under cover of darkness to spend the night.

The next day would be a long haul back to Ongha and in five days' time we were going home.

The C-130 took off from Ondangwa airbase and soon we were flying high over Botswana at about 30 000 feet in relative darkness.

I'll be back, I thought.

I knew I'd be back one day.

4

Forbidden fruit

Three months had passed since I sat in that office in the converted house in Oshakati with Captain Botha. I hardly remembered that I had applied to join Koevoet, and since I had returned from my three-month counter-insurgency border duty at Ongha in northern Namibia, life had returned to its boring old self in boring old Durban.

Well, not always that boring …

I was posted to the magistrate's court, where I became Court B's orderly. Court procedure fascinated me. I listened to so many trials that I began to think that I would be able to prosecute or defend in a case. I knew every lawyer's trick.

One of the lawyers, old man Louis Podbielski, said it was not the lawyer's knowledge of the law that made him a good lawyer, but a good deal of common sense and masterful control of the English language. Podbielski was old and wise and was reputed never to have lost a case. He stimulated my interest in the legal profession, but I was not going to become a lawyer.

Not even Magistrate Gus Brits could change my mind. He was outraged when I told him about my plans to go and fight.

'Don't become cannon fodder,' he said. 'Stay and study law. You have the potential to become a fine criminal lawyer.'

But it wasn't going to happen. My fate lay somewhere else.

I liked the magistrate, though. He made it tough for me in the beginning, but we got to the stage where he would even ask my opinion on what I thought the outcome of a trial would be – like the trial of the old professor who was accused of shoplifting.

Technically the professor was guilty. He had put a bottle of food colouring in his pocket and left the supermarket without paying for it. This was all the state needed to prove its case. The prosecutor could have let the case slide, but no, he wanted a conviction. It was his job. I could see that the case was heading for a guilty judgment, but I thought that in this instance one should just do the right thing and let the old man go free. The absent-minded professor had probably put the bottle of food colouring in his pocket to prevent it from falling through the holes of the supermarket trolley and had forgotten to pay for it at the till. It could have happened to anyone.

So, when I went down to Magistrate Brits's chambers to tell him that the court was ready for him, I was pleased when he asked my opinion on the case and what I thought the outcome should be. I told him that I believed the professor had made a simple mistake with dire consequences.

'He has no previous convictions,' I added. This information was something I was not allowed to tell the magistrate – it could be revealed only on sentencing – so technically I was defeating the course of justice. But what the fuck – I wasn't supposed to be discussing the case with him anyway.

Later that afternoon I was relieved to hear Gus Brits pronounce the professor not guilty. The old man was free.

After the verdict, with my court in recess, I stood outside in the great hall of justice watching … and waiting.

Lawyers and prosecutors, some wearing their black robes, passed. And so did the accused and the accusers. The guilty and the innocent. The witnesses and the witnessed. Interpreters and court staff. Everyone drawn here by one common cause: justice.

The great symbol of justice, old-fashioned scales, was engraved in the wooden panel behind the magistrate's desk in every courtroom, but, at the time, justice in South Africa was a strange animal.

Among a slew of unjust apartheid laws was the ban on mixed marriages, which in 1950 was followed by an amendment to the Immorality Act to ban all sexual relations between whites and people of other race groups, including Indian, coloured and black people. Sex across the colour line became a serious criminal offence.

Police kicked down doors to find and arrest mixed couples that they caught in bed. Bed linen and underwear were used as forensic evidence in court. On conviction, most couples were sentenced to imprisonment, and people of colour generally received harsher sentences than whites.

Here she came. She was alone this time and not chatting and giggling with her friend. We were almost friends by then and it had become a joke: she'd always ask me to show her where the court library was.

'Will you escort me to the library, please,' she said in a perfect English accent, laughter in her eyes.

'It would be a great honour,' I joked back, bowing.

She was beautiful. Her green eyes shone and her chocolate-brown skin glistened. Her long straight black hair flowed down to her lower back. She was sexy, sophisticated, had recently finished her law degree and was doing her articles. What the fuck was she trying to prove? She knew quite well where the library was and she knew that I was immensely attracted to her.

We walked through the great hall of justice, side by side. I felt comfortable with her, but uncomfortable about what anyone watching might think.

'What do you think of Advocate Jacob Meer?' I asked her, making small talk.

'He's a great lawyer,' she replied, 'one of the best.'

He was indeed a great lawyer, but I didn't like his methods. He often settled his cases out of court by getting the complainant to withdraw his or her case at the last moment.

'Why do you always ask me to show you to the library?' I finally asked her.

She was quiet for a while and then said, 'It's the only way I can get to talk to you and, besides, I like having a handsome man in uniform looking after me.'

We walked up the steps to turn right down the passage that would lead us to the library.

'Do you mind if I take your arm?' she said, and did so without waiting for a response. I nearly shat in my pants, but at the same time my body tingled with excitement. Her behaviour had taken me by surprise. I had imagined an Indian girl would be a lot more conservative.

This mutual attraction was something different. It was something dangerous. Our boundaries were set by custom, culture and law. What if we crossed those boundaries?

I opened the library door for her, but this time I did not leave immediately. I followed her in. What now? What the fuck am I doing?

'What books are you looking for?' I asked, although I didn't have a clue where to find a single book. I was just trying to find a reason not to leave. She looked at me without a word.

'I guess I'd better get back to court,' I said.

'Look, here is my number. Phone me.' She handed me a piece of paper and I quickly put it in my tunic pocket. She then turned to the books and I left her to it.

I walked back to my courtroom. I was excited. This was something dark and dangerous. Despite the little warning bell ringing in the back of my head, I was sorely tempted.

In that day and age, how would a white cop and an Indian article clerk ever be able to go on a date? There simply was no way we could be seen together in public. To have a relationship would be a criminal offence.

I thought about it for the rest of the day. The piece of paper in my pocket burnt like a red-hot coal and I felt a sense of guilt, like I was doing something dangerously wrong.

At the end of the day I walked to the barracks where I lived. The piece of paper seemed to have cooled down and I was excited again. I was in the comfort of my own space and I had to decide whether to call her or not.

With her number in my hand I stood at the payphone in the foyer, wrestling with the decision. It was tempting. On the one hand something was urging me on, on the other hand danger lights flickered. Should I, shouldn't I?

Someone walked past and I became nervous.

Finally I crumpled the piece of paper into a ball, threw it into the dustbin and made my way to the non-commissioned officers' (NCO) pub for a drink and a few games of darts with my friends. I knew I shouldn't mention my attraction to this Indian girl to anyone. Never. It was a sealed secret.

Brigadier Mouton was the reason I had been posted to this cushy office job at the Durban magistrate's court after my training at the police college. He was a rugby fanatic and had assumed that I would play rugby for his pride and joy, the Durban police team. But the day I had left school I had vowed I would never play another game of rugby.

Brigadier Mouton was always after my blood and, on occasion, had even sent officers to the barracks to fetch me to play. He had threatened to have me transferred to some remote outpost where I would never see my friends or family. Little did he know that I had bribed Sergeant Nortjé at HQ with two bottles of whisky to send me to remote Ongha.

One morning when I arrived for work, I saw the brigadier sitting in the control room. I thought he looked like a white vampire bat. I knew I had to disappear as quickly as possible, but to do so I had to get past the control room.

'Durand! The brigadier wants to see you. Now!'

I came to attention as smartly as I could and saluted Brigadier Mouton, who was going through a register. He looked up at me while I suppressed a smile. Never act too friendly; they tend to take it as disrespect. Always appear to be serious.

'It looks like I'll never get you to play rugby. I've decided to let you go. Your transfer to Koevoet has been approved. Remember one thing: in the war zone it's the survival of the fittest.'

After another big salute I turned and left for the tearoom, where we court orderlies gathered in the mornings. I was about to collect some prisoners and make my way to Court B when I was told to go and see Warrant Officer Strauss. He was a big, loud man, warm and friendly, and I liked him.

'So you've been transferred to Koevoet,' he said. 'Go to divisional HQ and find out what your orders are.'

'But what about Court B?' I asked.

'No, you need a few days off before you join Koevoet, so go and find out at HQ what you must do.' With that he stood up, shook my hand and said goodbye.

I walked out of the Durban court building for the last time, confused and not really understanding what was happening to my life. At divisional HQ they weren't very helpful. All they knew was what the book said, and the book said nothing about being transferred to Special Ops (K) at Oshakati in northern Namibia. I did get a one-way train ticket from Durban to Pretoria out of them though, and I walked out of there thinking, What the fuck! I've been there before and I'll get there again.

One evening, three days later, I took a drive out to Umhlanga Sands Disco, my favourite hang-out, saw a few old friends, got totally trashed and then drove home, saying goodbye to Durban all on my own. Okay, I thought, I've made up my mind; it's time to go. Fuck everyone, fuck this place and this life. Tomorrow a new life, a new adventure, will begin. With my head I will follow my heart; the key to life I will find in fate and destiny intertwined.

Some of my friends and family came to see me off at Durban's new railway station. In spite of all the warnings that 'Koevoet did not exist', in spite of all the secrecy when I applied at Oshakati, I soon realised that Koevoet was an open secret. My sister, who was by then a captain in the security branch in Durban, had helped me to get security clearance for Koevoet, and some of my friends who had been to the Border knew about the 'top secret' police unit. I told everyone I had joined Koevoet for five years. In truth I didn't really know for how long I was going or whether I would ever come back. My original plan had been to join for one year, but often it was better not to have a plan and just to let life take you wherever it wanted to.

I wasn't good at goodbyes, so instead of getting all sad and sentimental I played the fool, joking and kidding.

There was a final call and soon the train was pulling out of the station.

As my friends and family walked away, my mother heard Dougie Taft's cynical remark to Andy Woods: 'Arn will never make it. He'll never last in Koevoet.'

My mother didn't like Doug's tone and attitude, but she hoped he would be right, in which case I would soon be home again.

The train finally pulled into Pretoria station. The journey had been a nightmare, with drunken people making a noise all night and a drunken woman screaming from the toilet next to my compartment, 'I want a baby, I want a baby!'

With my kitbag I made my way from the train, wondering how I was going to get to the COIN transit division at the police college. From there I wanted to try to get onto a military flight from Waterkloof airbase to Ondangwa.

At a phone booth outside the station I decided to phone the duty room at the police college. I thought I might as well try my luck.

I dialled 1023 and got the number from enquiries, popped a coin into the box and dialled the duty-room number.

'Police college duty room, Warrant Officer Botha speaking, how can I help?'

'Hello, I've been transferred from Durban to Koevoet. Do you think it's possible that someone can come and give me a lift to the college? I'm at the station in Potgieter Street. I've just got off the train from Durban.'

'Yes, sure, I'll come and fetch you in about 15 minutes,' he replied.

Wow, now that was service!

About 20 minutes later a big black Chevrolet pulled up and, after we introduced ourselves, we were on our way.

'I just need to make a stop on the way. I hope you don't mind,' Warrant Officer Botha apologised, and I thought, fuck, this is strange, a warrant officer apologising to me while he's doing me a favour. We pulled up at a house and he climbed out of the car and went inside.

I realised why he was apologetic and a bit nervous, and why he had been willing to come and fetch me: he had wanted to make a little unauthorised detour past his house.

What the fuck did I care? Take your time, do what you like, as long as I get to the college. After all, he was the one doing me the favour and I had all the time in the world.

The South African Police College … how I hated that place! I had hated police training. The six months I'd spent there had seemed to drag on for an eternity.

Counter-insurgency training at Maloeskop had been good, though. I had enjoyed it so much that I'd stayed on for a mortar course, after which I'd volunteered for border duty. It was amazing how in six weeks of intensive COIN training they could prepare one for combat. Some guys cracked during training and I wondered how they would react in a real contact. And, yes, I wondered how I would react myself. Would I turn and run? Would I lie on the floor of the Casspir and cry for my mommy?

Now Warrant Officer Botha dropped me off at the hated college again, at the COIN transit division, and of all people in the police I least expected to see, it was my old instructor from Maloeskop who attended to my request for help in getting to Ondangwa. Sergeant Dozy Coetzee was a damn good instructor, one of the finest. 'Hello, Sergeant, I've been transferred to Koevoet and I was wondering if you could help me get there,' I asked him.

'Well, let's see … Koevoet! That's not our baby, but yes, I'll do whatever I can to help you.' He thought for a moment before saying, 'There's a COIN company flying out on Wednesday from Waterkloof to Ondangwa and I might be able to smuggle you on board with them.'

My next worry was also taken care of. 'Here's a key for a single room behind the barracks,' he said. 'You can eat in the NCOs' mess. If they ask, just say you're with COIN transit.' He paused briefly, then said, 'Oh, and here's the key to the Ford 350 standing at the back. Sorry I don't have anything smaller. We're going off now; we'll be back on Monday. You'll just have to sit it out.' And with that he was gone.

I was flabbergasted.

It's like a magic formula, I thought. All I said was that I had been transferred to Koevoet and asked whether they could help. I didn't expect them to roll out the red carpet.

On Monday morning I saw a Casspir parked outside the headquarters.

'Where is that Casspir going?' I asked someone.

'To Oshakati,' he replied.

I had an idea. 'Hey, can you give me a lift to Oshakati?' I asked the two guys who would be driving the Casspir there. 'I've been transferred to Koevoet.'

They looked at each other and I could see that they were unsure.

'Koevoet, you say?' one of them asked.

'Well,' the other replied, 'I suppose it's okay.'

'Okay, I'll just get my stuff.'

I rushed to Sergeant Dozy. 'Sergeant, don't worry about me. I'm going to hitch a ride with that Casspir. It's going all the way to Oshakati. Thanks for everything, but I don't want to sit around waiting.'

What I didn't realise was that I would have arrived in Oshakati much sooner had I waited for the flight on the Wednesday. Sergeants Greyling and Meiring were in no hurry whatsoever to get to Oshakati.

We spent the first night at the police barracks in Upington and then we proceeded to visit all their family members and long-lost relatives throughout Namibia.

I was getting pretty bored and frustrated with my two travelling companions, but I couldn't say anything because they were doing me a favour by giving me a lift.

At last, after about 2 000 kilometres, we were in Oshakati and I said goodbye to the two sergeants. The Casspir drove off and the dust settled. I stood in front of the gate to Onamwandi. People spoke of Onamwandi in hushed tones. For some it was a place of foreboding, a place that shouldn't exist, a place of great suffering, agony and even tortured death. It was a place where some simply went missing, never to be seen again. The name was whispered: *Onamwandi.*

For some, to go through this gate was like passing through the gates of hell to eternal misery. A shiver ran down my spine.

Onamwandi was the Koevoet base where prisoners were kept. They were called prisoners of war (POWs), but they were prisoners of Koevoet, captured by Koevoet and kept by Koevoet, fighters from SWAPO and its armed wing PLAN. They were the lucky ones, the important ones who survived the contacts, torture and interrogation in the field, the ones deemed to have valuable information.

The rehabilitation process began as soon as they had passed through that gate: solitary confinement in single galvanised-iron cells the size of an outhouse, for an indefinite period with little food and water at temperatures reaching 52 °C. The plan was to release them back into society eventually. Later I would learn about the process between entering the gates of hell and the final plan.

I stood at the gate with my brown kitbag next to me. I looked at the green bell button on the gate, trying to build up the courage to press it. My heart skipped a beat when the steel door inside the gate opened suddenly and a man came out.

Then I recognised him. It was Brigadier Hannes Dreyer, commanding officer of Special Ops (K). He was dressed in a police camouflage uniform and strode confidently with duck feet. He always looked as if he was about to fall over backwards.

He approached me and looked at me from behind black-rimmed spectacles, hawk-like. Three months had passed since my interview with him and I hardly expected him to remember me, but as soon as I started to introduce myself, he cut me short.

'Yes, we've been expecting you for some time. Where have you been? Come inside.' His voice was deep and rasping, calm and confident. I realised that this man was not to be fucked with.

This was the man who had started Koevoet. Back in 1978 he had taken a security-branch investigating unit and turned it into the finest fighting unit in the world. Statistically it was one of the most successful fighting units in the history of military conflict, with a kill ratio of 25 to 1.

His initial investigating unit drove around Ovamboland in

Ford bakkies, investigated SWAPO activities, took statements from locals, compiled reports for security HQ and gathered ammunition for government to use in Parliament and against the world, which was perpetually condemning South Africa.

After physically clashing with SWAPO on numerous occasions, Brigadier Dreyer gathered a few good men and launched a small paramilitary operation. They called their first venture Operation Koevoet and, after achieving great success, security HQ gave the green light and the unit Koevoet was born. A shoestring budget was channelled from secret government funds to finance the unit.

After the initial successful operations, Brigadier Dreyer called in a few big guns, guys like former recce and career soldier Frans Conradie, and 'Gene' (Eugene) de Kock, to put Koevoet on the road to success.

Counter-insurgency and anti-guerrilla warfare were revolutionised, and by the end of 1981 Frans Conradie was literally wearing the T-shirt, *Happiness is one hundred confirmed kills.*

Koevoet was made up of not more than 1 000 members, but it accounted for 85 per cent of SWAPO's losses within South West Africa, while the army, with about 50 000 soldiers deployed in the operational area, was accounting for 10 per cent. SAP COIN got the remaining 5 per cent.

Initially Koevoet and SAP COIN were not permitted to operate in Angola. This was a huge frustration for us. Once SWAPO insurgents knew that we were following them, they would often run straight for the border, as the pair we were following had done while I was based at Ongha. Once they crossed it, they knew they were safe. Obviously our orders not to cross into Angola were often ignored.

After the big infiltration by SWAPO PLAN in 1982, Koevoet

was formally recognised and we were officially allowed into Angola for the first time.

Even at the time of my arrival at the beginning of 1982, Koevoet did not officially exist, so who was taking the credit? Koevoet had become the army's biggest embarrassment, so the army despised Koevoet and Koevoet despised the army.

I realised that if Koevoet did not exist officially there would be no recognition, no honour and no glory in this fight. I was happy with that because, as I have said, I wasn't there to fight for God and country. It had also been decided that no medals would be awarded, simply because there wouldn't be enough to go around.

Fuck them, fuck SWAPO, I thought. There's a fight going on and I'm going to jump in. A fight is a fight. I'm on this side and they're on that side. I have to live and they have to die.

Brigadier Dreyer led the way into Onamwandi with me right behind him and I passed through those gates into a new life. At last I was a member of Koevoet. Would I be able to do it?

We walked through a mess room and into the open area inside the base. Behind high sand walls with steel sheets on top and barbed wire on top of that, we were cut off from the outside world.

Offices and sleeping quarters were housed in rows and rows of green bungalows. Iron sheds stood on the far side of the base and right in the middle of it all, in an enclosure made of logs, were two elephants, Ollie and Momphie. One was just a baby, the other a youngster.

The brigadier led me into a bungalow.

'Make yourself comfortable here. The task force have cleared out; they're gone.'

Little did I know that he had fired the top anti-terrorist unit in the country, told them to pack up and fuck off back home because Koevoet did not want them and did not need them.

'Report to the office tomorrow morning, to Captain Botha … and no firearms in here. We've got a lot of captured SWAPOs in the base, just waiting for a chance to grab a gun and kill us.'

Before I could explain that I had my service pistol, a Walther P38, with me, he was gone and I stood in a bungalow with eight beds, of which three had mattresses, but no linen or blankets. Luckily I had a sleeping bag, which I rolled out on one of the mattresses. There were six grey steel cupboards, and I thought it best to hide my pistol behind one of them.

I sat on the bed, wondering what to do next. I would've loved a beer. Sounds from people socialising and drinking drifted over from a bar close by, but I didn't dare join them. I was sure that the bar was for officers only.

I decided to go and have a look at the elephants. Nervously I stepped outside, expecting someone to shout at me while I looked over my shoulder to try to see who was in the pub. I thought it must be mostly officers – some seriously scary people.

'Hello, who are you?' Someone approached from behind me and I nearly jumped at the sound of his voice. He introduced himself as Koos and from him I learnt where I could eat, drink and shower. Then I asked him if he could get me a couple of beers.

'What for?' he asked. 'Why don't you go and have a beer in the pub?'

'But isn't it for officers only?'

'No. Here we all drink and eat together, so go have a beer or whatever you want.'

I just couldn't gather the courage to enter the pub, so I went back inside and climbed into my sleeping bag. At least I now knew where to wash, eat and drink. I had been on the road for days. I was tired, weary, hungry and in a strange place a long, long way from home: I was in Onamwandi, Oshakati, Ovamboland, Northern Namibia. I was in the operational area and I was now a member of Koevoet.

I didn't know a single soul in Koevoet and not a single soul knew me, but when I looked at the ops board the following morning, I saw a familiar name: Lieutenant David Baker in the Zulu Oscar team.

I had worked with his wife, Sergeant Linda Baker, in Durban. Because of her I knew that he was English-speaking. And then Linda Baker herself walked in. I did know someone in Koevoet after all!

Linda Baker worked in the ops room, manning the B25 SSB radio, which kept the ops room in contact with every team in the bush. The irony of a woman 'manning' the radio made me smile.

The board on the wall in the ops room listed each of the 20 Koevoet teams, which were divided into two groups. Half were the alpha teams, the other half were the bravo teams. While the alpha teams were in the bush, the bravo teams were in town and vice versa. They switched places on Wednesdays, so for everybody it was one week in the bush, one week in town.

The ops board also kept score, recording each group's total number of kills for the year. That morning I didn't get a chance to analyse it to see which group had the highest score, as Captain Botha was waiting for me.

'What happened to your friend? What was his name … Rob Mitchell?' Captain Botha asked.

'He decided not to come.'

'At least we've got one good man.'

Why did he say that? How did he know whether I would be any good?

The captain looked at me with his fat, owl-like features, thinking about what group to put me in.

'Zulu Oscar?' I suggested.

'No, they've got enough men. Zulu Golf. Yes, that's it,' he said. 'Go to Okavi and find Lieutenant Goosen. He'll be working on his Casspirs. Tell him you're working with him.'

I caught a lift on the back of a truck and arrived at Okavi base, where I nervously looked for Zulu Golf and its lieutenant.

Lieutenant André Goosen was quite dark, almost Roman-looking, a great and talented man. He was a loner, a non-drinker and a non-smoker. Honest and hard-working, he was determined to show that he could make a difference.

'Hi, my name is Arn,' I said. 'Captain Botha sent me to find you. Apparently I'm in your group.'

I felt awkward and nervous.

'Well, I don't know, we've got enough guys in our team, but I suppose it's all right,' he said. 'We're going to deploy on Wednesday.' He turned around and continued to work on his Casspir.

No 'Welcome to Zulu Golf.' No 'Let me introduce you to Jackie, Whitey, Greens and the rest of the team.'

I stood there feeling like a prick, not knowing what to do with myself, and wishing the ground would open up and swallow me.

Then trouble arrived. 'Hello, I'm Jackie and this is Whitey.'

I thought they should call themselves Blackie and Whitey, or Ebony and Ivory. Jackie was dark – dark-skinned, with dark hair and brown eyes. He was of medium build and medium height. His nose curved down. He could easily have passed as coloured or Indian.

Whitey was of the same build as Jackie, but there the similarity ended. Whitey had blond hair, blue eyes and a very fair skin.

I shook hands with both of them and introduced myself as Arn.

'What kind of a name is that?' Jackie asked. Whitey sniggered.

'Call me Jim,' I said.

Arn was my name, but every time I introduced myself or was introduced, people would ask about my name, and the Ovambos just didn't get it. It was time to change it. Also, a name change would shield me against any inquisitive interest from Durban. If anyone asked after me, no one would have heard of me. So I celebrated my new life with a new name.

'Jim – that's better,' Jackie grinned. Whitey just stared at me with a fuck-you look. Like their physical appearances, their characters were also completely opposite from each other. Jackie was the total extrovert, Whitey the total introvert. I immediately took to Jackie, but Whitey gave me a bad vibe.

'Why did they put you in Zulu Golf? We don't need more people.' Whitey was making me feel really welcome.

'Where are you staying?' Jackie asked.

'Across at Onamwandi.'

'No, you can't stay there. You must move across and stay with us here at Okavi,' he said. 'We're going to the bush on Wednesday. Have you got kit?'

'Yes, but I don't have a gun,' I replied. 'Where can I get a rifle?'

'We can try Uncle Bill at the stores at Ongwediva, but he'll give you fuck-all,' Jackie said. 'Don't worry, though, we'll get you an AK with our next contact.'

'How many contacts have you guys had?'

'Plenty,' Jackie told me. 'We've shot plenty of gooks. We are the best. The other guys think we're mugus, but we shoot more gooks than any of them.'

Then Lieutenant Goosen crapped on Jackie. 'Stop talking shit and come and help me with this.'

'I love you, Lieutenant. Hey! Have you met Jim? He's our new guy but he's first got to prove himself.' Jackie tried to kiss the lieutenant, who almost hit him with a shifting spanner. Then he asked Jackie if his Casspir was ready for the trip to the bush the following Wednesday.

Jackie tried to get out of work. 'Hey, Jim, go fetch your stuff from Onamwandi. You're moving in with us. Let me come and help you.'

Whitey mumbled something and left in a huff.

Fuck, I thought, are these guys moffies or are they just plain bosbefok? And I've got to move in with them!

At Onamwandi I looked at Ollie and Momphie. I wouldn't be staying with them, but I'd see them often because the guys from Okavi took their meals there.

There was a lot I had to get used to at Okavi. I shared a bungalow with five other guys and we were in the midst of dozens of bungalows occupied by more Koevoet members. I had to get used to country-and-western music, Dolly Parton and Kris Kristofferson, and to Jackie's singing and guitar playing. Or his attempts at singing and guitar playing. He believed that he could play and sing, and we had to endure it.

Luckily the generator that supplied the base's electricity switched off at ten o'clock every night.

Then there was the boeremusiek of some of the Afrikaans-speaking guys. The sound of concertina and accordion tortured me night after sleepless night. And the singing! I'm sure the fathers of the Afrikaans language never realised that some people might one day try to sing in it. Boeremusiek was, however, very close to the hearts of some white Afrikaners. God bless Chris Kristofferson and Dolly Parton!

On the far eastern side of the base, four former SWAPO PLAN soldiers and one black former Selous Scout from what had become Zimbabwe occupied a bungalow. They now all worked for Koevoet.

On my first night at Okavi I was awoken at around midnight by the rat-a-tat-tat of an AK-47 coming from the eastern end of the base.

'Who's making shit?' I heard someone shout. No one seemed too concerned about the shooting, thinking that it was probably a drunken member having some fun.

'Hey, guys, come and look here, here's shit!' someone shouted.

The former Selous Scout had had a disagreement and then a fight with the former SWAPO members, pulled out an AK-47 and shot them. He had simply killed them in cold blood and disappeared into the night, never to be seen or heard from again. He could have joined UNITA or found his way back home. Had he stayed, he probably would have got off lightly, because his four victims were former SWAPO and no one really gave a shit.

Wednesday morning came and it was time for the bravo teams to deploy while the alpha teams were returning to base.

Stores for our equipment were still under construction at the base and Zulu Golf was storing its equipment in a cell that was meant to serve as a holding cell for SWAPO prisoners.

Bennie was our black group commander. He had a squint, was a lot bigger than most Ovambos and a lot older than those in our group. He had a driver's licence and could drive a Casspir, so the lieutenant sent him off to Ondangwa to round up the group's Ovambos who lived there.

We did not yet have a Blesbok, which was a four-wheel-drive supply truck, designed like the Casspir but used to carry drums of diesel, ammunition, equipment, food supplies and sometimes aviation turpentine for the gunships. So Lieutenant Goosen borrowed an Albatross, a 25-ton supply truck that was not a four-wheel drive and therefore not suited for bush work, but was landmine protected. He sent Whitey, who was the only one of us with a licence to drive it, to Zulu 3 at Ongwediva to fetch our food supplies for the coming week as well as our Ovambo members who lived in that area.

Okavi was a hive of activity with Casspirs, cars, trucks and people coming and going. Vehicles were being loaded and off-loaded. Machine guns were being fitted to Casspirs and Blesboks.

Louw van Niekerk, one of the legends of Koevoet, had a warning for us when he saw that we were using an Albatross as a supply truck.

'Guys, whatever you do, don't try and take that thing off the road. If you get that vehicle stuck, there's no fucking way on earth to get it out again. Believe me, I've been there.'

He didn't elaborate, but the story went that he had taken an Albatross on a trip to the west and got horribly stuck on a narrow dirt strip near the Etosha National Park. A week later, with the help of the strongest recovery vehicles in the entire operational area, the Albatross was still stuck. Eventually it took a Super Frelon helicopter, the most powerful helicopter in our air force, to get the Albatross out.

Finally we were heading west on the main road that connects Oshakati to Ruacana. It was almost the end of a heavy rainy season, which had broken the severe drought of the previous few years. The rivers to the north had burst their banks and sent their water down to fill up Ovamboland's waterways and shonas, the pans that are dry in winter but fill up with water in the rainy season, all the way down to the Etosha Pan. The countryside was green and lush, unlike what I had seen the year before, when everything had looked like it was dying.

The heavy rains were over now and this signalled the start of SWAPO's infiltration period. Water was available, food was plentiful and the green vegetation gave them good ground cover.

This was bad news for us. Tracking had become more difficult in places, because the rain had hardened the soil, making it easy for our enemy to operate. But it was also good news: SWAPO was on its way and that was what we were there for – to find them and to kill them. If they didn't come, we couldn't kill them.

Let the games begin.

Because of three months of continuous rain, the road – if I could call it a road – had become one big mud bath, churned by the flow of heavy traffic. In places it had become impossible to use so we detoured or drove next to it. Our main concern was the Albatross that Whitey was driving.

Lieutenant Goosen turned around in the driver's seat and asked me if I could drive a Casspir.

I was the new guy and the Ovambos eyed me suspiciously. Jackie had warned me that it would take a lot before they would accept me. Some of them had been fighting for years and they didn't take kindly to a new shirumbu, the Ovambo name for a white person getting in their way or telling them what to do.

'Yes, sure, I can drive a Casspir,' I replied with faked confidence, hoping that I was right. I had never driven one before, but it looked pretty easy. A Casspir had a steering wheel, gear lever, clutch, brake and accelerator, just like any car. I was sure I could drive it.

'Do you have a licence?' the lieutenant asked. 'Do you have a code 10?'

'No, but I'll drive it if you like.'

'If you don't have a licence, we had better wait until we leave the road,' he said.

Fuck, did he think a traffic cop was going to jump out from behind a bush and check my licence? We were in the middle of a war zone in the middle of a major infiltration! I nevertheless thought it wise to keep quiet.

The guys at the SAP COIN base at Onesi were not very welcoming. We had to sleep on the hard concrete floor of the tribal office. The mosquitoes feasted on us, making it impossible to sleep. The next morning we all were very grumpy.

'I hope you guys have all taken anti-malaria tablets,' Lieutenant Goosen said.

'Fuck the malaria,' Jackie chirped, 'it's just like having a bad hangover; it's not that bad.

We left the Albatross at Onesi for the day, set off and started exploring the area.

We drove in convoy and then spread out as we reached the kraals where we wanted to question the locals. This was the west and the terrain was much harder than in the east, there was a lot less vegetation and a lot more water. The shonas were big and full, making it very difficult to get through or around them. Extracting information from the locals here had become almost impossible – this was the home of Sam Nujoma, SWAPO's president, and the locals were mostly of the Ongandjera tribe, staunch SWAPO supporters who refused to give us any information.

We pissed them off by driving over their fences and through their mahangu crops.

We stopped at a kraal complex and our Ovambos were getting very frustrated with the uncooperative locals. They grabbed some of the children and whipped them with sticks. To get a 12-year-old boy to talk, one of the guys, Tommy, grabbed him and put the boy's hand on the Casspir's exhaust. The boy screamed with pain and when Tommy pulled his hand off the silencer, he realised that the boy's hand had burnt severely. It was the last time Tommy tried that trick.

The locals cut down lots of trees, bushes and shrubs for firewood and building material for their kraals, and the exposed stumps gave us flat tyres, 14 of them by mid-morning. We got our Casspir bogged down about 10 times. We seemed to be getting nowhere slowly and it was getting very hot.

'Okay, let's see if you can drive,' Lieutenant Goosen said. He couldn't drive, plot our position, and talk on the RSA53 and his B25 radio at the same time. He got out of the driver's seat and I took the wheel.

Fuck, this clutch is stiff, I thought as I took off in second gear.

About 10 minutes later I thought it was a piece of cake. I knew I could do it. Let's rock 'n' roll.

An hour later I felt like I was going to pass out. The temperature outside had reached over 50 °C. Inside, and especially where I was sitting, it was a lot hotter, and I hoped we would soon get another flat tyre. I was closed in by armoured steel and bulletproof glass. The Mercedes diesel engine under the floorboards beneath me was pushing the temperature up to over 60 °C.

I need to get out, I wanted to shout. I need to get the fuck out of here.

I was claustrophobic and sweat was streaming out of every pore of my body. I refused to complain or to say anything, although I was about to black out.

After about two hours of burning hell, Lieutenant Goosen took over again.

'God bless you,' I felt like saying as I scrambled out of the seat to the back of the Casspir as though the devil himself had just released me from hell.

I was weak and two of the Ovambos helped me up to the hatch. The 'cooler' air, at 50 °C, felt like heaven.

What have I done? This was one big mistake. What on earth made me want to join Koevoet? I just wanted to go home and forget that it had ever happened.

It was Saturday and we got back to unfriendly Onesi early. It had been a hard and horrible day of heat, adversity and hatred.

Finally, as stubborn as he was, Lieutenant Goosen decided to pack up and move to Ombalantu, which was further north-east of us. Our plan was to leave the Albatross at the security police base at Ombalantu and operate above the main road closer to the Angolan border.

On Saturday night we set up a temporary base (TB) in the bush and slept on the ground in the open in a circle facing outwards between the four Casspirs, which were facing north, south, east and west.

A member of our group, Greens, a dark, fat guy, was a mystery. None of us knew what had brought him to Koevoet and he didn't seem to want to be there. He didn't talk much, and no one talked to him. He generally kept to himself and made sure that he did as little as possible. He had somehow put up a small tent on top of his Casspir, Zulu Golf 4, and that was where he slept.

'I would laugh if some gook shoots that fat slob off the roof of his Casspir,' Jackie said, and shouted, 'Hey, Greens, don't turn over in your sleep, it's a long way down!'

'Fuck off. Leave me alone,' Greens shouted back.

'It's going to rain,' one of the Ovambos said. The rainy season was over and the sky was clear, so we ignored Lieutenant Goosen's advice to put up our bivouacs. Besides, I didn't have one. The Ovambo was right. Soon it started to rain, lightly but continuously. We were in for a long wet night in the open. I was beginning to learn that the Ovambos were fully in tune with nature.

On Sunday I was driving again, while Lieutenant Goosen was in the gunner's seat next to me. It wasn't so hot that day – the night's rain had cooled the air a bit – but we stopped at 1 p.m. to take a break and to put our sleeping bags out to dry.

Two hours later we were on our way again. The sand was soft, so I was pumping the clutch and changing gears rapidly, and my left thigh muscles were beginning to ache.

The lieutenant and I were leading in Zulu Golf 1, Jackie was behind us in Zulu Golf 2, with Whitey behind him in Zulu Golf 3. Greens was bringing up the rear in Zulu Golf 4. We made our way along a pathway that took us to a kraal complex about 300 metres ahead.

My thoughts had taken me back to the Durban court building, to the Indian article clerk and some of the other girls who worked there. Why hadn't I had the courage to make a move on her and why had she taken me into the photostat room once and shown me how the machine worked by making a photocopy of her hand? What had she been up to? I'm sure she'd been trying to be kinky. God, I was stupid. Imagine what I could have got up to with her …

Then suddenly I am plucked from my fantasy. SWAPO is

behind us. We are in the middle of a contact. A huge surge of adrenalin pumps through my body as the bullets start to fly from assault rifles and LMGs. On full automatic, every weapon is sending thousands of rounds in every direction, finding their marks in the bodies of the enemy.

'SWAPO is behind us!' Greens shouts over the radio. A stupid thing to shout. Why not 'Contact, contact, contact!'? But the eruption of gunfire tells us that the shit is hitting the fan.

'Drive forward slowly, yes, good, that's right, keep it in second gear.' Lieutenant Goosen talks me through it. My right foot and leg shake uncontrollably and I worry that I won't be able to keep my foot on the accelerator.

Lieutenant Goosen suddenly swings the turret to the left and opens fire into a thicket about 20 metres away across a clearing. He has seen something. The LMG above him erupts and he twists the barrel in a small circular motion, spraying a circle of death into the thicket.

I watch as the 7.62-mm bullets fly at 850 metres per second from the barrel, 1 000 rounds per minute. Every fourth copper-coated lead bullet is a tracer that leaves a red streak through the air, showing the path they travel.

Slay the fucking devils! The bullets slam into their bodies, spraying and spitting splinters of bone, blood and brain flying through the air. One of them shits and pisses in his pants as his last breath leaves his body.

'Go forward, go through the kraal, there might be more. They would have run that way!'

I drive through the kraal and to the other side until the lieutenant tells me to turn around and return to the scene of the contact.

The liberators have been liberated to hell, or to meet their great Tate Kalunga, the Ovambo's supreme spirit.

It's over; the contact is over. I pull up, stop at the contact point and cut the engine by pushing the cut-out button with my left foot, which still shakes uncontrollably.

There's a scene of human carnage and great jubilation. I light a cigarette and it's never tasted so good. I feel different. I feel alive. I feel like I'm on a high.

The bodies are being stripped of all their equipment. The weapons are placed on one side: one RPG-7 (a rocket-propelled grenade launcher capable of taking out a Casspir), six RPG rockets, two AK-47s, two Soviet SKSs (which fire the same round as the AK but can fire a Heat Stream grenade with almost the same effect as the RPG-7), AK magazines and ammo, F1 hand grenades and three POMZ anti-personnel mines.

Apart from the weapons, there are scores of uniforms, equipment, pouches, medic bags and propaganda literature. 'We will win through to ultimate victory, my comrades, against the racist dogs of the evil apartheid regime. Victory is imminent. We must unite and drive apartheid from the land of our forefathers.'

Well, the only thing uniting these six is death.

Lieutenant Goosen radios the coordinates of the contact and all the relevant information through to Zulu HQ.

'We have to take the bodies in for identification – they need to screen the bodies and see if these are ground forces,' the lieutenant instructs. 'Load them up and let's get going.'

The Ovambos strip bark from the trees to make ropes for tying the bodies to the Casspirs. Now I find I have something in common with the Ovambos: they don't want to touch the dead bodies and neither do I. But for me there is no way out.

There's nothing I am more afraid of than a dead body and I don't know why. I don't mind killing them, but I don't want to play with them once they are dead.

'Come on, don't just fucking stand there, help load these bodies,' Jackie craps on the Ovambos. Most of them flatly refuse, so I set about helping to hoist the corpses up onto the spare wheels and bumpers of our Casspirs and fasten them so that they don't fall off.

Jackie has got the feet and I've got the hands of the last one and together we swing it up on top of the one already fastened to the spare wheel of Lieutenant Goosen's Casspir.

'The lieutenant says you drove very well during the contact,' Jackie says. 'Was that your first contact?'

I want to lie and tell him that I had one at Ongha, but I admit that it was my first one.

'Were you scared?'

'Yes,' I concede. 'But it was okay. I feel good now.'

'Fuck, I nearly crapped in my pants,' he tells me.

'Was it your first?' I ask him.

'No,' he says, 'I've been in a few.'

'Jackie, stop talking shit and let's get going,' Lieutenant Goosen interrupts. 'We've got a long way to go and it's getting late. We still need to fetch the Albatross from Ombalantu.'

I sat in the back of Lieutenant Goosen's Casspir while he drove us down to the main road so that we could get to Ombalantu and then back to Oshakati.

The Ovambos looked at me differently now. Was that the look of acceptance? Had this shirumbu proved himself?

My first contact was over. Little did I know that it was the first of 127 contacts to follow in years of fighting. Little did I know that Whitey was about to leave us because he was actually a COIN member and with Koevoet for only three months. I also didn't know that Jackie and I were about to become the best of friends and that he would often get us into serious trouble.

Sunset on the road back to Oshakati with the Albatross caught us, and soon I felt that the souls of our slain enemy and their great Tate Kalunga were trying to take revenge.

The others weren't coming. We couldn't see their headlights behind us any more, so Lieutenant Goosen stopped and waited. After half an hour we turned back to look for them. Then the Albatross, which Whitey was driving behind us, ran out of fuel and Lieutenant Goosen decided that I had to stay behind with it.

'You need to find a switch to engage the reserve tank, which will pump fuel into the main tank. Stay here and see if you can find it,' he ordered. Turning to Whitey, he said, 'Come, let's go and look for the others.' With that, he and Whitey left in the lieutenant's Casspir.

I was left alone with the Albatross, without a firearm and in total darkness. Then it started to rain. About an hour went by, during which I found a tap on the fuel line from the Albatross's reserve tank to its main tank. The main tank was empty and the electric pump needed to pump fuel to the main tank, but the risk was that the battery could go flat and the fuel line through the filters and into the injector pump would need to be bled.

Some god intervened and chased the great Tate Kalunga away. The engine started! I started the Albatross and the main tank was filling. I saw lights approaching from behind. Tommy was now driving Lieutenant Goosen's Casspir and drove slap bang into the back of the Albatross.

Greens' Casspir was giving trouble. Lieutenant Goosen had found him and the others and told Tommy to drive his Casspir, while he drove Greens' Casspir himself.

After crashing into the Albatross, the front of Lieutenant

Goosen's Casspir was smashed in a bit and the engine's fan was catching against something, but after another two hours we were on our way again to Oshakati.

We didn't have clearance from the army, but when they saw the dead bodies strung up on our Casspirs they stepped aside at the main entrance to the town.

At 1 a.m. we parked the Casspirs outside Onamwandi and Jackie, Whitey and I made our way to Okavi next door to try to get some sleep – but not before Jackie woke the entire base to relate the story of the contact – grossly exaggerated – to everyone.

The next morning, the identification done, we rode through Oshakati to the cemetery for blacks on the far side of town, the dead bodies strung over the spare wheels of our Casspirs, bodies shot to shit, mangled and broken, torn to pieces by bullets and thorn bushes.

We drove past children on their way to school, townsfolk on their way to work. Women drove past, all dressed up, hair and make-up perfect – bank tellers, secretaries and receptionists. They acted oblivious to the gruesome sight, looking away. They'd seen it before, Koevoet coming back into town with dead bodies hanging all over their Casspirs.

It was barbaric, but what could we do? We had to bring the bodies back for identification. If they weren't important, we would have left them to rot in the sun or be eaten by wild animals.

There was one single deep grave for all six bodies, dug by the POWs. I cut a body down from where it was hanging from the spare wheel on the side of the Casspir. It had been in the heat and sun for almost two days by this time and was unrecognisable. The face was blown away completely and, because of the heat, the body had already begun to decompose. It fell to the ground with a thud, releasing rotting stomach gases.

My nostrils filled with the stench. I breathed it in. It went down the back of my throat, filled my lungs, moved down to my stomach and descended into the bottomless pit I call my soul, never to escape again. Never to be forgotten.

5

My Casspir, my nightmare

That Sunday morning we were back at Okavi. The bodies had been identified and buried and the Casspirs cleaned, but our work was not done. Lieutenant Goosen decided to fix the Albatross and his Casspir under the shed at the back of the base and we had to help him, starting that morning.

We thought it was sheer madness and everyone told him so. 'Why not just replace your front grill and bumper? You can't fix panzer steel.'

'Why not give the Albatross back like it is?' Jackie wanted to know. 'Fuck it, it's not ours.'

A Casspir was made of armoured steel – panzer steel, it was called, after the original German armoured vehicles called Panzers. The steel was hard and the only weapons that could penetrate it were armour-piercing rounds of various big calibres, including the RPG-7 and the Heat Stream. These could penetrate almost anything, but that is another story.

The point is that one cannot panel-beat the body of an Albatross, let alone a Casspir, but don't tell Lieutenant Goosen that. He will just make sure that he'll prove you wrong.

And prove us wrong he did. For the next week he set about

fixing both of the vehicles. His favourite tools for this work were an arc welding machine, a heavy-duty angle grinder, an oxyacetylene set and a big sledgehammer. A week later he had won, right down to the final paint job. Both vehicles looked almost perfect and I had learnt to weld and to use a cutting torch and an angle grinder even better than when I'd used my dad's tools to make my Cardboard Gang sword. The repairs cost a lot of blood, sweat, tears, aching muscles, burns, bruises and cuts.

I now knew the most stubborn man I had ever met.

But by 6 p.m. that first Sunday there was a short respite. Jackie announced that there would be a braai at Onamwandi that night.

'Lieutenant, let's leave this for now,' he said. 'I promise we will all help you tomorrow. Come, let's go and get something to eat.'

The lieutenant continued to swing the sledgehammer. 'No, you guys go ahead. I need to work.'

'Where is Greens?' Jackie shouted suddenly. 'Greens just fucks off and does nothing. Where is that useless fuckhead?'

'He must fix his Casspir, that's all I know,' Lieutenant Goosen said.

For another 15 minutes Jackie tried to persuade the lieutenant to go to the braai. He pleaded and begged, and then gave up. 'Come Whitey, come Jim, let's go and see what's happening next door,' he said.

I felt bad for the lieutenant and didn't want to leave, but Jackie dragged me away.

About an hour later we had showered and changed and were standing in Onamwandi, where a huge fire was blazing. Soon it would turn into red-hot coals, ready to cook the steaks, lamb chops and boerewors.

I was worried about money and how I was going to pay for my share of the braai. Someone offered me a beer, but I declined because I would not be able to reciprocate later.

'Jackie, how much will this braai cost?' I asked, thinking that it would be like a bring and braai, or that we all would be expected to contribute towards the cost.

'Fuck, I don't know.'

'Seriously. I don't have much money on me.'

'What do you need money for?'

'To pay for the braai and buy some beers.'

Jackie packed up laughing. 'No, Jim, the state pays for everything and tonight even the drinks are on the house. Go and help yourself at the bar to anything you want. And bring me a beer.'

I returned with two beers to find Jackie reliving our contact once again. The way he was telling the story, I could have sworn that he and I were at two different contacts.

'Bring the guitar,' Jackie shouted. 'Let me play some songs for you guys.'

Hide the guitar, I thought, but Jackie got hold of it and started strumming the strings. It was time for me to move further away.

At Onamwandi baboons were kept as pets – the wild ones were locked in big cages while the tamer ones roamed freely. They were being a nuisance, trying to grab my beer and becoming aggressive when they didn't get what they wanted, so I walked across to the elephants, carrying two beers and a double whisky for myself.

'Here Ollie, take it.' Someone came up and gave Ollie a beer. He gently took the can in his trunk, put it in his mouth, crushed it and drank the beer.

He was given another beer and then another and soon Ollie

the elephant was drunk. Almost everyone was drunk, even the former SWAPO chefs in the kitchen.

I went back to where Jackie had by now gathered a small audience. He was trying so sing 'I Don't Wanna Dance' by Eddy Grant.

'Those are the wrong words,' I told him.

'What?'

'It's supposed to go, "I don't want to fight, fight with my Casspir no more … 'cause the Heat Stream is bad, the Heat Stream is sad".'

'Hey, Jim, that's good; you're going to become my songwriter. Tell them how we shot those gooks, man, it was incredible!' he shouted.

I gave my version. 'One day the Koevoet Long Knives, they came to our SWAPO village, riding steel ponies. They raped our cattle, killed our women and stole our children. I am Big Chief Running from Casspir; I no speak with forked AK.'

Now I had everyone in hysterics, but Jackie didn't like sharing the limelight.

The atmosphere in the base suddenly changed when Captain Eric Winter, Captain Ertjies Erwee and Warrant Officer Piet Stassen stormed into the base. They were pissed – and very pissed off. They headed directly for a member standing next to the elephant enclosure and attacked him violently. He did nothing to defend himself, except to try to cover his face with his hands. All three of them punched him and as he went down one of them shouted, 'We're going to fucking kill you! You can tell your brother and we will fucking kill him too!' They continued kicking him while he was on the ground, but they got tired and he tried to escape. He fled out of the base, with them after him.

We watched the scene in silence, shocked. So did the two

elephants. A tear rolled down from Ollie's eye, for he had seen the way of man. His entire herd had been wiped out by UNITA soldiers in Angola. They had been after the ivory, which they desperately needed in order to buy weapons to cause further death and destruction.

'What was that about, and why didn't anyone help him?' I asked. 'Fuck, even I wouldn't take that. I don't care, I would fight back. It's better to go down fighting than to go down a coward.' But everyone was dead quiet; no one said a word.

'No, Jim, stay out of it,' Jackie said. 'Come, let's get the fuck out of here. Someone's going to get killed tonight.' He put the guitar down and we left.

'What did that guy do?' I asked Jackie, but he just mumbled something about one of the men's wives.

We were feeling very down. Jackie, Whitey and I and our three roommates lay on our beds in silence. Then Captain Winter burst in.

'Where the fuck is he? I want to kill him!' he shouted.

From where I was lying I could smell the whisky on his breath and I could feel the anger in his voice.

'Don't you lot stand up for an officer?' he shouted. 'I'm a fucking officer! Come to attention right now!'

In an instant we were on our feet standing at attention next to our beds.

He decided to pick on Donkey, who slept in the far corner.

Donkey stood over two metres tall, weighed about 160 kilograms and wore thick spectacles. He could hardly fit on a bed, but he was as gentle as he was big. He was a builder in the SAP and stayed with us while he helped to build the base.

Captain Winter got stuck into Donkey, seriously abusing him verbally.

I saw an R1 rifle lying against the wall nearby and a silent rage started to build up deep inside me. I suppressed the temptation to grab the rifle and smash its butt into Captain Winter's face again and again until he would shut the fuck up and leave us alone. I was seriously tempted. I wanted to take him down, there and then.

'I'm going to fuck you lot up,' he said.

I started to calm down only when he left.

Captain Winter was a tough old bastard, a veteran of conflict, but by this stage he was over the hill. He had acquired a liking for what makes one drunk, then stupid – whisky. He had fought in the Rhodesian war and was captured by the Patriotic Front, tied to a wagon wheel and tortured. In the end he managed to escape. Now he was here, tormenting us.

Eventually he headed Koevoet's investigation team. He had a nervous breakdown when Frans Conradie played a very daring and horrible dirty trick on him. It involved blowing up a mole who gave information to SWAPO. The mole was in a bakkie just behind Winter's vehicle and they were on their way to an investigation near Etosha. After that Winter retired. I had very little sympathy for him.

It was Wednesday and it was deployment time again. We still didn't have a Blesbok, so the lieutenant borrowed the Albatross once again.

This time we were deploying to the east, the home of the Kwanyama people. Okavi was a hive of activity as the alpha teams were returning and our bravo teams were deploying.

'Where's Greens?' the lieutenant asked. No one knew. Greens had simply vanished. Then Jackie joined us. 'Greens has gone,' he announced.

'Gone where?' Whitey wanted to know.

'Gone home. They fired him. They put him on a plane this morning. He caused a lot of shit.'

According to Jackie, Greens had gone on a drunken rampage with some of his army buddies over the weekend. There was talk of him being involved in the rape of an Ovambo woman, together with his army buddies.

'Where is his Casspir?' the lieutenant asked. 'We need his bloody Casspir. Jackie, take your Casspir. You and Jim go and find Greens' Casspir.'

'It's probably at the SWA Police barracks,' Jackie said as we drove off. 'That's where Greens stayed.'

We indeed found Greens' dilapidated Casspir at the barracks, parked in a corner, dirty and in a disgraceful state.

I drove it through the town and back towards Okavi. Suddenly I realised what was about to hit me. No, please, no! Not this one. Not the worst fucked-up Casspir in the world. Please, I don't want it!

We headed out on the tarred road and about 40 kilometres further on we passed the town of Ondangwa. We stopped at Tony Banana, a small supermarket. A number of our teams were there and this was our chance to do a bit of last-minute shopping. I bought a carton of Chesterfield cigarettes. Several of the Ovambos were drinking, and so were the guys from Zulu Whisky.

From here we still needed to drive all the way up the dirt road to Eenhana. It was getting late.

'Have they swept the road today?' I heard someone ask. I realised that this was why no one wanted to leave – they didn't know whether the army sappers had checked the road for landmines. SWAPO knew that we deployed on Wednesdays and that a lot of our teams would be coming up the road to Eenhana every Wednesday, so they often made sure that there were a couple of anti-tank landmines waiting for us.

It became a game to see who would leave first from Tony Banana. To leave first meant that you would clear the road for those following. It also meant that you stood the greatest risk of detonating an anti-tank landmine.

Frans Conradie, commander of Zulu Foxtrot, had a trick. He would tell everyone that they were a bunch of faggots and he would leave first, only to turn off the road a few hundred metres ahead and then wait for the others to pass. They would think that he had cleared the road, but they would be the ones at risk. Once they had passed, he would drive along behind them, knowing that the road was safe.

'Come, let's go. Drive in my tracks and watch carefully,' Lieutenant Goosen said, leading the way north in Zulu Golf 1.

We reached Eenhana safely and parked outside the army base. We refuelled from the army's fuel dump and filled our Casspirs' water tanks with drinking water.

Food rations were dealt out from the back of the Albatross and the Ovambos made fires to braai the 50 kilograms of meat that were part of the rations.

The army had allowed Koevoet to establish a field operations HQ in the base and we reported to Captain John Adams.

He had an ego the size of an elephant. He always breathed heavily through his nose, which looked so much like a potato that we called him Potato Nose behind his back. His thin spindly arms stuck out from his camouflage uniform like the legs of a spider.

This was the part Lieutenant Goosen hated: to have to socialise with Captain Adams and the other officers. The drinking would start and the bullshit would follow. Lieutenant Goosen just didn't have time for this. He would prefer to stay outside and sleep next to his Casspir.

The lieutenant had to cope with Potato Nose; I had to cope with Potato Nose's assistant, Tom Boom. As if from nowhere he appeared next to me.

'Hey, ek sê my bro, my china. I hear you all come from Durban.' He knew my sister and some of my friends from Durban. He was one of the reasons why people from Durban had a bad reputation. He loved smoking marijuana, or *boom*, as it was also called, which earned him the nickname Tom Boom. He now offered me some 'good Durban poison'.

'No thanks, Tom. I don't smoke that stuff. Whisky works for me.'

Tom was surprised and disappointed that I didn't smoke dope. Luckily he quickly lost interest in me.

In the morning we left Eenhana and headed east along the road towards Elundu and Okongo.

The road was in a terrible condition and we progressed slowly. At 10 a.m. we left the road and followed a narrow track to the north, winding and weaving between tall kiaat trees.

Just as I thought I was getting the hang of driving Greens' old Casspir, suddenly, wham! I caught the right wheels against a huge kiaat tree. The damage was bad. I had snapped the bolts off the mounting consoles that held the springs and the differentials to the body both front and back. We would not be going anywhere for some time. Everyone was pissed off with me. Some of my Ovambos jumped ship.

Among those who stayed was Lakulya. He had appointed himself as my gunner. He was only about 17 years old, small and slender like a spider, with a complexion slightly lighter than those of the others. Apart from Tommy, who was always full of laughs and smiles, he had the most positive attitude.

Paulus was the oldest in my section, short and stocky with a deep, gruff voice. He was former UNITA and thought he knew everything. He crapped on me for driving into the tree.

'Do you want to drive? Can you drive a Casspir?' I asked him to shut him up.

'No, let Labanye drive – he can drive; he knows how to drive.' Paulus always had an answer.

The lieutenant, Jackie and Whitey had turned around and come back. I could see that the lieutenant was pissed off. He said nothing. He just stood there, looking at the damage and scratching his head.

'What happened, Jim, didn't you see the tree?' Jackie rubbed salt in my wounds. 'It's a big tree. How could you drive into it?' Then he gave his opinion. 'Hey Lieutenant, this looks bad. We won't be able to fix this. Look, all these bolts are broken off, the threads are stuck inside. We'll have to get a recovery vehicle. We don't have bolts like these.'

Finally Lieutenant Goosen came up with a plan. 'We take a few bolts from all the other consoles and use them to fix these.'

'But how do we get these out? They snapped off inside.' Jackie saw no light, but Lakulya loosened the shafts of the broken bolts with a steel punch and hammer and removed them one by one. Four hours later, after a lot of shouting, swearing and cursing, we were on our way. This time Labanye was driving. Paulus and another Ovambo, David, were no longer in my Casspir.

Labanye's attempt at driving failed hopelessly. Soon I was back behind the wheel.

Over the next few days, we patrolled, looked for spoor,

gathered information and questioned the locals, who were a lot more helpful and cooperative than those in the west.

The Odila is a long and ancient waterway that dried up when the climate changed. The Atlantic Ocean on the south-western side of Africa is cold, never warmer than about 15 °C. This is due to the Benguela current, which brings cold water from Antarctica along the south-western side of Africa all the way up to Angola, where it dissipates. Then the Atlantic Ocean becomes warm again. That is why the south-western sides of South Africa and Namibia are so arid. The cold water from the Atlantic does not evaporate easily, so the region receives little rain and contains the world's second-largest desert, the Namib, which runs along the coast of Namibia.

It wasn't always like this. Two million years ago the ocean was warm and the region was luscious and tropical. That's when the Odila flowed, connecting northern rivers like the Kunene with the Etosha Pan in the south. In prehistoric times the Etosha Pan was a huge lake. When the Benguela current started to push cold water up along south-western Africa, a catastrophic climate change took place and the entire area changed. Many animal and plant species died out as the area dried up.

Captain Joost Engelbrecht's favourite saying was that while he was in the bush he bathed only when the Odila flowed. It had not flowed for hundreds of thousands of years.

Now, at the end of the rainy season, we were driving down the Odila. It was one of SWAPO's favourite infiltration routes, on which they often planted a lot of anti-tank landmines. That is why the Odila was also known as Landmine Lane.

Late on Sunday afternoon I was bored and tired of driving. It was hot and where there were no roads we bundu-bashed through shrubs and smaller trees. Leaves, sticks, branches, insects and the occasional snake came tumbling down. If I opened the hatches for fresh air, it all fell down on top of me. With the hatches closed it was unbearably hot and sweat poured from my body. As I lost body fluid, I drank litres of water from one of the canvas water bags that we shared and passed around. We had no shortage of water, as our Casspirs' water tanks each carried about 150 litres of drinking water.

Food was never a problem either. Part of our food supply consisted of one ration pack per person per day. The Ovambos ate a lot, or else they stored their food to take back home for the week that we were in town – aside from their pay they received nothing from Koevoet during the weeks spent in town. Guinea fowl, steenbok, duiker and kudu were easy pickings, and sometimes the locals would be missing the odd cow, goat or chicken once we had passed.

The Ovambos had the most bizarre way of killing a chicken. They would pluck a strong feather from the wing and push the sharp point of the quill into the chicken's brain from the back, at the point where the neck and the skull meet. The chicken died almost instantly. The Ovambos believed that this method made it easier to pluck the dead bird's feathers.

We were heading south down the Odila and we were about to reach the main road. It was about 3 p.m.

'Drive in my tracks; we don't want to hit a landmine,' Lieutenant Goosen warned over the radio. I could see his Casspir ahead to my left, at the bottom of the Odila.

A sudden white-and-yellow light flashed under the lieutenant's Casspir, which was instantly engulfed in a black cloud. The explosion was deafening. Lieutenant Goosen and his guys were temporarily deafened, dizzy and disorientated, but they would be fine.

During the Rhodesian war anti-tank landmines were a valuable weapon and were used extensively by the Patriotic Front against the Rhodesian security forces and the civilian population. That led to the development of the anti-landmine vehicle. First sandbags were packed on the floor of a Bedford truck to absorb the impact from the explosion of a landmine. After that, one of the first actual anti-landmine vehicles was developed, called the Spook. It looked like a dustbin on a Volkswagen chassis.

Those who designed anti-landmine vehicles soon realised it would be of no help to try to absorb the impact of a landmine. It should rather be deflected. One of the early successful South African inventions that did just that was the Hippo. The problem was that the Hippo ran on petrol and not diesel. The advantages of a diesel-driven vehicle in combat are pretty obvious, especially if one is going to detonate a landmine with a tank full of fuel.

Then South Africa's weapons giant Armscor – the Armaments Corporation of South Africa – came up with the Buffel, which was based on a Unimog (a Mercedes 4×4 truck) and used Unimog components. At the same time Dr Vernon Joynt at South Africa's Council for Scientific and Industrial Research (CSIR) developed the Casspir. He used a Mercedes engine, gearbox, transfer case and differentials. The Casspir was unique; it did not have a chassis. Instead the differentials and spring blades were bolted to cast-iron consoles, which were in turn bolted directly to the armour- or panzer-steel body of the vehicle. The body was built in a V-shape so that when a landmine was detonated by one of the wheels the blast would be deflected outwards and upwards, with very little damage to the rest of the vehicle.

The army chose the Buffel, but the police chose the Casspir, mostly because it was the choice of Frans Conradie, who revolutionised modern anti-guerrilla bush warfare.

The Buffel was lighter than the Casspir and it was top-heavy. It gave its occupants little protection, as it was open on top. The Casspir, whose name is made up of the letters of the abbreviations CSIR and SAP, was far superior to the Buffel in too many ways to mention. This was one of the factors that gave Koevoet an advantage over the army.

Our superiority was put to the test after the big infiltration in 1982, when the authorities were forced to recognise Koevoet officially and allowed us to go into Angola for the first time, on condition that the army accompanied us with their Buffels. We left them behind when they couldn't keep up.

After the landmine explosion in the Odila, we cautiously pulled up near Lieutenant Goosen and Zulu Golf 1 to protect them and to see if they had survived the blast. Don't be in a hurry to get out, I remembered having been taught. Instinctively one would try to get out as quickly as possible, but it was a lot safer to stay put. A landmine detonation like this could be accompanied by an ambush. Anti-personnel mines – mines intended to harm people, rather than vehicles and buildings – could be planted in the area around the landmine.

Be careful, take it slowly, be alert, I thought. Let the Ovambos get out first – not to put them a risk, but because their eyesight and senses are far better than ours. They are the masters of the bush.

The area was now secure and we assessed the damage. The right rear wheel had been blown off, but that was about all. A normal truck the size of a Casspir would have been blown to pieces and the occupants would have been dead. Lieutenant

Goosen and his guys were unscathed. The lieutenant could have passed for an Ovambo though – he was covered in black dirt.

'Look, we have to take what is left of the rim off, jack up this Casspir, put the spare wheel on and we'll be mobile again,' he said optimistically.

About an hour later we were indeed mobile, but not for long. Twenty metres on, the wheel attached to the drum came out together with the diff's drive shaft.

Lieutenant Goosen requested a recovery team and vehicle. It was late and it was obvious that they would never reach us before sunset. We were going to be there until the next day.

But first the lieutenant tried to persuade Zulu HQ to get a Puma helicopter to drop a diff. This request was denied, although it had been done before on a number of occasions and those Casspirs had been repaired on the spot.

'Guys, we are stuck on a major infiltration route,' the lieutenant said. 'We must dig in and wait this one out until tomorrow. Put claymore mines out to the north and set an ambush to the south,' he ordered. 'They reckon there could be a group heading up the Odila, coming our way.' After a pause, he said, 'Come on, Jackie, put the claymores out.'

'I don't know how to,' Jackie protested, shaking his head, and Whitey too shook his head. Either they didn't know how to do it or they didn't want to.

'Okay, I'll do it,' I volunteered.

A claymore mine is an anti-personnel mine consisting of a slab of plastic explosive covered with ball bearings and then coated with plastic or Bakelite. Two holes are left open on the top for one or two electrical detonators to be inserted. Under the claymore there are two metal bipods to plant it on the ground. On the face of the claymore is written, 'This side facing enemy' in raised plastic lettering so that one can feel the letters in the dark.

I placed the first claymore in front of a big kiaat tree and faced it to the north. Now came the tricky part: inserting the detonator, which can be sensitive if it's been in the sun a lot, and more so if it's been in a vehicle that has endured a landmine explosion. It would take only half a volt to detonate the detonator, and that created my next problem: attaching the electric cable to the wires of the detonator.

I kept the two wires of the detonator and both ends of the cable crossed. The cable could build up enough static to give the detonator sufficient charge to detonate the moment I connected them.

Next came the worst part: uncrossing both the detonator's wires and the wires of the cable and joining them. I was doing this from behind the tree with my hands and arms stretched out around the tree. I couldn't see the mine so it was as if I were blindfolded.

With a deep sigh I mumbled 'fuck it' and got up. I moved to the front of the tree and attached the two ends of the cable to the two ends of the detonators, then I ran the cable back about 20 metres to a point where I plugged the end of the cable into the hand-held plunger. When pressed, the plunger would send an electrical current down the cable to the detonator, which would set off the explosive charge and send hundreds of ball bearings flying into the face of any approaching enemy. Eventually I had placed six claymores out in a semi-circle facing northwards in order to stop any advance from that direction. Mission accomplished. I needed a cigarette.

The cigarette tasted better than usual. It felt good to be alive. We'd had one contact and we had hit one landmine since I had joined Zulu Golf. The future looked good, but I hated my Casspir. I must say, though, that at least at that moment Lieutenant Goosen's Casspir looked a bit worse than mine.

I joined the others on the southern side of our TB. We lay on top of a bank looking down over the road below and the bush on the other side. We could see for about 300 metres down the road to our left and for another 300 metres up the road to our right. It was a perfect ambush. Our rear was guarded to the north by my claymores. Let them come.

'Maintain absolute silence, no noise,' Lieutenant Goosen instructed. 'Jim, stop smoking.'

'But your radio is making a noise,' Jackie pointed out. 'Anyone will hear it from a mile off.' Radio contact was essential, but Jackie had a point, and the lieutenant turned down his radio, staying close to it.

Koevoet and COIN operated on the same long-distance frequency, which led to complications. The airwaves became jammed with nonsense, especially nonsense from the COIN base. Radio procedure and protocol was a complex issue. I had learnt radio procedure at Maloeskop, where radio secrecy, radio codes and Slidex were drilled into us. COIN still adhered to those procedures. The situation report given by every COIN base every morning to COIN HQ drove us crazy. If a casualty evacuation (casevac) was needed after a contact, it would often be impossible to use the airwaves.

We had to endure frustrating hours of listening to long coded messages, which would often end with '... and back to base', meaning, 'Okay, you're going on patrol and then you're going back to your fucking base to the tomato sauce and toilet paper that you have just requested.'

Captain Eugene de Kock, commander of Zulu Delta, once

got his message through to Sergeant Willie Nortjé just after some ridiculous message from a COIN base. 'Hey, we're at Ohangwena tonight. Bring some Red Heart rum; the rum here is fucking shit,' he said over the air to Willie, who was obviously on his way to join them.

At our TB on the Odila, an hour went by, two hours ... All I could hear was the buzzing of insects and the occasional bird in a tree. An Ovambo drove his Ford F250 past on the road below. Boredom set in. In another hour the sun would give us a beautiful display in the west as it went down.

'I'm fucking hungry!' Jackie shouted. Clearly he'd had enough. Finally, with enough complaining and manipulation, he got his way.

'Okay, but no fires tonight,' Lieutenant Goosen said, giving in. We spent the rest of the day eating and talking a lot of shit.

'Hey, so this is your last week with us,' Jackie said to Whitey.

'Yes, when we get back, I'm going home.'

'Why don't you stay and become a permanent member like me?' Jackie asked. 'You're my friend. I'm going to miss you.'

'Not a fuck. I'm going home.'

Only then did I realise that Whitey was a temp and that soon it would be just the lieutenant, Jackie and me.

'What will happen to our Ovambos if we have to leave and go home?' Jackie asked Lieutenant Goosen. 'What will become of Tommy, Bennie, David and all the others?'

'They have been promised that if we withdraw, or if they have elections and SWAPO wins, no matter what happens they can come back to South Africa with us,' he replied. 'They will be looked after.'

'Do you mean that all of them will be allowed to come back with us?' Jackie asked, wanting to make sure.

'Well, only those who want to. It will be their choice.'

Now the Ovambos were interested and wanted to know all about life in South Africa. I realised just how little they knew about the outside world. Most of them had never been outside Ovamboland and had never even seen a double-storey building, a train, a city or much of modern civilisation.

Into the night we exchanged stories with the Ovambos about our cultures and our homes and our different ways of life.

Their biggest concern about South Africa was our cattle. They had heard that most of our cattle didn't have big horns and that some didn't have horns at all. This was unacceptable. To the Ovambo, cattle is the most important aspect of life. Ownership of cattle is status – the bigger the horns of the cattle, the higher the status of the owner. Their cattle may be dying of sickness and starvation, but if they have big horns, they are good cattle.

That night, after we'd gone to sleep, something coming down the road woke me. It was the army, a sapper team sweeping the road for landmines. It was early morning and they had already come a long way from Eenhana. They were making their way towards Elundu, while a team from Elundu was making its way towards Eenhana. The two teams would meet halfway. What a shit job, I thought, and dangerous too. There was a soldier in front on their left flank and one on their right flank. They were on point duty. Then there were about five guys carrying the metal detectors, walking in a staggered line down the road with earphones over their ears, focusing on the pitch of the sound. A sudden change of pitch would indicate that the plate had passed over a metal object. Behind them a couple of Buffels followed.

I sure didn't want that job. It made you an easy target for an ambush. From our position we could annihilate them in about 20 seconds. If they discovered a landmine, they would have to lift it and it could be booby-trapped. The army's sapper teams had the difficult, dangerous and thankless job of sweeping the roads in the operational area. Having to walk long distances carrying a metal detector all day in the heat and in the open at great risk was not fun.

They were doing us a huge favour by trying to clear the roads of mines and make it safe for us and the army to travel, but some of our teams would still brush thousands of empty bullet casings out of the back of their Casspirs when they came out of the bush onto a road after a contact. Imagine what it was like for those poor sapper teams with their metal detectors suddenly to have a few thousand empty metal casings scattered for some kilometres down a road.

The recovery team eventually arrived, under the command of Warrant Officer Nel. He was in a hurry and didn't waste any time. He hooked up Lieutenant Goosen's Casspir and left for the police garage at Ondangwa.

We packed up and I retrieved the claymore mines, going through the same stress as when I set them up.

Lieutenant Goosen wanted us to stay and finish the week with just three Casspirs, but his was the only one with a built-in long-distance radio and we were left with only a portable TR28. Our remaining three Casspirs were now overcrowded and his had to be fixed.

We packed up and headed for the Ondangwa police garage. I also needed to fix my Casspir. At the garage the mechanics offered to repair Lieutenant Goosen's Casspir, but the lieutenant was adamant that, because it was his fault that he had detonated the mine, he had to fix it himself. He immediately set about replacing the rear diff on his Casspir while I tried to fix mine.

The storeman at the garage became a real pain in the butt, as he wouldn't issue any part until he had been given the old one.

I had to replace two of the cast-iron consoles on my Casspir, but before going to all the trouble of removing the old ones, I made my way to the store to get two new ones so that I could check if they were going to fit.

I asked the storeman politely for two rear-right consoles.

'Where is your job card?' he replied in a strong German accent. 'I must have your job card first.'

'Sorry, but where do I get a job card from?' I was feeling a little frustrated.

He handed me a form and I tried to figure out how to fill it in. I asked to borrow his pen.

'No,' he replied, 'it will never come back.'

I eventually found a pen, filled in the job card and handed it to him. He looked at it and gave it back to me, saying, 'No, you must fill it in properly.' I started to get pissed off, but I said nothing and made the corrections to the form.

'Okay,' I asked, 'can I now have the two right-rear consoles?'

'No, you must bring me the old ones first.' He was adamant. He was a typical storeman who believed that everything in the store belonged to him. To part with anything was like parting with a prized possession.

'But what if the new ones don't fit?' I asked. 'It's a very old Casspir.'

He just looked at me and said, 'I want the old ones. I cannot release the new ones until you bring me the old ones.'

I walked away, muttering, 'No wonder you fucking Germans lost the war. Typical bloody storeman.'

'What was that? What did you say?' I heard as I walked away.

Eventually, after an hour of running back and forth borrowing tools from Lieutenant Goosen, where he was replacing the diff on his Casspir, I got both consoles off and made my way to the store.

The storeman kept me waiting for 20 minutes before he gave me the two new consoles.

I wanted to fit them quickly and get the hell out of there. It had become almost impossible to work there and I didn't have much in the way of tools.

They didn't fit. The new ones were not the same size as the old ones, so I took the new ones back.

'Are you sure you asked for the correct ones, both right rears?'

Obviously it was going to be my fault.

'Look, I brought the old ones, so compare them. They are not the same,' I said.

After half an hour of comparing the old consoles with every console in the store he said, 'No, we don't have any like these.'

I was really pissed off. 'You mean I went to all the trouble to take the old ones out and now I have to put the old broken ones back again? Do you realise what a mission it was to remove these? I asked you in the beginning if I could first go and compare the new ones with the old ones.'

'Yes, but I have to have the old ones before I can release the new ones,' he said.

'And what do you do with the old ones? You dump them with all the rubbish. You don't need the old ones; you just need to make life difficult for me.' I'd raised my voice and attracted some attention from the lieutenant in charge as well as another mechanic, who came to my rescue and helped me.

Eventually we got my Casspir fixed in the best way we could, with a few modifications to the old consoles and a lot of sweat.

Not a good job, but the best that could be done under the circumstances.

It was a nightmare to work at the COIN garage at Ondangwa, which was 40 kilometres from Oshakati. They were never helpful and often didn't want us there at all. Some of our guys had given us a bad reputation by stealing from the garage and from other Casspirs that were sometimes left there for repairs. My Casspir was old and had been neglected, so it needed a lot of repairs. Trying to fix it became my biggest nightmare and I had to take the blame for its condition. This frustration brought me to the brink of quitting.

Back at Okavi we were offloading the Albatross and the Casspirs. Okavi had become Koevoet's headquarters and Jackie and I had been kicked out of our bungalow, which was now the ops room. The bungalow opposite it had become the main administrative office and next to it was Brigadier Dreyer's office.

I carried a case of claymore mines from the Casspirs to the prison cell that served as our temporary store. It was opposite the ops room and admin office.

I placed the box of claymores on the floor, turned and left the store. BANG! One of the claymores' detonators suddenly went off. Luckily no one was in the store and it didn't detonate a claymore.

The small explosion echoed through the base as Captain Winter walked past.

'What the fuck is going on?' he shouted. 'I'm still going to fuck you lot up!'

Just then Captain Gene de Kock passed Captain Winter and said, 'What, who are you going to fuck up? You couldn't even fuck yourself up,' and walked on.

Captain De Kock was scary and I learnt to avoid him. He was

just not the type of person I wanted to be near to. He had a reputation for losing his temper and beating up anyone near him.

A few years later Brigadier Dreyer sent Captain De Kock back to Pretoria after a disagreement. I liked the way he shut up Captain Winter, but I made sure I got out of the base to the Casspirs as quickly as possible.

That Wednesday we were called to one of Brigadier Dreyer's famous crapping sessions under the tree behind the ops room.

A fight had taken place in the pub at the International Guest House, one of many between Koevoet and the army, and it had got out of hand. After they had come off second best in the first round, the army had called in reinforcements. Two Buffel-loads of armed army members had arrived, and that was when the fight had really got violent. A number of army rifles had been broken and had had their barrels bent by our guys. Someone had also driven a Buffel through a civilian house, causing extensive damage. An army guy had a broken neck, was paralysed and had been casevaced. Several others were in a critical condition in hospital.

When the brigadier came out, he got straight to the point and asked, 'Who was at the Guest House last night?' A number of guys put up their hands.

'These are the injuries and this is the damage.' He gave a rundown of everything. Then he raised his voice. 'All of you, the whole lot of you, are banned from the Guest House for ever. Is that clear? The next one of you who puts one foot through that door will be on the first plane home. Did you all hear me?'

As he turned to walk away, he asked in a quieter voice, but so that we could all hear, 'And who won?'

'We did,' someone said.

He chuckled to himself as he walked on.

'Hey, Jim, tonight we have to go to the Guest House for a drink,' Jackie said.

'Are you mad? Did you hear what he just said?' I replied.

'No, every time he bans us we all go back on the same night of the day he banned us.' Jackie was confident. 'He can't fire all of us. He can't put all of us on a plane back home. Don't worry, he's bluffing.'

That night about 20 of us sat in the bar of the Guest House, defying the brigadier's order. Whitey was on his way home.

For Jackie and me the Guest House in Oshakati became a favourite hangout. It was where Jackie one night set himself alight when he tried to drink flaming Escorial. The two of us became best friends.

6

Hot pursuit

Our next temporary base was at Elundu, home to the Kwanyama, the biggest and most cooperative of the seven Ovambo tribes. Elundu, with its thick bush and soft white sand, is 10 kilometres south of the Angolan border in the north-east of Ovamboland, on the road between Eenhana and Okongo. The rainy season was over and everything was drying up.

Our Ovambos were very unhappy. They didn't like operating from Elundu. They believed that the place was cursed after a dispute between the army and a witch-doctor chief who had lived there when the army built the base. Elundu was where Zulu Mike had got fucked up in an ambush.

The water at Elundu comes from deep under the ground and tastes like soap. It is useless for washing, too, because soap won't dissolve in it.

We made our TB outside the army base against the northern sand wall and parked our Casspirs in a row, facing north, about 20 metres apart. We were going to sleep on the ground in the open between the Casspirs.

Food rations were being handed out and the Ovambos were making fires for cooking. Our supply of 50 kilograms of frozen meat had almost defrosted after the long drive from Oshakati.

Refuelling our Casspirs and the Blesbok from the 200-litre drums of diesel on the back of the Blesbok became a major mission. The hand pump was broken, so we had to siphon the diesel from the drums into the Casspirs' fuel tanks, which meant manoeuvring the Casspirs as close to the Blesbok as possible.

I took a turn to suck on the end of the pipe in order to try to get the diesel to flow, but I ended up with a mouthful of diesel.

'Fuck, this tastes vile,' I cursed, coughing. I spat and cleared my throat before lighting a cigarette to try to get rid of the taste.

'Don't blow yourself up,' Jackie joked. 'You drank so much diesel you might explode.'

Finally the Casspirs were refuelled and their water tanks were full of Elundu's putrid water. I hoped that the water wouldn't carry Elundu's curse with us for the next week.

I stank of diesel and could still taste it. I sat down on my rolled-out sleeping bag next to my Casspir, Zulu Golf 4, to eat some cold bully beef, tinned sweetcorn and raw onion.

'Lakulya, come and tell me about this base,' I asked. 'You guys say it's haunted.' Lakulya and some of the other Ovambos were standing at the fire. Tommy turned and laughed. 'The oshilulu is coming tonight to get him,' he said.

'Isssh.' Lakulya said something to Tommy in Oshivambo, obviously angry and upset.

Some of the Ovambos came closer and sat on the ground with me. David brought me some sausage from the fire and when he sat down I asked him what an oshilulu was. He was the youngest Ovambo; I guessed he was about 15. I wondered how he had got into Koevoet at his age.

Tommy joined us and became very serious as he began to explain. 'An oshilulu is a devil–demon that comes during the night to torment and torture us.'

'Like the tokoloshe?' I asked. They looked at me blankly.

'The black people in South Africa, the Zulu and the Xhosa, believe in the tokoloshe,' I explained. 'He is an evil demon that comes at night to play tricks on people and torment them. He has a very long penis, which he wraps three times around his body or else he carries it over his shoulder.'

They laughed at my description and I asked them where and when the oshilulu came.

'Many places, but especially here. This is an evil place,' Tommy said. 'You will see; it will come for some of us tonight. This war started when the army came here long ago and shot one of the holy birds of Ovamboland.'

I'd heard that story before, like the time when I tried to shoot a turkey buzzard at Ongha. The Ovambos went ballistic and, when I missed, they said it was because the bird was invincible and holy. I knew better, off course. I was just a shit shot.

'What does the army shooting a holy bird have to do with the oshilulu coming here tonight?' I asked.

'When the army came to Elundu there was a kraal here. A very powerful and important chief, who was also a witch doctor, lived in the kraal,' Tommy explained. 'The army wanted to build this base and said the chief must move and so there was a dispute. The chief died. No one knows how he died. Maybe the army killed him or maybe he just died.

'When he died, he put a curse on this base and this place. That's why the water is so bad and that's why the oshilulu comes to torment us at night.'

'There is no such thing as an oshilulu,' I protested. That upset them and I realised I might be getting out of line, so I said, 'Okay, if the oshilulu comes tonight, wake me up and I will fight it.'

'You can't do that. You can't see the demon, but we can. He

is real to us. You're not one of us and you don't understand our culture.'

I had obviously upset them.

I left it at that and changed the subject with a joke that had worked before.

'Tommy,' I said, 'you're an Ondonga and you come from the Ondangwa area, don't you?' I asked.

'Yes, I'm an Ondonga,' he replied proudly.

'So you eat donkeys?' I teased him.

They all packed up laughing and they too teased Tommy until we crept into our sleeping bags for the night.

The next morning we were up before sunrise. Spirits were high and I wondered what the day had in store for us.

'We must take supplies for two days,' Lieutenant Goosen instructed. 'We might need to TB in the bush.'

He preferred the solitude of the bush over the protocol and formalities of the officers at the bases. He was such an introvert; he didn't drink like Jackie and I did. Our priority when we first reached a base was to find the pub.

'Hey, Tommy, did the oshilulu come last night?' I shouted.

'No,' he shouted back, and I realised that the Ovambos were more than happy to be leaving Elundu and its curses behind.

'Make sure you've got enough supplies for two days,' Lieutenant Goosen reminded us once more. 'We're leaving the Blesbok here.'

'What if we need diesel?' Jackie protested.

'No, we don't have enough drivers,' he said tersely, cutting Jackie short. 'I need Tommy to drive for me. I can't drive and do everything myself.'

The sun was just rising as we drove out, heading in a north-easterly direction.

Why did I have to inherit this piece of shit from Greens, I wondered as I climbed into my Casspir. The old relic must have been the oldest Casspir in Koevoet. It was an original prototype and the speedometer had stopped working long ago. I didn't even know what mileage it had done. The steering wheel was horizontal, not tilted like the others, and a lot of the spare parts didn't fit that model, as I'd discovered at the Ondangwa police garage. I decided that the next thing I had to do was to cut the roof open with an angle grinder, because there was no fucking air in there.

Suddenly my Casspir lost power, the engine cut out and we came to a grinding halt. I pushed the starter button and pumped the accelerator. The Casspir started and then cut out again.

I watched the other Casspirs disappearing ahead of me.

Another three attempts brought no joy.

'Lieutenant Goosen, Jim,' I called on the RSA53 radio.

'Go,' he replied.

'This Casspir has cut out; it won't start,' I called back.

There was no reply so I opened the hatch above me and climbed out, not realising that my troubles had just begun. Some of the Ovambos helped to open the bonnet. I looked inside, not knowing what I was looking for.

Lieutenant Goosen and Jackie arrived. The lieutenant looked pissed off and I felt shit. Jackie came to my defence. 'Greens really fucked up this Casspir,' he said.

'I told him to drain the diesel tank – there's water in the diesel,' Lieutenant Goosen shouted. He took a screwdriver, unscrewed a grub screw, unscrewed the hand pump and bled the fuel line. 'Right, try and start it,' he ordered.

I jumped behind the wheel, hit the starter button and pumped the accelerator. The Casspir roared to life and black smoke billowed from the exhaust. The others were back in their Casspirs and off before I could say anything. I'd just follow them, I thought.

About an hour later we arrived at a kraal. I pulled up away from the others and opened the bonnet of my Casspir to reassure myself that I would know what to do if the same problem occurred again.

An old man came out of the kraal. Lieutenant Goosen's Ovambos talked to him. The man, dressed in tatters, was excited; he pointed and waved wildly.

'Tell him he's mad,' Jackie shouted in Afrikaans. The old man understood the language. 'No, I'm not mad. Come, come with me. I'll show you. There were many of them, more than all of you, three times as many. They had a meeting over here yesterday.'

We followed the old man in a north-westerly direction with the Ovambos laughing and chatting. Obviously no one was taking him seriously. After about 400 metres we reached a clearing. The mood suddenly changed, as did our attitude towards the old man.

The Ovambos are born trackers. Some are better than others, but they all have the most incredible ability to track – not only to see the tracks but to interpret them. They had tried to teach me in the past, but what they read like a book was a blank page to me. Now even my ignorant eye could see hundreds of tracks left by Soviet combat boots.

We asked the big questions: How many were there? When were they there? Where were they heading?

'Three times as many as you are,' the old man repeated, annoyed.

There were 45 of us. Three times that is almost 150. That's a big group, a fucking big group.

'The night before last,' the old man said, 'they met here and left yesterday morning. They went south.'

It was almost 8 a.m., so if they had left at sunrise the day before, we were about 26 or 27 hours behind them. We were about two kilometres from the Angolan border. I wondered how far into Angola their bases were, and whether they walked all the way or whether Cuban trucks would have daringly transported them closer down to the Namibian border. Much would have depended on the situation in Angola and what our army and UNITA were doing.

With Operation Protea and Operation Quicksilver our defence force had cleared southern Angola of the Cuban and the Angolan FAPLA presence all the way up to the Kunene River at Xangongo. About 200 kilometres of southern Angola would have been a no-go zone for the Cubans and FAPLA to assist SWAPO to get this far south. How had a group of 150 insurgents made it here? And, more importantly, where were they heading and what was their mission?

We were going to chase them. In one fluid movement the follow-up fell into place and we took up our positions. I was on the left flank behind Jackie, while Bennie was on the right flank behind Lieutenant Goosen. There were about 15 trackers on the ground between Jackie and me, and Lieutenant Goosen and Bennie. Lieutenant Goosen ordered most of the trackers back to the Casspirs.

'It's going to be a long and hard follow-up, so save your energy. The tracks are so easy it's like driving down a highway. Not more than five trackers on the ground at one time. We have to move fast – they can move at night, we can't. Watch out for booby traps, POMZs, Jumping Jacks and Black Widows. If we hit one with too many trackers on the ground, there'll be a lot of casualties.'

Countless possible dangers lay ahead: an ambush, traps, or just driving slap bang into the enemy. We were possibly outnumbered three to one.

Jackie wanted to form one front instead of us driving single file, so I moved alongside him to his left and Bennie drew up alongside Lieutenant Goosen to his right. I thought it was stupid, as it meant we had to drive through the vegetation, which would cause a lot of wear and tear to the vehicles, and the enemy was still far ahead of us.

We progressed as quickly as possible. The vegetation was dense. While some of the trees could be pushed over with the Casspirs, the bigger ones had to be avoided.

It was hot and my leg muscles throbbed, especially those in my left leg from pumping the clutch all the time. I kept Jackie and the rest in sight out of the corner of my right eye, doing my best to keep in line.

The trackers picked up an East German combat helmet that the enemy had discarded.

At every kraal we passed, the locals confirmed that we were chasing a very big group.

Lieutenant Goosen kept Zulu HQ updated on our position, with all the relevant information he could give them, but he tried to downplay the size of the group we were following, telling HQ that there were probably about 50 insurgents.

The size of the group was always disputed, even after they infiltrated. Because of its size, it was difficult for our trackers to tell from the spoor exactly how big this group was, as the insurgents were walking over each other's spoor. Some might have thought that 150 was a gross exaggeration, but at this stage all the information we were obtaining from the locals indicated that the group was about three times as big as ours.

Other Koevoet groups were making their way towards us to join our follow-up. Zulu Yankee was the closest and would probably be the first to reach us.

No, please, no! My Casspir came to a grinding halt. The engine died. It didn't want to start, so I got out and bled it.

'Jim, Jim, Jim. Jackie,' he called over the radio. 'Where are you?'

I quickly explained. Lieutenant Goosen ordered me over the radio to make my way back to Elundu, where our new Blesbok had been left, to sort out my Casspir's fuel troubles.

'You've got water in your fuel,' he said, diagnosing the problem. 'You need to drain your fuel tank, refuel it and clean out your fuel line. I told Greens to do it but he didn't.'

Go back to Elundu and leave the guys? Not a fuck. Even if I had to carry my cursed Casspir, I was not turning back, so I didn't reply. I could always say that I never got the message, that my radio had packed up.

I had made the decision, so I jumped out and once again bled the fuel line with the hand pump. Then we were on our way and I was driving like a deranged demon, following their vehicle tracks and trying to catch up.

How far could they have gone? It shouldn't take long for me to catch up, I thought. Half an hour went by and I saw no sign of them. My Casspir broke down again and I got it going again.

Then it cut out again, and while I was bleeding the fuel line once more, I noticed a glass bowl with a small filter under the hand pump. It was full of water. I opened it up and cleaned out the filter while I stood over the engine.

What was that? Something had fallen down the side of the engine but I couldn't see down there as it was dark. I decided that it couldn't be important. I replaced the glass bowl and filter and pumped the hand pump, but diesel now sprayed out from the top of the glass bowl. Whatever fell down there must have been important after all, I thought to myself.

'Lakulya, something fell down here. See if you can find it,' I said.

Lakulya went in from the bottom through a hole behind the bumper and stuck his hand in along the V of the body. He pulled out a handful of dirt, leaves and twigs, mixed with diesel. The pile had just been waiting to reach the right temperature to ignite – and set our Casspir alight. Lakulya got a stick and sifted through the muck as he scraped it out.

My arm was longer than his, so I pushed my hand in and scraped out as much as possible. Then I pushed my arm in as far as I could and … hey, what was this? I felt something and grabbed it, but then couldn't pull my arm out. I manoeuvred the object slowly and out it came – it was a washer. I took my shirt off and wiped the muck off my arm and hand and cleaned the washer. I realised that it fitted between the glass bowl and the hand pump.

How could such a small and insignificant rubber washer be so important to our future? Without it we would never have got to wherever fate was about to take us. Was I getting drunk from all these diesel fumes or was I going insane?

My shirt was dirty and covered with diesel; I threw it on the floor, slammed the key down and pushed the starter button while I pumped the accelerator. The Casspir sprang to life. With a roar we took off and I prayed that the bad beast wouldn't give any more trouble. As I drove fast and furiously, it bounced, bucked and banged along. I needed to catch up, but we were far behind. I couldn't even hear the others on the radio any more. If we were out of radio contact, we were at least 15 to 20 kilometres behind.

For the rest of the day we desperately fought to catch up. The Casspir broke down continually. Sometimes we would drive for as long as an hour and sometimes we would move just a few metres before it ground to a halt again.

Without radio contact it was important for me not to lose the vehicle tracks, but it soon started to get dark.

Zulu Yankee finally caught up with me, only to drive past and tell me that I must have water in my diesel and that I needed to drain my fuel tank. If I drained the tank it would be empty, and since we had left the Blesbok at Elundu their advice didn't help one bit.

I wondered whether the other Casspirs would be able to follow the spoor at night. If so, I stood little chance of ever catching up.

Lieutenant Goosen must have considered this option, but it would have been foolish. Under cover of darkness the enemy would have had an advantage over us if we bumped into them.

What would the enemy do at night? Would they sleep or would they walk through the night? At some stage they would have to sleep. The big mystery was where they were heading to.

As it got dark I had to slow down so that I did not lose the tracks. Finally, at 10 p.m., someone waved a torch ahead.

I had caught up.

I was exhausted and dehydrated, my hands were cut and full of blisters and the diesel made them stiff and sore.

Lakulya rolled out my sleeping bag next to our Casspir and offered me a new rat pack.

'No thanks. You can have it; I'm not hungry,' I said. 'I've still got enough in the old one. Please clean the LMG.'

He looked at me and said, 'Yes, Tate Kuru.' Tate Kuru means 'My Grandfather' in Ovambo. To call someone 'Grandfather' was to show respect. I was 20 years old. Then I slept.

The sound of a Casspir starting up woke me. I jumped up, rolled up my sleeping bag and tied it, and got into the driver's seat of my Casspir. The Ovambos had a fire going and were making coffee. Fuck that, I needed to get the bitch going.

I slammed the key down and hit the starter button. The engine turned and turned while I pumped the accelerator. I wanted to cry, scream and shout. I could feel tears welling up in my eyes. I climbed out and heaved the bonnet open.

I saw Jackie climbing into his Casspir, and he saw me.

Why don't you help, I thought. Why don't you and Lieutenant Goosen help me sort this shit out for once and for all and then we can all be on our way again? I'm not going to ask for help, so fuck you all. I hope you all get shot.

'What's wrong, Jim?' It was Johnny Enslin from Zulu Yankee.

'I've got water in my diesel and need to drain the diesel tank but I don't even know where the drain plug is. There must be a drain plug somewhere. Even if I drain it, we don't have diesel to fill it. Surely at some stage all the water will have worked its way out.'

'We had the same problem. Come, let me show you,' he said. 'Here is the drain plug, under the back step, which swings up like this. All you need is a number-14 socket. You should do it now. Water is heavier than diesel and will lie at the bottom of the tank, so now, after the Casspir stood still over night, the water will have settled at the bottom. Open the drain plug and tap the water off,' he instructed. 'Water will come out first. As soon as diesel starts coming out, the water should be out and you can put the plug back.'

'I don't have a number-14 socket. The tools are with Lieutenant Goosen and he's fucked off. Do you have one that I could borrow? Please, Johnny,' I begged.

'No, sorry,' he replied, and he was off.

When I finally got the bitch going again, I was way behind the follow-up. It was time to pray for some luck in trying to catch up. I noticed that I had only five Ovambos left with me. The others had deserted by jumping into the other Casspirs.

At some stage we would all run out of diesel, food and water. I wondered what the plan was and for how long we would be able to keep going. We would catch up with the enemy at some point. How was this all going to turn out? I didn't want to miss the action – in fact, I was determined not to miss out.

I spent another day trying desperately to catch up, my Casspir breaking down constantly.

Lieutenant Goosen soon realised that the trackers didn't need to be on the ground at all and that it was possible to follow the spoor from his vehicle.

Stiripo was our best tracker. He was tall, pitch black, young and good-looking, and had joined Koevoet having come over from UNITA. He could hardly speak a word of Afrikaans or English, but he was always on the spoor during a follow-up operation, coordinating things on the ground with his whistle.

At first Stiripo had sat on the bonnet of the Casspir and signalled to the lieutenant, who was driving. This was plain suicidal. Not only could he have fallen off, but imagine driving into an ambush or a contact while sitting on the bonnet of the leading Casspir.

Later Lieutenant Goosen had called Stiripo in to try to follow the spoor from the gunner's seat next him. As a result, the follow-up was going a lot faster. They were gaining on the enemy quite rapidly – and leaving me behind even more rapidly. I was once more so far behind that I had lost radio contact with Zulu Golf.

It was dead quiet, apart from the noise my Casspir was making.

'What's that?' I whispered suddenly. I heard something coming from behind: it was the sound of Casspir engines.

A Blesbok approached. It was Sergeant Terblanche, commander of Zulu Tango. What was he doing driving a Blesbok? He pulled up next to me while I was under the bonnet of my Casspir.

'I heard you guys need diesel,' he called to me. 'Where's the follow-up?'

'Just follow the tracks and you'll find them,' I shouted back. 'I've run out of diesel and soon the others will too,' I added. I was lying, but by that point I would have done anything to get some diesel.

The back of the Blesbok fell open and three Ovambos tossed a 200-litre drum of diesel onto the ground. It landed with a thud.

'Do you have a number-14 socket?' I called, but either Sergeant Terblanche didn't hear me or he didn't care. He drove off, shouting, 'Don't use all of it; there's not enough for everyone.'

Now we were stuck with a problem. We had diesel, but no way to get it out of the drum and into the fuel tank. We also didn't have a number-14 socket to drain the tank.

Somebody might come along with a spanner at some stage, I thought. But what if that didn't happen? I considered the amount of water that could be in our tank, weighing up the pros and cons. I decided that we needed to fill the tank.

We had no way of opening the drum, but eventually I found that I could open it with our tyre lever. We tried to lift up the drum and pour the diesel into the tank, but we nearly killed Lakulya in the process when the drum slipped and almost squashed him.

Eventually the rest of Zulu Tango passed. Then Zulu Bravo passed. And still we had no spanner. By now a couple of my Ovambos had lost interest and had wandered off.

They returned later with a bucket, which we flattened slightly. We proceeded to pour the diesel into the fuel tank, bucket by bucket, until it was almost full. There was still some diesel in the drum and I felt like leaving it behind, but we or someone else might need it, so we pushed it into the Casspir. After bleeding it one more time, we were off.

I raced as fast as possible to try to catch up. It was dark by the time we did so and the groups had already set up TB. There were four groups on the follow-up now, which meant a total of 16 Casspirs with about 180 men. Now we outnumbered the enemy.

I pulled up in the tracks, stopped and cut the engine. I was finished, and so was our water.

Lakulya offered me a rat pack, but I traded him for the last bit of his water. I folded my arms over the steering wheel, put my head down and fell asleep in a sitting position.

The third day of the follow-up started just before sunrise. I woke to the sound of Casspirs starting, so I climbed out of my vehicle and tried to urinate behind a tree. It burned. I looked down and saw a thick stream of red urine coming out. Had I caught a disease?

I had heard of sexually transmitted diseases – they had taught us about them at the college. But I hadn't been with a woman. Sharing the water bag with the Ovambos perhaps?

Eventually it turned out to be nothing serious – it was probably the result of extreme dehydration.

It was cold and I felt goose pimples prickling all over my body. It hadn't been possible to wash, shave, brush my teeth or change clothes for a few days, and I didn't even have a shirt to wear any more. I stank of sweat and diesel. I rubbed the back of my neck and my shoulders and a thick layer of black grime came off in my grubby hand.

I was happy that my fuel problems were over and I joined Zulu Golf's row of Casspirs at the back, behind Bennie.

'Today, we are going to get them; today we will kill many enemy. Later the gunships must come,' Lakulya, the eternal optimist, said next to me with a smile.

The Ovambos were totally in tune with their surroundings. This was their territory, their home environment. A lot is always said about the Bushmen and their incredible tracking ability, but they couldn't compete with the Ovambo in Ovamboland.

The Ovambos were the worst racists I had ever encountered and they treated Bushmen with scorn. If a Bushman tried to gather information from the local Ovambos, they would simply tell him to fuck off. The seven Ovambo tribes didn't get on with each other either. The Kwanyama and Kwambi would seldom mix and would almost never intermarry.

Koevoet was made up of about 90 per cent Ovambos, while SWAPO was almost 100 per cent Ovambo. Politically we could justify helping the Ovambo people to defend their country against the evil communist infiltrators coming in from Angola. It was better to help the good Ovambos to kill the bad Ovambos. This was their fight and we were there to help them – or so we often indoctrinated them.

The Bushmen were not good soldiers. Some of the Koevoet teams had tried to use them, but as soon as the spoor became hot and a contact was imminent, the Bushmen trackers would slow down. Often they would run as soon as rockets and bullets started to fly.

I was told that Zulu Delta had once used a Bushman tracker who was good, but would run away at the first sign of a contact. They had tied a rope around his neck and led him like a dog to stop him from escaping the contact.

Tracking didn't simply mean following spoor. The spoor was a key to the mind of the enemy, to his identity, what he was doing and where he was going.

At this stage of our follow-up all we knew was that the enemy was leading us further and further south. The Etosha National Park lay to the south of Ovamboland, but that would not be their objective. The town of Tsumeb and the surrounding white farming community could perhaps be their goal.

The spoor was warming up and Major Tickly, a Namibian farmer and a member of the citizen force, decided to come and assist us by flying some top cover with his own private Cessna. The major had become a legend with Koevoet.

Only the previous week we had been hot on three sets of spoor, but the sunset was about to stop us. Major Tickly was flying to Eenhana at the time and was passing quite close by. He picked up our conversations on our RSA53s and offered help.

He came in from behind and during a quick flyover he opened up with two AKMs, which he had just had mounted under the wings of his Cessna, in the projected direction of the spoor.

Nightfall stopped our follow-up, but the next morning our Ovambos could clearly see from the spoor that Major Tickly had very nearly scored a lucky direct hit on the three that we were following.

He was now flying as a spotter for us, just as the air force would fly the Bosbok as air support. The Bosbok had no armaments, but its air support was of great value. It would put pressure on the enemy. It might spot the enemy and then guide us to them. It also helped to coordinate the follow-up.

The enemy probably now knew that we were following, unless they assumed that Major Tickly's private plane was just a civilian plane. They would eventually find out that we were after them, anyway.

At some stage Lieutenant Goosen would try to call in some gunships – Alouette helicopters flown by a pilot and an engineer–gunner, armed with a 20-mm cannon. They always flew in pairs.

A pair of gunships was available at Ondangwa, and another at Eenhana, both very far from our follow-up. To reach us would take some time and, once they had reached us, they would not be able to stay airborne for long before they would have to go back to refuel. Although we sometimes carried two 200-litre drums on our Blesbok so that the gunships could refuel in the field, none of the groups present was carrying any aviation turpentine.

When calling in the gunships, timing was crucial to secure an element of surprise and to maximise the time that they would be able to stay airborne. The enemy should realise that we were following them only once we were close and the gunships were arriving.

That moment came. Lieutenant Goosen scrambled the first pair of gunships from Eenhana, indicating that the spoor was getting hot. But the instant it looked like there was going to be some action, my beast wanted to back down. Please, no, it can't be possible, I thought desperately. My Casspir is afraid; it's a fucking coward.

I lost about 15 minutes after jumping out and bleeding the fuel line for about the fiftieth time in three days. After that I broke down another three times while I heard that the second pair of gunships had joined the follow-up. Major Tickly had climbed to a higher altitude to oversee the entire operation. One pair of gunships circled ahead of the follow-up by five kilometres, the other pair by five to 10 kilometres.

That far south the vegetation was not so dense. A group as big as the one we were following couldn't be missed from the air, but the pilots and gunners saw nothing. They believed that the enemy was much further ahead. The trackers were adamant, however, that they were close. The gunships extended their flying radius to 20 kilometres to the south. One pair of gunships returned to base to refuel, then went back to relieve the other pair, and so they alternated.

I got left so far behind that I lost radio contact with the other vehicles, but I still had contact with the gunships and the spotter.

I raced forward as fast as I could get my Casspir to move. She rocked, rolled and bounced along as I raced up and down through the gears. I had to make up time because I couldn't miss this one.

We started to pick up the other vehicles on the radio and I heard someone call: 'We are close. The Ovambos say it's any moment now. Can't the gunships see anything?'

Then, suddenly: 'Maintain radio silence. I must make a forced landing …' It was Major Tickly. His Cessna's engine cut out and down he went into a mahangu field. He landed on the furrows crossways, so his wheels caught and the nose went straight down. He was killed on impact.

Two gunships had gone to refuel and the remaining two, who didn't yet know that Major Tickly was dead, withdrew to assist him.

He had crash-landed quite near to me and the gunship pilots saw that I was close. They called to try to make contact with me before landing at the crash site, but I ignored them – I had to get to where the action was about to happen.

Then, suddenly, 'Contact, contact, contact!'

7

Death in 60 seconds

Stiripo with his keen eyesight sees movement; he sees one of them. He rises up in his seat and cocks the LMG. As he does so Lieutenant Goosen, while driving, looks to his left at Stiripo.

Just then the insurgent pulls the trigger. The rocket leaves the tube of the RPG with a deafening bang. With another earth-shattering bang it hits its target 20 metres away – the side of the Casspir, just above the side window next to Lieutenant Goosen's head.

On impact the nose of the rocket crushes against the panzer steel. A crystal in the nose smashes and sends an electrical impulse along two wires to an explosive charge behind the parabola-shaped cone made of a copper and lead alloy in the head of the missile. The explosive charge detonates and it explodes and melts against the panzer steel, melting the steel and flying through the Casspir with a terrible bang. It detonates just a few centimetres from Lieutenant Goosen's head, bursting his right eardrum.

The RPG's white-hot molten metal slug cuts through the Casspir like a bullet slicing through a paper bag. It strikes Lieutenant Goosen on the right side of his head in front of his temple as he looks to the left, blowing away a piece of his skull and melting his skin and his hair.

Shrapnel from melted panzer steel and the RPG spray through the inside of the Casspir, hungry for human flesh. A piece of the slug breaks off and flies down through the console and through the engine of the Casspir. The rest of the slug passes through Stiripo's head, in through the right side of his skull, through his brain and out through the left side of his skull, sending Stiripo to meet his great Tate Kalunga and his ancestors who have cattle with horns that are two metres long.

The slug passes out of the Casspir and slices through the air, eventually falling and coming to rest on the ground, where it cools down and is to remain for eternity.

All of this happens in just a fraction of a second.

In an act of self-sacrifice, 20 insurgents stayed behind to ambush us while their comrades continued. They had to buy time for the rest of their group in order for them to achieve their objective.

Zulu Golf 1 is immobilised, out of the fight. Stiripo is dead, the lieutenant severely injured. The rest of its occupants are deafened and dazed.

To counter the enemy gunfire 12 Casspirs surge forward past Zulu Golf 1, with 12 LMGs that have 200- to 300-round belts of ammo. One hundred and twenty Koevoet members open fire, every assault rifle and machine gun on automatic. Ten thousand rounds of 7.62-mm ammo erupt in retaliation, spewing death in every direction.

Some of the insurgents start to flee; they are no match for this kind of firepower.

The Casspirs race forward. The enemy are shot over and over and over again and the nine-ton Casspirs drive over them, mangle and mash them.

It is all over in 60 seconds.

The ambush was a greater success for SWAPO than it was for us. They achieved their objective and we did not.

Their objective was to take a big group south and penetrate the white farming area around Tsumeb. They left 20 of their comrades behind in order to delay us so that the rest could achieve that objective. They did that, and lost only nine men.

Our objective was simple: to kill the enemy. We had killed only nine men.

We had been following this group for three days. Our Casspirs were breaking down. Three Casspirs never made it to the contact, including mine. Several of the LMGs and many of the rifles jammed during the contact because of dirt, dust, leaves and twigs from three days of bundu-bashing. By the time of the contact we had lost air support because the gunships had withdrawn to assist Major Tickly after his crash. If they hadn't withdrawn, the gunships with their 20-mm cannon and deadly accurate optical sights could have killed many more enemy.

Koevoet had a 25 to 1 kill ratio; during this contact we achieved a 9 to 1 ratio. But it wasn't over yet.

The ambush was over and the follow-up was over, but the infiltration wasn't. The SWAPO infiltrators were heading south and so was Koevoet. Our alpha teams were already deploying from Oshakati. They were racing down the main road to reach the town of Tsumeb and to start hunting down each and every one of the infiltrators. Some of the bravo teams were also heading for Tsumeb while others were on their way to Oshakati to rebunker, repair and prepare to redeploy.

Warrant Officer 'Snakes' Greyling, commander of Zulu Yankee, was a stout man with goldfish eyes. He was a bit of a nutter, a veteran of years of conflict, right from the days of the Rhodesian war. I had never taken to him. Somehow Zulu Yankee just didn't seem to get kills and this must have frustrated the man so much that on a few occasions we felt that he had tried to undermine our follow-ups.

There was the time when Zulu Yankee had not reported that they were following any insurgents. We had, and we were indeed on spoor that was becoming very hot. Lieutenant Goosen had called for gunship support.

Just then Warrant Officer Greyling had suddenly reported that he was hot on the tracks of a group of insurgents and that he now needed the air support. Lieutenant Goosen had given in. When the gunships had arrived at Warrant Officer Greyling's location, he had suddenly lost the spoor. Later on, some of Zulu Yankee's Ovambos told us that they had not even been following spoor at the time. There were more incidents like this.

But it was different the day Lieutenant Goosen was wounded. Warrant Officer Greyling earned my respect and admiration when he took over command of the operation after the contact. He displayed courage, bravery and leadership and pulled us through one of the toughest times I've ever been through. His action was worthy of the highest award, but awards were not what Koevoet was about. Koevoet was about killing SWAPO.

Snakes pulls up next to Lieutenant Goosen's Casspir knowing that it's been shot out. His first priority is to ascertain how many casualties there are and the nature and extent of the injuries.

He calls a ceasefire over the small radio, the RSA53.

He leaps over the side of his Casspir and lands firmly on the ground while there is still some sporadic firing. Some of the Casspirs are emptying rounds into the already dead enemy as if they are not dead enough.

Snakes gets into the back of Zulu Golf 1 and gets Lieutenant

Goosen out. There's nothing he can do for Stiripo, who is watching his big-horned cattle in the sky.

He stabilises Lieutenant Goosen and then calls for an immediate casevac from his big radio – the B25 – in his Casspir. He supplies Zulu HQ with his coordinates and the nature of Lieutenant Goosen's wounds, as well as the fact that we have lost one member.

Zulu HQ starts asking a lot of questions and requests information.

'Listen, Zulu, we have been ambushed and we have casualties. We need a casevac as soon as possible. I repeat our coordinates ...'

'Zulu Yankee, Zulu Yankee, Zulu,' they call.

'Zulu Yankee, go,' he replies.

'Yes, but the brigadier wants to know ...'

'Zulu, you tell the brigadier to go fuck himself. I've got casualties and priorities to deal with,' Snakes shouts into the mic. 'We can deal with the bullshit later.'

The brigadier is listening on the other side, concerned about the situation. He smiles at what Snakes has just said about him. The brigadier fully understands, and about 45 minutes later he speaks to Snakes over the radio in his calm and collected way, congratulating him for handling the situation on the ground.

'Zulu Yankee, Zulu Yankee, Giant.' The Puma helicopter approaches the contact site from the east for the casevac.

'This is Zulu Yankee, go Giant,' Snakes replies.

'From your coordinates we're two minutes out,' the pilot calls. 'Listen and look out for us. Get some smoke ready.'

'Roger, copy that.'

'There they are, we hear them coming!' some of the Ovambos shout.

'Here.' Snakes tosses a white phosphorous grenade to an Ovambo and, pointing, says, 'Okay, go and throw it over there.'

To bring in a helicopter accurately depends on the accuracy of how well you have plotted yourself, but plotting your position in Ovamboland was not easy; there was always room for error. When the chopper was within a five-kilometre range, it would be able to see a smoke grenade.

Smoke grenades came in three different colours: a dirty white, orange and green. Green was useless against the background of the green vegetation. It was far more effective to use a white phosphorous grenade, which instantly gave off the best white cloud of smoke. It was also dangerous, though.

The grenade thrown by the Ovambo explodes and in a beautiful display of glowing phosphorus it releases a huge cloud of white smoke.

The pilot sees it and comes in to land.

Lieutenant Goosen walks! With a piece of his skull blown off he actually walks to the Puma helicopter with the assistance of Snakes.

Stiripo's corpse and those of the dead insurgents are loaded into the Puma. It takes off and heads at full speed for the primary trauma centre at Ondangwa airbase.

When I finally arrived on the scene and stopped behind Zulu Golf 1, Jackie was sitting on the roof of his Casspir. He was emotionally and physically traumatised and was crying with his face in his hands.

'Jackie, what happened?' I asked.

'The lieutenant got shot out and I got shot out, Stiripo is dead and the lieutenant's head got blown away,' he said. 'He's still alive, but I don't think he'll make it.'

Another one of our teams arrived, but all the other teams decided to leave. Zulu Yankee and what was left of Zulu Golf were left behind to sort out the shit.

Why the other teams didn't continue with the remaining spoor, I couldn't understand. It was probably because the enemy had scattered and the general decision was to deal with the infiltration from Tsumeb.

Snakes started to bring some order and put a plan into action.

'How many Casspirs are out of action and how many are mobile?' he wanted to know.

'Lieutenant Goosen's was shot out, and mine also,' Jackie replied. 'We both got shot out.'

'Where was your Casspir shot out?' Snakes asked, trying not to upset Jackie. 'Show me.'

'Here in the front, somewhere over here.' Jackie pointed in the general direction of the front of his Casspir.

'Where is the damage?' Snakes wanted to know. 'There must be a hole or something.'

'No, it must have gone through the grill and through my engine,' Jackie maintained. 'My engine is fucked. It can't even start.'

'Okay, will you go and see if Lieutenant Goosen's Casspir will start?' Snakes knew better than to push Jackie too far at that stage. But I worried. It was not the right time for Jackie to get into a cabin of death with Stiripo's blood and brains sprayed all over its inside. So I said I'd do it, but Tommy got there first. I followed him into Zulu Golf 1.

I could smell death and I could feel death inside the Casspir. Hesitantly I moved forward as if something was warning me to get out.

Tommy got behind the wheel and I watched as he pushed the key down. The alternator light came on. He pushed the starter button. Nothing.

'Come, Tommy, let's go and open the bonnet,' I said.

Before he could move, Tommy noticed that a white phosphorus grenade on the dash was leaking. A piece of shrapnel had punctured it. It was smouldering and becoming unstable.

Tommy grabbed the grenade with his left hand and tossed it out of the Casspir through the hatch above him, onto the ground. He shouted a warning in Oshivambo and the Ovambos outside scattered.

Some of the phosphorous had leaked out onto Tommy's left hand and in pain he grabbed it with his right hand. I got hold of him from behind and helped him out.

Outside Snakes dived into the tool box at the back of his Casspir, grabbed a jar of grease, opened it, scooped some out in his hand and smeared it on Tommy's burning hand.

'You have to starve it of oxygen,' he said, 'or it will never stop eating into your flesh until they cut it out.'

Snakes then picked up a stick and turned on the smouldering can of the white phosphorous grenade.

He danced around it as if he were dealing with a deadly snake, tapping it with the stick, breaking it up while the phosphorus bubbled and burnt as it made contact with the oxygen in the air.

If the detonator went off, so would the charge, and in an instant it would explode, sending a burst of phosphorus into the air. We would all be covered with white phosphorus, which would eat our flesh away while we screamed and died in sheer agony.

I was mesmerised by the way Snakes dealt with the grenade

and I didn't bother to run for cover. Finally it broke up after all the phosphorus had burnt away. Snakes had defeated it.

He smeared more grease onto Tommy's hand and wrapped it in a bandage.

'Keep it sealed,' he said.

'Right, let's hook up the Casspirs that are out of action and get the hell out of here.' Snakes was looking at a map. 'We need to head east until we reach the 17/30 cut line and then we take that line all the way down to Miershoop, where we'll find the army's 61 Mechanised Brigade. There we can get onto the tar road and make it to Oshivelo gate, where help from Oshakati will be waiting for us.' The 17/30 cut line was a crude, very bad dirt road running north–south at 17 degrees 30 minutes east of zero longitude.

'No, we're going back to Elundu,' Jackie protested. 'It's closer and our Blesbok is still there, we need to fetch our Blesbok.'

Snakes was patient and calm with him. 'Look, Jackie, Elundu is slightly closer, but what are you going to do when we get there? You will still have to go all the way back to Oshakati. Leave your Blesbok. Someone else can bring it back for us. Come now, we need to get moving.'

Now it was my turn to complain. 'My Casspir is fucked; it's been breaking down for the last few days. It's got water in the diesel—'

Snakes cut me short. 'Can it start? If you can start it, hook up Lieutenant Goosen's Casspir and let's get moving. It's getting late.'

Without another word I hooked up Lieutenant Goosen's Casspir and put Rabane behind the wheel. The engine of Zulu Golf 1 still wouldn't start, so Rabane was in for a tough time with no power steering. This also meant that we could not take any sharp corners.

Snakes was in the lead, towing one of Zulu Yankee's Casspirs, followed by Johnny Enslin, towing another of their Casspirs.

I then followed, towing Lieutenant Goosen's Casspir, with Bennie behind me towing Jackie. Our column progressed at a snail's pace. I couldn't get into third gear so we moved in first and second gear in four-wheel drive, heading east.

The vegetation and landscape were changing, there were fewer trees and much more open grassland. At the same time the sand was getting softer.

Finding the 17/30 cut line was a blessing and a curse. I was relieved to know that we knew exactly where we were and that it would be a straight haul to the south, albeit a long one. Yet while the cut line looked like a good dirt road inviting us to use it, it was very soft and we got stuck a few times as a result. I suggested that, seeing that the road was straight, we hook all the Casspirs together like a train and pull together, but no one liked my idea.

I hadn't eaten for a few days and I hadn't had water the whole of that day. Fatigue, dehydration, hunger and irritation were bringing me to breaking point.

Suddenly Jackie called over the radio, saying he wanted to stop. He needed to get unhitched from Bennie, as his Casspir had miraculously come back to life.

My tongue had swollen up in my mouth; I couldn't speak. I felt dizzy and nauseous and I could no longer think straight. I suddenly realised that my Casspir had not given any problems since we left the ambush site.

'Fucking coward, you're a fucking bitch!' I screamed out loud, but the words came out slurred.

'What's wrong, Tate?' asked Labanye, who was next to me in the gunner's seat. He looked at me strangely.

I ignored him.

Labanye took the telehand of the radio and called: 'Sergeant Jimmy, he's going crazy.'

In the distance we saw some cattle. Where there are cattle there must be water. Then, alongside the road, I saw a waterhole. We stopped. I scraped the green slime and the cow shit away and scooped up some water in my hands. It tasted good and I didn't care that it might make me sick. After drinking too much I climbed out of the pit and vomited it all up again, only to go back down and drink some more.

The Ovambos filled our water bags and were filling our tanks when Snakes stopped them. 'Come, that's enough now. That's all we'll need. It's another 30 kilometres to 61 Mech and it's going to get dark soon. We'll be passing their artillery shooting range and we don't want to become their target practice. Let's go.'

It was indeed dark when we reached 61 Mechanised Brigade. The 17/30 cut line took us straight into their base. We rode through unchallenged. Snakes must have let them know via Zulu HQ that we were coming.

The army stared at us and we ignored them. I saw Ratel ARVs – armoured fighting vehicles – lined up in rows, G5 artillery cannon and Oliphant tanks. These were the guys who had fought in Angola during Operations Quicksilver, Protea and Daisy. What did they know about hunting down groups of SWAPO insurgents who infiltrated into South West Africa? These guys were not geared for that. They were geared for conventional war.

We left for Oshivelo, the gate between the operational area in Ovamboland and the rest of South West Africa. There was an army base on the eastern side of the road and a police COIN base on the western side, with a Koevoet post. Access through the gate from the south was restricted. Civilians were required to have a permit in order to pass through the gate, which controlled the media's access to the operational area, while locals leaving the operational area needed identification papers.

There was a corrugated-iron shed at the checkpoint in which POWs from Onamwandi sat during the day to screen the locals passing through. On the odd occasion, a SWAPO enemy would be caught when a POW recognised him.

We arrived at Oshivelo at about 10 p.m. There was a reception waiting for us. Captain Winter and a few of the jam stealers were there – mostly officers and men who didn't fight like us but did administrative work, yet were always there to take credit for our successes.

'Boys, well done, well done, come and get a beer or whatever you want to drink.' Brigadier Dreyer had sent a truckload of food and drinks as a gift for us. Now the jam stealers were trying to sell it to us. They were expecting us to pay for the drinks and they themselves were already getting pissed on our account.

Jackie asked about Lieutenant Goosen, believing that he was dead.

'All we know is that they stabilised him at the primary trauma centre at Ondangwa and put him on a C-130 to 1 Military Hospital in Pretoria,' Captain Winter told us. 'He's on that plane right now. He'll get excellent treatment.'

'You mean he's alive?' Jackie was surprised.

I turned to Captain Van der Merwe, who was in command of Onamwandi and the Koevoet post at Oshivelo. 'Captain, I have a request, please.'

Captain Van der Merwe walked with a limp in his left leg, the result of an encounter with a poisoned Bushman arrow years before. How that arrow got into his Achilles heel I never found out, but it must have been a good story.

I needed help for Tommy. 'One of our Ovambos got white phosphorous on his hand during the contact,' I said. 'Please, we need to get him to a hospital. Can we borrow a vehicle and get some medical treatment for him?'

The captain refused. 'No, you know the road is closed at night. You can't go driving around at night – you'll get yourself shot.'

'What about Tsumeb then? There must be a hospital there. We'll drive him through to Tsumeb; it can't be that far.'

He wasn't interested and he was adamant that the hospital at Tsumeb would not help. Jackie and I walked away with Tommy, who was holding his hand in pain. He was trying to be brave while the phosphorous was eating away his flesh. I tried to comfort him. 'Tommy, you are going to have to hold out until tomorrow. When we get to Oshakati, I'll take you to the doctors at Sector 10.'

He looked at me with that permanent smile on his lips, his eyes masking his pain and suffering. 'It's okay, it can wait,' he said.

Jackie, Tommy and I walked away, disgusted with the officers' attitude.

'Fuck them,' Jackie said, 'I want nothing to do with those wankers, let's go and sleep with the Ovambos next to our Casspirs.'

I rolled out my sleeping bag on the ground, on the side of the road, next to my Casspir. I climbed into my sleeping bag, tired, thirsty, hungry, greasy, dirty and upset. 'Fuck them. If Tommy has to suffer, so will I,' I said to myself.

Over the past few days we had travelled the length of Ovamboland through the bush. We had started at the Angolan border and had ended up at Oshivelo gate.

I looked up at my Casspir and said, 'Fuck you, too. You're a scared bitch.' And I was asleep.

In 1981 an entry was made in the Guinness World Records. The most highly trained dog in the world was Roman, a bloodhound from the SAP dog school in Pretoria. He was the only dog in the world that could walk up a ladder and along a tightrope, turn around, walk back and climb down, blindfolded.

The entry, with a photograph of the dog, did not mention who the trainers were. One of the trainers did not want his name in the book for his own stubborn, personal reasons. Had the entry mentioned the names of the trainers, Lieutenant André Goosen's name would have been in the Guinness World Records.

Lieutenant Goosen had for many years served in the war in Rhodesia. He then joined the SAP dog school and became one of the world's top dog trainers.

Hollywood film companies had offered him a fortune to train dogs for their films, but being the humble introvert that he was, he had turned them down. I think his fear of the English language also had something to do with it, but the less I say about that the better.

Instead of pursuing a career as the world's top dog trainer, he had left the dog school and joined Koevoet out of a sense of duty to serve God and country.

He also believed that his ability to train dogs would be better put to use in combating SWAPO insurgents infiltrating South West Africa from Angola. He believed that somehow there would be a use for dogs in this conflict, especially in tracking down the enemy.

At the beginning of 1981 Lieutenant Goosen had joined Koevoet and later established Zulu Golf.

But now he lay unconscious and in a critical condition in 1 Military Hospital in Pretoria, with a burst eardrum and part of his skull blown away. The damage to his brain still had to be determined.

After a few days the doctors performed surgery. His eardrum was repaired with plastic parts and the missing piece of his skull was replaced with a piece of metal. Had he not been unconscious, he probably would have tried to perform the operation himself.

After surgery he lay awake in his hospital bed, confused, disorientated and uncomfortable. As soon as he was strong enough he disconnected his drip and all the medical apparatus connected to his body. He got out of bed and found some clothes and money that had been left there for him.

He walked out of the hospital and onto the streets of Pretoria. He didn't have a plan and he had no idea where he was going or what he was going to do. In his dazed state he saw a reflection of himself in a shop window. He saw his deformed head, covered with bandages. He felt that he was being stared at and decided he needed to cover his head.

He walked into the first clothing shop he could find. It did not bother him that it was a ladies' clothing store. The only hat he could find that would fit over his swollen head and bandages was a lady's hat, the type that a nice big fat boeretannie would have worn to church a decade or so earlier, when boeretannies still wore hats to church. What he particularly liked about this hat was the fact that he could pull the brim down over his eyes so that no one would recognise him.

He paid for the hat and left the shop. He was back on the streets walking around aimlessly and a bit dizzily. At least he was free. When he pulled the brim of the floppy hat down over his eyes, all he could see as he walked was the pavement stretching unevenly before him.

The hospital staff soon realised that he was missing. After a search of the hospital, a manhunt started across Pretoria. The police were notified and eventually Lieutenant Goosen was back in his hospital bed, minus his floppy hat.

8

Running wild

Long before Lieutenant Goosen donned his ladies' hat and took to the streets of Pretoria, we had to begin the long haul back to Oshakati, all the way across Ovamboland once again. At least this time we travelled on a tar road. I towed Lieutenant Goosen's Casspir Zulu Golf 1 all the way. My Casspir gave no trouble for the entire journey.

After a long stretch, we stopped at the SAP COIN garage at Ondangwa to unhitch Zulu Golf 1. This time we weren't going to fix it ourselves, oh no. We booked it in and left it for the mechanics to fix.

Jackie kept an audience of mechanics enthralled for half an hour with his account of the ambush. He was such a good storyteller that he had them fighting over who would have the honour of repairing the famous Casspir.

I was determined to make sure that my Casspir would never again give me the sort of trouble that it had given over the past few days. Somehow I needed to get the oshilulu out of her.

I completed a job card and in the section that read 'spares required', I wrote in clear bold letters, 'DIESEL FILTERS × 4, OIL FILTERS × 2, GLASS BOWL UNDER HAND PUMP

× 2, FILTER FOR GLASS BOWL × 2, LITTLE RUBBER WASHER FOR GLASS BOWL × 2'.

I handed the job card to the storeman and looked at him eagerly, expecting him to give me what I needed.

'I want the old parts first. Bring me the old ones and I will give you the new ones,' he said arrogantly in his German accent.

My mother always told me that more flies are caught with honey than with vinegar, but I was about to spray this fly with Doom.

'Just give me the fucking parts before I fucking kill you!' I shouted. He took a step back.

Jackie's stories suddenly stopped and the jovial mood changed. Everyone looked at me. I was still without a shirt, as black as an Ovambo, and covered with dirt and grime. My dirty hair and beard had grown long, my eyes were red, I was worn out and I looked a mess. I was also threatening to kill the storeman.

'What's the problem?' the lieutenant in charge asked in a calm but concerned way as he approached me.

'Please, just listen to me. We have been through shit. I've got water in my diesel, I need to drain the diesel tank, flush out the fuel system and replace the filters, and then fill the tank again. I can't do this here. I can't empty a tank in the middle of your garage. I need to go and park my Casspir on a steep slope and empty the tank, and before I fill the tank I want to replace the diesel filters. How can I give him the old ones before I go and do that?'

'Klaus, give him want he needs,' the lieutenant ordered.

'But why does he want double of everything?' the storeman asked.

'I want spares. If my Casspir breaks down during a follow-up in the middle of nowhere, do you expect me to walk here, bring you the old ones, get the new ones and then walk back?' I asked, wanting to add, 'and shove the old ones up your arse'.

Eventually I walked away with a box full of filters, one glass bowl and rubber washers. Klaus made me promise to bring the old ones back once I had finished the job. He also reminded me that they don't usually just give spare parts out.

'Hey, Jim, you're crazy, man,' Jackie said.

We stripped the LMG and the Browning and removed all the equipment from Zulu Golf 1 while Bennie was dropping off our Ovambos, who lived in the Ondangwa area. Before he took them we told them to be back on Wednesday, because we didn't know what the future held.

Our next priority was to get home to Oshakati and to get Tommy treated. When we got to Okavi, I took Tommy to the army doctors at Sector 10, where his hand was seen to.

The only news of Lieutenant Goosen was that he was in a stable but critical condition.

We then offloaded the vehicles and packed everything into the cell that we still used as our storeroom, although we had been told that we had to vacate it, probably because of the claymore detonator going off. Jackie and I had had to break the padlock to get in, because we couldn't find the key, which was kept by Lieutenant Goosen.

'Hey, Jim, come, let's get cleaned up, we need to drink,' Jackie said when we were finished. 'We need to drown our sorrows.'

'Go ahead, I'll see you later. I must still do something.'

'What?'

'I need to drain my fuel tank.'

'No, Jim, come, leave it until tomorrow. I'll help you tomorrow.'

I said nothing and just sat on the side of my bed, wanting to lie down and sleep for ever. Jackie disappeared.

Okavi was almost deserted. Everyone was either in Tsumeb or on their way to Tsumeb to hunt down the infiltrators.

After a while I wondered where Jackie was. Just then he walked into our bungalow with a six-pack of beers. He opened one for me and one for himself and sat on the bed opposite me. I finished the beer in one go and suddenly we both packed up laughing. We didn't know why, but we laughed.

'What do we do now?' I asked Jackie when he became serious again.

'We're going to deploy on Wednesday, to Tsumeb,' he replied. 'You and I, Jim, we're going to Tsumeb. We'll show them. You and I, we can do it.'

We each finished our third beer and the six-pack was gone.

'I'm fucking hungry, Jackie. Do you know how hungry I am?' I asked.

'Okay, before we drink tonight we will eat,' he promised.

It took me half an hour in the shower to get clean with a cake of soap and a bottle of shampoo, another half an hour to clean my teeth, brush my hair and cut my nails. Finally I was dressed and I added the finishing touch with some deodorant, which smelt potent because I hadn't used any of the stuff for quite some time.

'I'm good and clean and fresh, tra la la,' I sang. Luckily no one could hear me. 'Hey, Jackie, I'm ready to rock the town,' I called, walking back into the bungalow from the showers. 'Where are we going?'

'Let's go to the Guest House,' suggested Jackie.

'How are we going to get there? It's too far to walk.'

'We'll take my Casspir.'

I was doubtful. 'Can we do that? Can we just take a Casspir to the Guest House?'

'Hey, I'm giving us permission. The lieutenant's not here, so now I'm in charge of Zulu Golf. So I give us permission. Hey, no, sorry Jim. Let's do this together, you and I. So we both are in charge, but if there's any shit, I'll take the blame.'

'Where did you get those beers from?' I asked. 'I feel like another.'

'No, come,' he said, 'let's go.'

We drove Jackie's Casspir through the town. Jackie had somehow got hold of another six-pack and we got stuck into it.

Then I noticed that we were going the wrong way.

'Hey, where are we going?' I said, confused.

Just then we pulled into the SWA Police barracks.

'Come, Jim, let's eat in the mess,' Jackie said. 'I hear the food's not too bad here.' He dragged me along, but I pulled back.

'We don't stay here, Jackie, so how can we just come and eat here?'

'The auntie in charge of cooking here is nice,' he said. 'If she gives us shit, we say that we've just moved in. Don't worry.'

The food was good. Anything would have tasted good that evening, and I said to Jackie, 'I haven't eaten for 10 years.'

We heard a noise in the kitchen and a short fat lady marched in like a sergeant major.

'I've seen you before,' she said to Jackie, and then looked at me, 'but who are you? I've never seen you before.'

Jackie covered. 'He's new here, Auntie, he arrived yesterday. He's in room 105, I'm in 104.'

'Well, boys, I hope you're hungry. I made all this food but there doesn't seem to be anyone around, so eat well.' She went through the kitchen and out through the back door.

Afterwards Jackie parked the Casspir behind the Guest House so that no one driving past would see it from the road.

I don't know why it was called the International Guest House and not the Oshakati Hotel or something like that. It was the only accommodation in the town available to the public, it looked like a hotel and it was run just like a hotel.

One came in through the entrance on the side and could go left down a passage to the rooms at the back, second-left into the bar, or right into the dining room.

It was still early and the Guest House was empty. I met Lobo, the manager, for the first time. He was a Portuguese man who had fled Angola after independence from Portugal in the mid-1970s, and he had a wife and five children. Two of his sons often worked behind the bar counter, especially when it got busy. One son's name was Fernando.

It was rumoured that Lobo was heavily into diamond smuggling, as were several other people in the town. Someone once told me that he kept a stash of uncut diamonds in the bottom of a fire bucket, covered with sand, on the front balcony of his house. I was once tempted to go and look late one evening.

Many Ovambos went to work on the diamond mines far to the south. They worked as migrant labourers and some would smuggle uncut diamonds back to Ovamboland to try to sell them.

Jackie and I were sitting at the bar and Lobo tended to us.

'I don't want any trouble tonight, hey boys,' he said in his Portuguese accent.

I looked around. There was no one in sight. I wondered how just the two of us could make any trouble.

Jackie ordered two beers.

'And two double whiskies, J&B,' I added.

Lobo looked at us strangely.

Jackie looked at me and said, 'No, I drink rum, Red Heart rum.'

'Sorry, Lobo, cancel the beers. One double J&B and one double Red Heart rum.' I placed the final order.

About four rounds later Jackie and I were getting pissed and talking the biggest load of crap. Jackie started to get sad and sentimental. Just when I realised he needed an audience, in walked Johnny Enslin from Zulu Yankee.

'I knew I'd find you guys here,' he said, joining us.

Johnny was small and scrawny. He was from a wealthy former Rhodesian family who lived in Pretoria, where he had been a policeman before he joined Koevoet. The last thing he had done before leaving Pretoria was to burn down a night club while on duty. He could get full of shit, and he was a naughty guy.

After another 15 minutes of drinking, Mike walked in. He worked at the security branch in Oshakati. His father was a general in the police. Mike had always wanted to join Koevoet, but his father had forbidden it.

'Right, let's play 7-14-21,' Johnny said. 'Lobo, can we have the poker dice please?'

'You guys carry on,' I said, attempting to withdraw. 'I don't know how to play.'

They insisted, and I asked how it worked.

'We go clockwise,' Johnny explained. 'I'll go first.' He threw the dice – two aces; he threw again – one ace; he threw again – no aces. 'The first person who reaches seven aces orders a drink, any drink,' he continued. 'The person who reaches 14 aces pays for the drink, and the person who reaches 21 aces drinks the drink. Right! We're on three aces, I just threw nothing, so now it's Jackie's turn.'

The next morning I woke up at nine and I felt terrible. Jackie was snoring away and I got up with a hangover of biblical proportions. I walked into the ops room and looked at the scoreboard. Zulu Golf: 14 kills for the year so far. Not too bad, I thought.

Captain Maritz was on duty. He was short and plump, but he was always smiling and he always seemed happy. I liked him.

'Morning Captain,' I greeted him. Then, suddenly, I remembered our Blesbok.

'Captain, our Blesbok is still at Elundu. How can we get it back?'

Just then Jackie walked in. He looked dik babbelas after the previous night's drinking.

'Go and fetch it,' the captain replied.

Jackie got into a heavy argument with him. I didn't want to get caught in the middle of it, so I left and went back to the bungalow. After a while Jackie came in, fuming mad after the argument with Captain Maritz.

'Come, let's go and fetch our Blesbok, just you and I,' I said. 'Let's take your Casspir, an LMG, two AKs, drive to Elundu and bring the fucking Blesbok back.'

'Okay, yes, let's do it and see what they say,' Jackie agreed.

As we walked past the ops room, Captain Maritz came out. 'Where do you two think you're going?' he called.

'To fetch our Blesbok from Elundu,' Jackie shouted back.

'Hey, boys, who's going with you? You can't …'

Jackie and I drove to Elundu, fetched our Blesbok and drove all the way back again, right through the operational area during a major infiltration. It was crazy – almost suicidal – but by now nothing mattered any more. We just wanted to get the job done and prove that we were as good as anyone in Koevoet.

Late that same afternoon we were back at Okavi. We were in deep shit. Captain Maritz was waiting for us.

'Where the fuck have you two been?'

'We fetched our Blesbok from Elundu,' Jackie replied.

'The brigadier has heard about this. He says I must put both of you on the first plane home,' he exploded.

'Then we're going to tell him that you sent us. You told us to fetch it ourselves. You did. When Jim asked you, you said "Go fetch it yourselves," and that's what we did. Where is the brigadier? I'll tell him myself,' Jackie said casually.

Captain Maritz walked away shaking his head, but even from behind I could see he was smiling.

'Come, Jim, let's go to the Guest House again tonight,' Jackie said.

'No, Jackie, I must drain my Casspir's diesel tank and you promised to help. It'll be a lot easier now that we have the Blesbok,' I said. 'Come give me a hand or I won't come with you.'

Outside Okavi, I drove my Casspir up the side of a bulldozed sand wall while Jackie parked the Blesbok next to me. I had the tool box with me. I took a number-14 socket and the wrench, heaved the back step up and loosened the drain plug until I could remove it by hand. With the drain plug out, I jumped aside. Out came the diesel, dirt, muck and water. There didn't seem to be much water but it all gushed out so fast that it was hard to tell.

I opened the bonnet and replaced the diesel filters, the glass bowl and its filter as well as the rubber washer. I then went back and replaced the drain plug, fastening it with the socket and wrench. Jackie helped me to fill my Casspir from the Blesbok.

I bled the fuel system, checked everything, climbed behind the wheel and pushed the key down before taking a deep breath and pressing the starter button.

The Casspir started.

The oshilulu was dead; the demons were gone … I hoped.

'Jackie, let's go and celebrate,' I said happily.

A few days later Jackie, Bennie and I deployed to Tsumeb, driving three Casspirs southwards. We stopped at the garage at Ondangwa to check on Lieutenant Goosen's Casspir and to see which of our Ovambos wanted to come with us. With only three Casspirs, there was not enough space for the whole team.

To our surprise, Lieutenant Goosen's Casspir was ready. There had not been much damage. The piece of the RPG slug had damaged the injector pump, which the mechanics had simply replaced.

Tommy was still in hospital, so with no one to drive the lieutenant's Casspir we were forced to leave it at the garage. We were already pushing it by letting Rabane drive the Blesbok. He didn't have a driver's licence, but Jackie and I weren't much better off – we didn't have code-10 licences to drive Casspirs.

We passed Oshivelo gate and then the turn-off to Namutoni, the northern camp of the Etosha National Park.

It was late afternoon when we reached Tsumeb, which was outside the operational area, a mining town renowned for a wealth of rare and unusual minerals.

But now Tsumeb was in total chaos. The army, the air force and Koevoet had descended on the town to deal with the infiltrators we had tracked and who had ambushed us. The local population didn't know what had hit them as the town was being turned upside down. Things got so bad, in fact, that the locals, who initially welcomed us, later signed a petition requesting us to leave.

We didn't know where to go until we saw another Koevoet Casspir. The driver told us to head for the airfield on the southern side of the town. We made it to the airfield without incident. Most of our Ovambos were seeing traffic lights and double-storey buildings for the first time in their lives.

The airfield had been converted into a military base. The army took up most of the base, while Koevoet occupied a small area at the top near the landing strip, where a field ops room had been set up as well as a couple of tents. Tents with beds in them had been erected for us and a mobile kitchen was taking care of our meals. Someone had been working hard, and quickly. More important than anything else, though, there was a pub and it was well stocked.

The South African Air Force (SAAF) had settled in just down the runway from us. The airfield had become a home for one big happy family. The SADF, the SAAF and we were all going to get along just fine.

After parking our Casspirs neatly next to each other, Jackie and I reported to Captain Potato Nose Adams at the ops room. There was a briefing going on and we joined to listen.

'Guys, this is not Ovamboland. We can't just go driving over the farmers' fences. I know it will be difficult to operate here, but we need the locals' support. The farm labourers will look for spoor and if they find any they will tell the farmers, who will phone us,' Captain Adams said, eyeing Jackie and me suspiciously.

'There is one farmer who is totally against us. His name is Van Rooyen and he has said that if we set foot on his farm, he will open fire at us with his high-powered rifles.' Captain Adams pointed to the map on a board and outlined Mr Van Rooyen's farm while some of the guys muttered, 'Fuck him. He'll get himself killed.'

Ironically, Mr Van Rooyen was taken care of the next morning by SWAPO. That night, possibly even while we spoke of him, they planted an anti-tank landmine in his driveway. Early the following morning Mr Van Rooyen died in a landmine explosion.

'Right, tomorrow morning we meet back here again for a final briefing. I will assign each group to an area,' the captain said. 'One more thing. Some of you might have heard that the army was ambushed yesterday near Tsintsabis. A Ratel was shot out by an RPG and all eight occupants were killed. So be careful out there. The enemy wants to fight; these are tough bastards. They could be Typhoon forces. We haven't captured one, so please, if you get a chance, we need to interrogate one. We need to know more about this group.'

The next morning all the groups were deployed. All except us, Zulu Golf. Jackie and I took it as a personal insult.

Jackie stormed into the ops room and confronted Potato Nose while I hung back.

'Where are we going?' Jackie demanded to know.

'Oh, you guys can hang around,' he replied. 'I'll find something for you to do.'

'Like what? Take the garbage out?' Jackie exploded.

'Don't get clever with me.'

'Captain, we were the ones who picked up the spoor at the Angolan border and chased the group all the way across Ovamboland,' Jackie shouted. 'We were the ones who got ambushed. If it wasn't for us, no one would have known they were coming and SWAPO would have been sitting in the pub in town having a drink right now.'

The captain tried to calm him with bullshit so Jackie left in a huff, determined that we would prove ourselves.

I led him to the briefing room and showed him the map. 'Look here, Jackie,' I said. 'This cut line divides Ovamboland from the rest of South West Africa. Let's drive up the tar road and just before Oshivelo, over here, we turn off the road and head east along this cut line to look for spoor. I'm sure some of them are still coming and some are already trying to head back. This would be a perfect place to search for spoor and we won't have to worry about the farmers. Look, this cut line goes all the way to Tsintsabis. I'm sure no one has thought of doing this.'

Jackie was impressed. 'Jim, you are not so stupid. You're quite clever.'

'No, Jackie, I'm not clever; I'm intelligent,' I joked.

We gathered our men and left without telling anyone.

Between the turn-offs to Namutoni and Oshivelo we turned off the road to the east and stopped in the bush. I climbed onto Jackie's Casspir.

Jackie had the portable TR28 radio out. It was our only long-distance radio and our only communication with the ops room at the airbase. Lieutenant Goosen's Casspir had the fitted B25 radio, the only other long-distance radio Zulu Golf had, and his Casspir was still at Ondangwa.

As I climbed up, Jackie was trying to figure out how to tune the TR28.

'Hey, Jim, do you know how to tune this thing?' he asked, looking a bit confused. He tried to touch my ear with the antenna, but I knew that trick. If you touch the antenna and press the mic at the same time, the antenna will give you quite an electric shock.

'Hey, stop that! Give it here.' I took the radio from him, tuned it in and gave it back while we listened to what was happening. Luckily we were out of range of the COIN bases to the north. Jackie took the mic and called, 'Zulu 2, Zulu 2, Zulu Golf.'

'Zulu Golf, this is Zulu 2, where the hell are you? We've been looking for you all morning,' Tom Boom said.

'We only have a portable TR28, so we can't be on the air all the time,' Jackie said. 'We'll call you in about two hours.'

Tom wanted our coordinates. That had us stumped. Jackie hadn't been keeping our position and neither of us thought to plot ourselves before we called them. Jackie looked at me and I looked at him.

'Just tell them that we're on the road almost at Oshivelo,' I said to Jackie.

Jackie was getting rattled. 'No, that will sound stupid,' he said.

'Just give me a moment, Zulu 2, I'll come back to you with those coordinates,' he said. He studied a map of the area and then really looked confused.

'Hey, Jim, look, we're over here,' he said, pointing to the map. He marked our position with a pencil.

'Yes, I know exactly where we are – we're just off the road near Oshivelo,' I said again. 'Why don't you just tell them that?'

'Can you plot our coordinates?' he asked.

'Yes, I think so,' I said confidently. 'It's been a long time, but I think I can.'

I took the map and looked at it, trying to remember everything they taught me at Maloeskop, but I got it mixed up with what I remembered from Mr Visser's geography lessons at school.

Instead of the eight-digit grid-reference coordinate system Koevoet used, I plotted our position in degrees, minutes and seconds east and south. Zulu 2 was calling us all the time.

'Come on, Jim, hurry up,' Jackie pushed me.

I wrote down the numbers and gave them to Jackie. He called them through.

'That will shut them up,' he said triumphantly. 'Come, let's go and look for spoor.'

But before he could turn the radio off, they called again.

'Zulu Golf, Zulu Golf, Zulu 2.'

'Zulu Golf, go,' Jackie shouted back.

'Zulu Golf, according to those coordinates you are somewhere in the Kaokoland, over a thousand kilometres away,' Tom said over the radio.

'Zulu Golf, return to base immediately, right now, come back!'

That was Captain Adams.

Jackie needed to save face and he thought quickly.

'We've just picked up three hot spoor, south of Oshivelo, heading east. We are following them and might need gunships.'

'Turn that fucking thing off,' he said to me. 'We need to find some spoor soon or we'll be even deeper in the shit.'

'We can always lose the spoor later,' I said. 'Fuck, Jackie, we could sit here all day and say we're chasing terrs all over the country. How would they know we're bullshitting? If other guys can do it, so can we.'

I had the map. 'Look here. From here we cut across to the cut line up here. Then we drive east along the cut line looking for spoor until we reach Tsintsabis here. Then we take this road back to Tsumeb. What do you think?'

'Come, let's go,' Jackie said. We turned the radio off as quickly as possible.

We had got not even 500 metres when God sent us greetings. We picked up three fresh spoor, just as Jackie had said we had. We started a follow-up and moved fast on the spoor for about two hours.

Then ... what the fuck! Army Buffels were ahead of us. They

had cut in on us and were trying to interfere with our follow-up. A competition developed between their trackers and ours, but they just couldn't keep up. Instead they kept loading their trackers and driving them ahead to offload them on the spoor. They were soon going to fuck up the spoor.

Jackie and I were getting totally pissed off, so I loaded my Ovambos and decided to go far ahead to try to pick up the spoor. I changed my mind when I saw the army right in front of me on the ground, so I tried to drive them down with my Casspir.

I stopped next to an army Buffel, threw my hatch open, stood up, pushed my head through the hatch, grabbed the LMG and swung it, pointing it at them.

'Fuck off before we fucking kill you!' I shouted. 'Take your guys and go before we kill you!'

At the same time Jackie was having a fight with an army lieutenant in another Buffel behind me. Jackie told them that he was Captain Winter. That got them to withdraw and leave us to do the job.

The sun was about to go down. Luckily the enemy didn't head into the sunset, which made it easy for us to chase them. My trackers reckoned we couldn't be more than 300 metres behind them. We gave it all we had.

I caught a movement out of the corner of my eye. What was that? About 200 metres to my left something was moving through the bush, gliding along like a silent elephant. And then another one, about 200 metres to my right. They were keeping a distance, but they were definitely moving with us. Ratels, army Ratels. Moving steadily along as though they were aliens just observing us.

The sun was setting and we had to stop and TB for the night.

Jackie and I agreed that we should carry on with those spoor in the morning. It would be worthwhile, because the enemy had nowhere to go, even if they ran through the night. In that terrain we could catch up quite quickly. We didn't want to go back to the airfield and face Captain Potato Nose.

What we didn't know was that a charge of attempted murder and assault had been laid against Captain Winter because of what we had done to the army earlier. (He hadn't been formally charged, and the case was later dropped.)

Although we didn't know about any of this yet, I was still worried. 'Jackie, we're in deep shit. Perhaps we should contact Zulu 2 and tell them what we're doing,' I suggested.

'No, Jim, let's get these three tomorrow. We'll give it all we've got and see if we can even catch one. That should get us out of the shit. We almost had them.'

'Something's out there,' I said. 'I can feel it.' I wanted to tell the Ovambo trackers to put the fires out.

'It's the army, the Ratels that have been following us,' Jackie said.

'No, listen. Someone's coming on foot. Perhaps it's the terrs coming to surrender,' I laughed, and picked up a rifle.

'Hello, can we come closer? Please don't shoot,' someone shouted out of the darkness. I heard the rustling of leaves.

'What do you want?' Jackie asked.

'I'm Captain Johnson from 61 Mech. Can we come and talk?' a very anxious voice said.

'Okay, but just be careful. Our Ovambos are trigger-happy and if they don't trust you, they'll shoot you,' Jackie shouted back.

Two very jittery guys appeared out of the darkness, emerging in the light of our fires.

'You're lucky to be alive. You shouldn't sneak up on us like that. You could get yourselves killed,' Jackie warned.

Shaken and nervous, the captain spoke. 'Look we don't want trouble. Is there any way we can help you guys? We don't want to interfere with your follow-up; we will stay out on your flanks and out of your way. We'll be there for back-up or to help in any way.'

Don't say it, Jackie ... I thought Jackie was going to tell him to fuck off, but I liked the captain's attitude and the way he was thinking.

Jackie put his hand out, 'Hi, I'm Jackie and this is Jim,' he introduced us.

'What are your ranks?' the captain asked.

'I am group commander and Jim is second in command, but we are both of the same rank. We are both commanders.'

That's telling them, Jackie. Yes, we are both fucking important commanders, so don't try that rank thing with us or we might just have to shoot you, I thought, smiling.

'Can our guys come closer?' they asked. 'They're interested to see how you guys operate. I mean this is crazy: you've got fires going and you don't even put guards out.'

Do you think this is a zoo? I felt like saying, but it was time to be hospitable and friendly. These guys were okay.

Eventually they made a TB with us and we exchanged stories late into the night. Some of them knew a friend of mine, Mark Whitson from Durban. I knew he had been serving with the Ratels in 61 Mech.

The next morning we were ready to roll while it was still dark. Jackie gave the Ovambos a talk and somehow he motivated them. I could see that they were now willing to do their best. He was brutally frank with them and told them that he and I were in the shit and that we needed them to pull us out. Nothing works better than pure honesty. We had built a special bond with them by showing them that we were different but equal and that we cared about them.

In the soft pre-dawn the trackers tried to take the spoor, slowly at first. Then sunlight started to filter through the trees and the follow-up gained momentum.

After two hours of chasing I realised that we could still be hopelessly far behind the enemy. I took a chance. I picked up my trackers from the spoor and shot ahead in a big arc to the left for about 10 kilometres. Then I turned sharp right and moved slowly across the enemy's path.

'Stop, stop, stop, Tate!' my trackers suddenly shouted. I stopped and they jumped out. Soon they said, 'Tell the others they can come; we have the spoor.'

'Jackie, Jim,' I said over the radio. 'Load the trackers and come about 10 kilometres forward. If you don't find us, tell me and I'll shoot a flare. I don't want them to see how far we are behind them by shooting a flare at this stage.'

'Okay Jim, we're on our way, well done.'

When Jackie arrived, I picked up my trackers and was off to see if I could find the spoor again and save some more time. This time we had no luck. I could have been ahead of them, but that was unlikely. I returned to the follow-up.

I had never seen our Ovambos put so much effort into their tracking. We had never before worked so much like a team.

Half an hour later I tried again and hit the jackpot. We saved another 10 kilometres and I noticed that one of the Ratels had followed me. It's a pleasure to work with these guys, I thought. They know how to operate and how to fit in.

We were still on the air force's radio frequency and I heard a spotter plane giving air support to someone who was also on a follow-up. We were moving at great speed on the spoor and soon we picked up a Casspir's radio transmissions. It was Zulu Lima and it was Captain Winter. What was he doing back out in the bush?

'Jackie, it's Captain Winter,' he said over the air. 'I believe that you are following the same spoor as us. We are way ahead of you so you might as well pack up.'

I pulled up next to Jackie, stopped and stood up out of my hatch so that we could speak in person and not over the radio.

'Jim, fuck him,' Jackie said. 'He's poached our spoor from us.'

'Let's poach it back from him,' I suggested. 'Let's go past him and see if we can steal it back.'

'No, let's first catch up with him; he can't just chase us away. Look, we've been catching up with him the whole time, which means that our trackers are better than his, so let's show him – let's go right past him.'

Our Ovambos loved the idea.

We followed the general direction of the spoor and the spotter, which we could now see, until we found their vehicle tracks.

As we caught up, just when we were about 20 metres behind them, we heard 'Contact, contact, contact!' And then I couldn't believe it. My Casspir suddenly cut out and died, leaving me to watch the contact 100 metres ahead.

Captain Winter was going to try to cut us out of this one. It was obvious that he wanted to claim this one for himself and say that we weren't present. We wouldn't be able to do anything about it.

Jackie saved the day. He raced forward and by chance found a gook who stood up in front of him. Jackie's gunner pumped a belt of LMG rounds into the insurgent as Jackie connected the front of his Casspir with him and flattened him.

I quickly jumped out, bled my Casspir and got going to stop next to Jackie. He and his Ovambos quickly stripped the body of the dead insurgent. Jackie grabbed the AK as well as the webbing and the items stripped from the corpse, ran across to where Captain Winter's team had made a small pile of the weapons and equipment from the enemy they had killed, and dumped his with theirs.

He ran back and shouted at me, 'Come, Jim, help me – we need to get this one loaded.' He grabbed the arms of the insurgent he had killed, and we loaded him onto Jackie's Casspir.

I thought Jackie had gone mad, that he just wanted a trophy on his spare wheel so that he could ride through Tsumeb and scare the locals. But then Captain Winter approached us. 'I'm going to fuck both of you up. What are you doing here?'

He called Jackie to one side, but I could hear their conversation. 'Don't ever use my name again. I've possibly got an attempted murder and assault charge against me in Tsumeb all because of you.' Suddenly he took Jackie's hand and shook it. He turned to me and shook mine too.

He walked away, shaking his head and said, 'Captain Adams wants to see the two of you.' Then I understood why Jackie had put the body of the insurgent on the spare wheel of Zulu Golf 2. It was Jackie's proof of our involvement in the follow-up.

9

Into Angola

We headed for the airfield at Tsumeb. Moments before the contact, my Casspir had broken down with the same old problem: water in the diesel. It kept cutting out on the way back to Tsumeb and eventually I was delaying everyone, so one of the Ratels towed my Casspir, which gave me the opportunity to compare a Casspir to a Ratel.

My Casspir bounced and banged along behind the Ratel, which was cruising effortlessly, smoothly. It was going too fast for the Casspir though, with the result that the Casspir's front bumper was ripped off. To prevent further damage, we unhitched the Casspir from the Ratel. I bled the fuel system and made it back to base on my own steam.

'Don't worry. Our mechanics will fix it for you,' the army guys assured me.

It was early evening and still light when we arrived at the airfield. A huge reception of high-ranking officers, politicians and the press awaited the returning Koevoet teams and army.

I parked near to Jackie and helped him to dump the corpse of the insurgent with the corpses the other teams had brought back. I was hungry and I found a rat pack lying on the floor of my Casspir. I was after its three small tins of food, in this case bully beef, baked beans and potato salad.

I sat on the back step of my Casspir, opened the tins with my knife and ate the contents, drinking water from a canvas bag. I finally got to the last one, my favourite – potato salad. Using my knife to scoop it up, I started devouring it, totally unaware of what was going on around me.

I was interrupted by a young army corporal. I realised that we were alone and I wondered where everyone else was. Then I remembered the media briefing. The media were for the most part kept out of the operational area, but the officials obviously didn't want to prevent them from hearing about this story of a major SWAPO infiltration that had been stemmed by the army and Koevoet.

'Hello,' the corporal said. 'Did you shoot those terrs?' He looked at the corpses Koevoet had brought back to Tsumeb after the successful operation.

'We did.'

'Won't you cut off one of their ears for me?'

I couldn't believe what I'd heard, but I controlled my temper.

'No, we don't do that. If you want an ear, cut it off yourself.'

He turned pale and walked off, shaking his head and mumbling as though I had done something wrong. I was tempted to call him back and cut an ear off with my knife, then put my 9-mm to his head and make him eat it, the little shit.

The cutting off of ears, fingers and even scrotums was practised by some members of the armed forces and Koevoet, but not by us. In all the years of my service I never saw someone cut off body parts. I heard a lot about it – including a number of guys who used the scrotums of slain enemy as gear-knob covers in their cars – but in the groups I fought with it was strictly forbidden.

Later, while I served with Frans Conradie, three new recruits were fired for carrying out this practice after a contact. It was fine to execute captives, but Frans did not tolerate the mutilation of their bodies. He had his own code of conduct and ethics that he adhered to strictly. But each group played by its own rules.

My next task was to get my Casspir fixed. The army mechanics welded the bumper back into place. They didn't have diesel filters that would fit, so we drained the fuel tank, cleaned out the filters and replaced them.

A lot of water came out with the diesel. I couldn't understand how it was getting into the diesel. The other Casspirs were running on the same diesel as mine, so the water wasn't coming from the diesel with which we were filling up. It must have been finding its way into my tank from somewhere else.

I started to wonder where I could get a couple of landmines. If I blew up my own Casspir, I thought, they would have to give me a new one.

'Captain Adams wants to see us,' Jackie said.

Yes, we still had to deal with Potato Nose.

'Where the fuck have the two of you been?' He was calm but angry. I could see through him, though. Deep down he wanted to smile.

'Shooting gooks,' Jackie said. 'We've already shot 17 this year. That's better than most teams.'

'Jackie, can you plot the position of Tsintsabis on the map?' he asked, pointing to the map on the wall.

He was going to make fools of us in front of everyone in the ops room. He was going to humiliate us.

Jackie stared at the map and someone sniggered.

'How many kills have you guys got this year?' he snarled at them. That shut them up.

'Jim, come here. You can read a map, can't you?'

I tried to stay out of it and was hanging back near the entrance, but now I had to step forward to the map. I looked at it and read out the coordinates perfectly – in degrees, minutes and seconds.

'No, that's not how we do it. You need to know how to read the grid-reference coordinates. What if you needed a casevac?' Captain Adams asked. 'How would you call in a casevac if you don't know how to read a map? Tom, take them out of here and show them how to read a map before they get someone killed.

'From now on you will work with Zulu Lima and Captain Winter,' he added. 'He'll keep an eye on the two of you. Now go! Get out!'

And fuck you too, I felt like saying.

Tom took us to the briefing tent. 'Jim, you were quite right, but that's not the way we work,' he said, and gave us a crash course in map reading. It all came back to me. The system they used was a lot easier than what I had been doing.

For the rest of the week we found ourselves following Captain Winter around. We followed up on a couple of reports from some farmers and chased a few spoor, with no results.

The town was in a state of chaos and the locals had had enough. They didn't realise that they were in danger, as they couldn't see the enemy out there. They only saw the dead ones hanging from our bumpers and spare wheels when we drove back through the town.

Fights between our guys and the army guys were breaking out in every pub in town, especially at the country club, which had become a major battleground. Even after we were banned from it, our guys just kept going back.

The local population wanted us to go away. What they needed

was an enemy attack on the town to wake them up to the reality of the situation and to make them appreciate our presence. However, the possibility of an attack on the town was fading quickly as our teams were hunting the insurgents down and annihilating them.

After Jackie and I had returned to Oshakati, we had a week to relax. I took Lieutenant Goosen's .30 Browning and an LMG to the shooting range and compared them to determine which one was the superior weapon. I put about 1 000 rounds through each weapon. I had to take my shirt off and wrap it around the barrel of the Browning as it became too hot to hold.

The Browning was a much older design by John M. Browning. He was a great weapons inventor and also created my favourite handgun, which today would still be my personal choice, the 9-mm Browning Hi-Power.

A lot of .30 Brownings had been imported from the USA and modified by Armscor to fire the NATO 7.62-mm round. The .30 Browning was of simple design and worked on a recoil system. It had a slower fixed cycle rate of about 600 rounds per minute. This was good, as one did not want to use all of one's ammo in a hurry.

The LMG, as we called it, was smaller, lighter and invented more recently. It was imported from a factory in Belgium. It fired the same 7.62-mm round, but worked on a more complex gas-operated system. It had a lot more moving parts. Its cyclic rate could be adjusted to 800, 900 or 1 000 rounds per minute. The gas adjustment was a problem, as it would often get bumped or knocked by tree branches when it was mounted in the turret of a Casspir, causing it to malfunction or jam.

The police had chosen the LMG, while the army had chosen the Browning. In my opinion (and there are differing views) the

Browning was a better choice. I decided that we needed some more Brownings, but didn't know where they were going to come from. The army, I thought. We needed to either steal them or bribe an army storeman to let us have some.

'Where do you two think you are going?' Captain Winter caught Jackie and me as we passed the ops room. 'I need you two to take my Nissan Skyline to Tsumeb,' he said. 'It's full of things that must go to Captain Adams at the ops room and then it needs to go for a service at the Nissan garage in Tsumeb.'

Cool! We had a car for the weekend and we could go and play in Tsumeb.

'There's one more thing,' Captain Winter added. 'Take this prisoner and give him to the security police at Tsumeb police station. They can keep him in a police cell.'

Jackie and I were ready in 10 minutes.

The car was packed full of shit. We didn't know what was in the boxes and we didn't really care. The back seat was so full that there was no place for our prisoner.

'We will have to put him in the boot,' I said to Jackie.

The boot was also full. After a bit of rearranging, we squeezed our captive into the boot by wedging him in so that he had to lie on his side. I saw the fear in his eyes and he cooperated fully, like an obedient well-trained dog. The fighting is over for you, my friend, and your future does not look good. You would probably be better off dead, I thought.

The countryside flashed past as Jackie drove at 180 kilometres per hour. We dodged the cattle, goats and donkeys and flew past the slower-moving traffic. Soon we reached Oshivelo and made a stop. We had completely forgotten about our prisoner in the boot, but suddenly I remembered.

'Hey, we'd better check on him,' I said to Jackie. I opened the boot and told him to get out.

'Are you okay, Tate?' I asked him. He didn't understand any English or Afrikaans, but he lifted up his shirt and showed us a burn mark on his right side. We were puzzled, but then Jackie realised what had caused it.

'He's been lying on top of the exhaust pipe and it gets hot. Shit, he's burnt himself.'

I started to feel sorry for him and looked through the car for some food. I found a box of tinned food with no labels and I opened one with my knife. Fuck, it's dog food, but maybe he's hungry. I offered him the tin. He attacked the food, eating it with his bare hand, scooping it out of the tin. He finished the whole tin and I gave him some water.

'Do you want to piss?' I gestured to him. He urinated at the side of the road.

'Let's shoot him,' Jackie suddenly said next to me.

'Why?'

'I feel sorry for him,' Jackie replied. 'He's better off dead. There is no future for him.'

'That's strange, I feel the same way.'

'What? Do you want to shoot him?' Jackie asked.

'No, Jackie, I don't want to shoot him. While he's still alive there will always be hope for him. I just feel sorry for him.'

'So let's let him go,' Jackie said. 'Let's let him run away. We can say that he escaped.'

'No, then we'll get into shit. We'll look stupid. Think, Jackie!'

We put a blanket on the floor of the boot to stop our prisoner from burning, loaded him back into the boot and took off for Tsumeb, with me driving this time.

We eventually found the Tsumeb police station and I pulled up outside the charge office. The charge office sergeant was fat, stubborn and dumb. He refused to take our prisoner because we didn't have any papers for him and neither Jackie nor I had our appointment certificates with us. We were dressed in civilian clothes and obviously looked suspicious. I had long hair and a bushy beard.

Jackie could never grow a beard. As much as he wanted to and tried, his beard would not grow. We teased him and told him that if he washed his face with his own piss, his beard would grow.

Jackie ran out of patience with the police sergeant. 'Do you have a mortuary here at this police station?' he asked.

'Yes, around the back,' the sergeant replied.

'I'm going to take this SWAPO terrorist outside and shoot him. Then you'll have to put him in your mortuary, won't you?' Jackie said as he led the prisoner outside. I heard him cocking his 9-mm.

'Wait, wait guys.' The fat sergeant jumped up from behind his desk and rushed out. He and Jackie walked back in with our prisoner and Jackie handed him over to the sergeant.

'Be careful. This guy is a terrorist. He has killed a lot of people and won't hesitate to kill you if he gets a chance,' Jackie said as we left.

I parked the car outside the ops tent, where we offloaded it. A pair of Koevoet guys, John Tate and Buks van der Berg, approached. Buks was a former middleweight professional boxer and not the type of guy with whom you would want to get into a fight.

'You fucking little prick. You're a newcomer. Who are you to be driving a car like this around? I'll fuck you up!' he shouted in my face.

There was no point in arguing and I didn't feel like getting into a fight with Buks. I simply held out the keys and he took them. He and John Tate drove off in the Nissan.

I wished I had said, 'You could just have asked, and, by the way, it's supposed to go for a service.' I also would have liked to have said, 'Fuck you, too.'

'Hey, don't worry, bro,' Tom Boom said from behind us. 'I've got a car. Let's go to town.'

Jackie and I drove with Tom Boom into town. He stopped to smoke a joint and the car stank so badly that I had to get out and wait for him to finish smoking.

'Don't you want some?' he asked me through his open window.

'No thanks, Tom, the smell alone makes me sick, but you carry on. I don't mind.'

'Let's go to the country club,' Jackie suggested.

'No, there's too much shit there and we're banned,' Tom replied. 'If we go there, we'll have to lie about who we are, but it will be useless. They'll know who Jim is. Just look at his beard.'

Koevoet members were known for having long hair and big bushy beards. Shaving while in the bush was almost impossible and to shave a week's growth off when out of the bush was a mission. The solution was simply to let it grow – it was a lot easier. Jackie couldn't because he hadn't washed his face with his own urine yet.

We found a hotel and had quite a few drinks and a couple of steaks in the bar. The locals ignored us completely.

Our night on the town did not turn out to be exciting at all and eventually we returned to the base. Tom was stoned and Jackie and I were pissed.

We found some colleagues in the tents and bought a dozen

beers from the bar. Jackie decided to try to play a guitar and sing. In between songs he once more made us relive his version of the ambush. In this latest version the ambush was set off with a landmine. One of the terrs lay waiting and as Lieutenant Goosen's Casspir approached, the terr set off the landmine with a remote device.

I had to sit and listen without saying a word. If I'd opened my mouth to set a fact straight, Jackie would have told his audience that I was not at the ambush.

The next morning the Nissan was back. It was Sunday and the Nissan garage was closed. Eventually Tom got hold of Captain Winter and Jackie and I were told to leave the car and get a lift back to Oshakati.

On Monday morning Captain Winter sent us on another little mission.

'Take an Albatross and 10 POWs from Onamwandi,' he ordered. 'Drive out towards Ruacana. Just before the town you will find a lot of rocks at the side of the road. Load the Albatross with rocks and bring them back. I specifically need a big flat rock as well.'

'What about our group?' Jackie objected. 'We need to deploy on Wednesday.'

'You guys are not going anywhere until I tell you.'

'Okay, but we need an AK.'

The captain gave Jackie an AK-47 and said, 'Watch out for those POWs. Some of them are fresh and will run away at the first opportunity. So don't come back without them. By the way, we are looking for a new leader for your group.'

With 10 POWs on the back of the Albatross we headed out on the road to Ruacana. I drove, with Jackie sitting next to me with the AK.

'Fuck, what does he think we are? His personal slaves or what?' Jackie complained. 'And no one is going to take over Zulu Golf. It's Lieutenant Goosen's team. He started Zulu Golf. I wonder how he's doing and whether he'll ever come back. I'm not going to let someone else take over the group.'

It took us about two hours to load the truck with rocks. Finally we found one huge flat rock that matched the captain's specifications.

'Hey guys,' I challenged the POWs. 'Do you think you could load that one?'

They couldn't get it up quite high enough to slide it onto the bed of the truck, but one of them was really big and muscular like a bodybuilder. He got under the rock as the others held it and with his shoulders he pushed it high enough to slide it onto the truck.

'Where did you get those muscles from?' Jackie asked.

'In Angola there is a little animal, I don't know what you call it,' he explained. 'It lives under the ground. I used to catch it and eat it. That's what made me strong.'

'Do you mean a mole?' I asked.

We questioned him a bit, but we couldn't really figure out what this animal was, so we left it at that. 'Hey, Jim, stop over there at those Cuca shops,' Jackie said. 'Let's buy these guys a drink.'

'Do you guys want to have a drink?' he asked them through the open hatch above us. Their faces lit up.

Jackie and I got out and as we walked towards the shops he called the big POW. 'Come here, Tate.'

Jackie handed him the AK. Yes, he gave the AK to the POW to carry!

I suddenly turned cold. All this guy had to do was simply to turn the AK on us. It was loaded and cocked. He just had to point it and pull the trigger and he and the rest of the POWs would be free. Angola was only a few kilometres away.

But he slung it over his shoulder, walked off with his buddies and went inside a Cuca shop. Why didn't he use it against us?

I considered running or jumping back into the truck and taking off. Instead, I just looked at Jackie, thinking he'd gone mad. He was fucking insane. Those guys were SWAPO, our enemy. They were hunted down, captured and tortured. Their comrades were killed. They would kill us at the first opportunity, and Jackie had just given them the AK so that they could kill us and escape.

'Watch, they won't do anything; I'm just testing them,' Jackie said confidently. 'Come, let's go and get some beers.'

'Hila, Tate, hila.' They called Jackie and me and, producing two jugs of mahangu beer, they invited us to drink it with them.

Okay, so they want to make us drunk before they kill us, I thought. The beer tasted like warm sour piss and I battled to finish it. I decided to take a walk and get as far away as possible from Jackie and his madness.

I walked past a shop and looked inside. I saw the most beautiful Ovambo woman I had ever seen standing behind the shop counter. She just looked at me and I walked on.

After some time I got back to Jackie. It was almost time to get shot or to leave.

'Hey, Jackie, I've just seen a really beautiful Ovambo woman,' I told him. 'I mean, she is really hot.'

'So why don't you go and make a move?'

'Now you've gone off the deep end,' I said. 'Please get the AK back and let's get the fuck out of here.'

Our 10 prisoners returned and the strong man gave the AK back to Jackie.

I felt lucky to be alive.

'I want to drive,' Jackie said, and I was glad to trade the keys for the AK.

We drove with the hatch open. Some of our prisoners were sitting on the roof above me. One of them handed me an open bottle of White Horse whisky. I drank out of the bottle and handed it to Jackie, who took a swig and handed it back.

'Where did they get money for the whisky?' I asked Jackie.

'They get paid while they are kept at Onamwandi. They get money, food and clothing. They are well looked after.'

Some things can never be explained; they have to remain a mystery. I will never understand why Jackie handed the POW the AK and why they didn't kill us and escape when they had the chance. Two weeks later Jackie told me that the POW to whom he had given the AK had vanished. Jackie claimed he had been shot and executed. Although I had learnt not to believe everything Jackie told me, I knew this was quite possible.

Warrant Officer Charles Louw was tall, thin and ugly as hell. His false teeth were too big for his mouth. He had long red hair and a bushy red beard.

'I am your new group leader,' he said, introducing himself to Jackie and me. Initially I didn't take to him and Jackie gave him a hard time. I summed him up as being a total idiot, but I was wrong. He turned out to be one of the nicest guys on earth.

'Look, guys, it's going to be just as difficult for me as it is for you, but somehow we need to work together,' he said to us. 'Zulu Golf is Lieutenant Goosen's team, but he's not here. So please, let me try and help, if I can. You guys know a lot more than I do, but you can't run this group on your own. They won't let you.'

We had a new member, Wessie. He was a fat slob who drooled and looked like a mommy's boy. We assigned him to drive the Blesbok. It was a simple job and he was happy with the arrangement.

We deployed on Wednesday and headed for Eenhana. The Tsumeb infiltration was over. The size of the SWAPO group that made it to Tsumeb remained in dispute. On that first follow-up, when we chased them from Elundu, the locals kept telling both Jackie and me that there were about 150 in the group. In the end it was claimed that there were about 70 and that only three of them made it back to Angola. The rest were hunted down and killed. Nearly all of them were killed by Koevoet, but the army took all the credit.

After the Tsumeb infiltration the South African minister of defence was asked in Parliament who or what Koevoet was. He was unable to answer the question. He said he believed that Koevoet had something to do with the police. The minister of police was also unable to explain Koevoet's existence until he got some answers from the head of the security police.

Some Koevoet guys lived in various houses in Oshakati. We occupied four such houses in a dead-end street known as Little Angola. Portuguese refugees from Angola lived in some houses in between, as well as Heinie Becker, who owned the Toyota garage; a member of the army, whom we called Pinocchio; and a priest.

One day some security policemen were sent to find out who the Koevoet members living in the houses were. Cassie Kruger, the commander of Zulu Charlie, pulled out an AK-47 and fired it into the air. Famous for his bad temper, Cassie once almost killed a guy during a fight at the Guest House pub. That was the first and last time that they came asking questions.

As a result of our success with the Tsumeb infiltration, Koevoet was forced out into the open. A television documentary, *The Second Arm*, was made about Koevoet and its activities. For the making of the documentary Frans Conradie was able to get 14 kills in one contact. We were accounting for about 80 per cent of the kills internally while the army was accounting for only 10 per cent. It made no sense to label us the 'second arm' and not the first.

We were no longer a secret operation, but at least now the money started to roll in and we were receiving equipment. I still did not have a rifle, but I hoped that I would soon be able to get one.

As a result of the publicity, our proving that we could do the job and successful negotiations, we were going to be allowed to deploy into Angola for the first time. The army also wanted to learn how we operated.

We paid a price, though. A huge propaganda campaign was launched against us by all of our enemies. We did nothing to counteract the campaign and it nearly led to the disbandment of Koevoet.

It was Sunday and we had been looking for the enemy in the bush for four days, with no luck. We reached Ohangwena, where we spent the night outside the COIN base at the tribal office together with Captain Joost Engelbrecht and his group.

At 2 a.m. I woke to the distant rumble of what sounded like a thunderstorm. The rainy season had been over for some time, so I didn't know what it could be. The others woke up too.

'Someone's getting revved,' one guy said as we lay listening to the explosions.

'Who could it be? What bases are there north of here?' someone asked. Another person wondered if it could be coming from Angola. The border was only a few kilometres away.

'Must be Alpha Tower,' someone else suggested. 'They must be revving Alpha Tower. Come, let's go and help them.'

'No, there is nothing we can do at night,' Captain Engelbrecht responded. 'By the time we get there, SWAPO will be on the move, running back to Angola, and we can't chase them in the dark. We need to be there in the morning before sunrise.'

A few hours later I started my Casspir as we got ready to move out. The four-wheel drive was not working: at the transfer case a banjo bolt, which allowed compressed air to be pumped into a cylinder to engage four-wheel drive, had snapped off. I had to replace the bolt, but we didn't have a spare. I started asking around for one.

'This is what you need.' The captain dangled his key ring with a spare bolt on it as he walked towards his Casspir, smiling cruelly. He wasn't going to give it to me.

Everyone started to drive off and I had to decide whether to go or stay. Let me see what happens, I thought, and I followed the rest.

Alpha Tower was guarded by the army, and that morning it was a scene of chaos. The safest place during the attack had been up at the top of the tower, where there was the protection of thick reinforced concrete as well as the water in the tank at the top. Nothing could have penetrated that, not even an RPG-7, but the two guys on duty at the top had jumped off during the attack and had nearly killed themselves in the process. They had already been casevaced.

Apart from the two who had jumped, no one else was hurt. A number of unexploded 60-mm mortar bombs lay half-buried in the sand in the camp, unstable and dangerous. They were waiting for sappers from Etale down the road to come and render them harmless.

'Come and look!' A young corporal showed me one of the Soviet 60-mm bombs stuck in the ground with its tail fin sticking out.

Instinct told me to get away from it. The vibrations from our footsteps would be enough to set it off.

'Pick it up and throw it away,' I jokingly said to the corporal.

We started to leave to go and look for the enemy spoor to the north-east, the direction from which they had attacked.

As I drove off, I heard an explosion coming from the base at Alpha Tower. Curiosity killed the cat – the corporal had taken my advice. He had decided to pick up the bomb and, as he did so, it had exploded in his hands, almost killing him. He survived to live the rest of his life deaf, blind and without arms.

For the first time we were given permission to go into Angola to chase this group. Their spoor took us across the border before they headed east for the whole day.

Why east, we wondered. Why not north? It would be logical to head north. We didn't know that they were heading for a FAPLA base to the east, where they hoped that they would find safe sanctuary.

The terrain was hard and we were moving fast. We came to a big open shona and on the far side of the dry pan I could see some kraals.

The locals in this part of southern Angola were Kwanyama, and they were extremely poor. The country had been ravaged by years and years of war, and the Kwanyama were helpful but afraid. Some of the men came running out of their kraals willingly to give us information about our enemy, who had just passed by.

Suddenly there was movement ahead and Bennie's Casspir Zulu Golf 3 raced on and opened fire, spraying automatic gunfire as it charged.

'Contact, contact, contact!' someone called over the radio.

We all charged forwards, but it was a fuck up. It was some of the locals who had seen the Casspirs coming and run for the safety of their kraal.

We passed the kraal and looked for the spoor on the other side, where we picked it up and continued with the follow-up. It was time to call in the gunships.

One of the guys signalled to me to stop as he caught up from behind. I halted and climbed out of my Casspir. I could see that he needed to talk.

'They shot some of the locals back there by accident,' he told me, trembling and looking pale.

'Tough shit,' I said, 'this is Angola.'

'There were two children, a boy and a girl aged about five and eight,' he went on. 'They were badly wounded. There was nothing that I could do for them. I shot them with my 9-mm; I put them out of their misery. I killed them.'

I didn't know what to say. I just stared at him. I could see pain and sorrow deep in his soul, but there was nothing I could have said that would have eased this.

'Have you told anyone?' I finally asked. 'Did you tell Zulu or Zulu 2?'

'No, you are the first person. Only Bennie's and my guys know what happened.

'Leave it. Just forget that it ever happened. Don't tell anyone. Don't ever talk about it again. Come, let's move on. The gunships are coming; the spoor must be hot,' I said as I climbed back into my Casspir.

The human brain is not like a computer hard drive, from which a memory like this can simply be deleted. No matter how hard one tries, memories remain at the bottom of your soul and, when you least expect it, they creep up to haunt you.

The gunships passed over us and flew ahead of the follow-up. Arthur Walker, the best of the gunship pilots in my opinion, was flying air cover for us that day. He was twice awarded the Honoris Crux medal for bravery. He was an ace in the air, we all thought, but an arsehole on the ground.

By late afternoon the follow-up was called off. We were less than a kilometre from a FAPLA base and high command didn't want a fight to break out between us and FAPLA. SWAPO had obviously made it to the base and had won the day. Jackie was furious and burnt down a hut that belonged to the local chief at the kraal where we had stopped.

It was time to withdraw and to get out of Angola. If we headed south we would come out somewhere between Okongo and Elundu.

The sand was soft and I didn't have four-wheel drive. I got stuck and burnt out my clutch. The sun was about to set, so we had no option but to dig in and wait until the morning. We hoped that FAPLA was not planning to attack us. Under cover of darkness they would have had the advantage.

With the hut nearby smouldering away, Jackie dug a shallow hole in the ground to sleep in. I refused to do the same – I was not prepared to sleep in my own grave. Warrant Officer Louw spoke to Bennie and decided that we should take turns to stand guard during the night. By midnight, however, we were all asleep. Guard duty with the Ovambos never worked, as they were never able to stay awake. But a sleeping Ovambo was a better guard than a white man from the city peering out into the dark night.

I was once caught in a hot spot under similar circumstances and put some claymore mines out for the night. Long after midnight I was awake, listening to the sounds of the night, when I heard movement about 50 metres from our TB. I took the hand-held plunger and was considering detonating a claymore when the snoring Ovambo next to me stirred in his sleep and said, 'Ondjamba, Tate' (It's elephant passing) and went back to sleep.

On numerous occasions our Ovambos would wake in the morning and tell us that if we travelled for five kilometres in a certain direction we would reach a kraal where we would find enemy spoor. They had heard the locals' dogs bark during the night.

The next morning we got out of our sandy TB after quite a battle. Wessie towed my Casspir behind the Blesbok all the way back to Oshakati. I was hoping to get rid of it. I had had enough of my Casspir.

10

Back from the dead

Warrant Officer Louw decided to leave us to join another team. He probably found it too much responsibility to command our group, or perhaps Jackie and I were too much for him to handle. Maybe someone higher up decided.

Our next group commander was Warrant Officer Pieter, whose surname I can't remember. He lasted only two weeks with us before having a nervous breakdown and finding himself a softer job as yet another jam stealer.

The new stores outside Okavi were being completed and we finally had one of our own. This was where we first encountered Warrant Officer Pieter. He found Jackie and me with some of our Ovambos. We had just said goodbye to Warrant Officer Louw.

Warrant Officer Pieter had been shown the ropes by Captain Erwee from Zulu Alpha and had been advised to take command of the group by asserting his control immediately. This was bad advice and soon Jackie, our Ovambos and I broke him without even a single contact. He came in with much gusto and left with his tail between his legs.

'Right,' he demanded immediately after introducing himself to us, 'we need to get this store cleaned up. Pack everything outside and let me see what we need. We can throw away what we don't need.'

Then he made all the Ovambos line up in front of him and asked the first one, 'What's your name?' He checked it against the list in his hand and asked, 'Are you a tracker or a gunner?'

The Ovambo looked at him as though he was mad.

'I'm asking you a fucking question! Are you a tracker or what are you?' he shouted.

Rule number one: don't swear at an Ovambo. Rule number two: don't shout at an Ovambo. All Warrant Officer Pieter needed to do then was to break rule number three and hit an Ovambo. Then he would certainly have got himself killed.

I had to intervene, as there seemed to be no communication.

'Sir.' I said the word with difficulty. 'All of our Ovambos are trackers and all of them are gunners, but not all of them can drive. We are short of drivers. Here we all do whatever we can to help. We work together because we want to.'

The Ovambos nodded their heads in agreement with what I said but continued to look at Warrant Officer Pieter as though he were mad.

At the time we were indeed short of drivers. Tommy could not drive because his hand had still not been treated properly. The doctors at Sector 10 had done their best, but Tommy needed to be sent to 1 Military Hospital in Pretoria for proper treatment. By now for some reason the white phosphorus had caused his ring finger and his middle finger to grow together, he was still in pain and he was unable to drive. His new nickname was Paddapoot – 'frog paw'.

One didn't want to get wounded or badly injured while in Koevoet, especially in the early years when we did not exist officially. My friend Kallie Calitz from Zulu Sierra told me what had happened to him after he stepped on a POMZ anti-personnel mine while chasing a SWAPO group on a follow-up. He was hit in several places by pieces of shrapnel. He was casevaced to the primary trauma unit at Ondangwa and then transferred to 1 Military Hospital.

He ended up lying on a stretcher in a passage for three days. The doctors were not prepared to treat him as he was not in the army. His wounds became septic, especially one in his side, and the smell became so bad that finally he was treated, but he lost both of his little toes. It took him a while to recover, but eventually he was back on the job, hoping never to get hurt again and being a lot more careful of booby traps.

I remember what happened to a friend of mine once when he got physical with his group. After assaulting one or two of his guys, they looked at him and said, 'Tate, next time we have a contact, be careful. Someone might just shoot you in the back.'

After that he was unable to work with that group. It was bad enough worrying about the enemy trying to kill you, but to have to watch out for your own guys was too much. Who in his right mind would want to go into a contact or an ambush with a group that felt that way about him? It was so easy to get rid of someone in a contact. Accidents happened.

Warrant Officer Pieter had another problem. He wasn't prepared to drink water from the same bag as the Ovambos. He got his own water bag and clearly marked it, forbidding the Ovambos to drink from it.

He even went so far as to make everyone get his own cup for drinking water from the tap on the outside of the Casspir. He wouldn't drink the water if an Ovambo's mouth had touched the tap. Imagine a follow-up when our trackers run on the spoor all day and the temperature reaches 50 °C. They run up to the side of the Casspir to drink some water from the tap quickly, but now, under Warrant Officer Pieter, they must first find their cup and fill it while the Casspir is moving, drink, put the cup away and then go back on the spoor.

We deployed to the east for one week with Warrant Officer Pieter in command, and for one week Jackie, Wessie, the Ovambos and I fucked him around without him realising it. We also pushed his nerves to the limit by telling him the scariest stories we could think of.

The final straw for Jackie and me was when we reached Eenhana and Warrant Officer Pieter announced that we were forbidden to go to the army pub as we were not allowed any alcohol. He reckoned that, while we were on duty, drinking alcohol was a serious offence. He also would not allow the Ovambos to go off as they always did to the Cuca shops nearby to drink their traditional mahangu beer. It was a form of socialising for them and a way of gathering information from the locals and from colleagues in other groups.

Like some other group leaders, Warrant Officer Pieter tried to force religion on us by making the group pray every morning. I explained to him as tactfully as possible that I had no religion and that I was fighting for myself, not for a god.

We returned to Oshakati after one unsuccessful week in the bush and that was the end of our new group leader. He went off to have his heart attack, nervous breakdown or whatever. Once again they were looking for a new group leader to take control of us.

Out of desperation they put Sergeant Kallie Calitz in charge of Zulu Golf. And finally we were happy.

Kallie was a veteran of Koevoet. He had blond hair, was of

medium height, was very muscular and wore thick glasses. He didn't drink or smoke and he was a fitness and sports fanatic. This didn't stop him from being our kind of guy.

Kallie had been in the special task force that the brigadier had fired and sent back to Pretoria. He had then left the task force to become a permanent member of Koevoet, together with his friend Koen Marais.

Finally we had someone who was experienced, whom we accepted and whom we were prepared to follow. I got to know and understand Kallie. He became a very close friend of mine and helped me to find better opportunities. He was also a damn good operator.

I had been in Koevoet for over six months by this stage. We were given 14 rest days every three months, apart from the three weeks' leave we were allocated each year. If we didn't use the rest days, we lost them.

My sister Jean was getting married, so I decided to take a two-week break to go to the wedding in Durban. After a flight from Ondangwa to Waterkloof and a bus ride to Jan Smuts Airport, I took a South African Airways flight to Durban. Jean and Wayne were at the airport in Durban to meet me and they drove me home through the city. The city lights had never been so bright – my eyes had grown accustomed to the green, grey, brown and white of the bush.

My father thought I looked like Fidel Castro, so I had my hair cut and I shaved. I bought some new clothes and used deodorant and aftershave for the first time in months. There had been no use for that stuff in the bush.

Durban was the same as always and held very little attraction for me, except for the fact that my family lived there. I had not missed the city, but one thing I had missed was girls. Soon I realised that I had changed. I had gained a lot of self-esteem and confidence. I was no longer shy and I felt like a pig on heat.

I made a move on every pretty girl I came across, including those on whom I had not made moves before because I'd lacked the courage. Trying to score as many girls in Durban as I could was like trying to get as many kills as possible in Koevoet.

It was a lot of fun, but I had only two weeks and soon I was on my way back to Oshakati. My sister was now married and I had acquired a lot of girlfriends in Durban, though I didn't want a permanent relationship with any of them. At least I knew I had something to go back to one day.

The C-130 landed at Ondangwa and there to meet me were Jackie and Lieutenant Goosen. Yes, Lieutenant Goosen was back. He had a scar on his head where they had performed a skin graft to cover the piece of steel in his skull. He also had a plastic eardrum, but even with it he couldn't hear properly with his right ear. He looked good, but there was something different about him. He was not the same as before. I guess the type of trauma that he had gone through was enough to change a man for life.

We drove back to Oshakati and on the way Jackie had more good news. They had had another contact and had shot two more SWAPO enemy. That brought our total to 19 kills and zero captured for the year so far, and the year wasn't nearly over.

When we drove into Okavi, Lieutenant Goosen caught sight of my Casspir. 'What happened to your Casspir?' he said. 'Did you hit a landmine or what?'

'No, I burnt the clutch out,' I replied, and explained what had happened.

'We will have to fix it,' he said as we walked across to look at it.

Here we go again, I thought.

'We must get an Albatross. If we park it over here, we can pull your engine out with the Albatross's hydraulic arm and replace the clutch. Or what if we take the gearbox out from the back? Then we won't have to take the engine out.'

He was planning some blood, sweat and tears.

'Look here, Lieutenant. This must be a very old Casspir. These consoles are different to the other Casspirs' consoles, and look at the position of the steering wheel. Another problem is that it keeps getting water in the diesel. I don't know how, but it's not coming in with the diesel when we fill her – there must be a hole or something in the tank. This Casspir just keeps breaking down and I can't get it fixed.'

The rest of the day we spent trying to get the gearbox out from the back, but it didn't work.

'Lieutenant, please can't I have Zulu Golf 3? I promise I'll look after it. Give me Zulu Golf 3 and I'll be happy. They can scrap this one.' Zulu Golf 3 was Whitey's Casspir, but he had left and Bennie was driving it in the meantime.

'I don't think so,' Lieutenant Goosen said. 'Your Casspir hasn't done much mileage.'

'Lieutenant, the speedometer hasn't worked since I inherited it from Greens, so no one knows what mileage it's done.'

'I'll think about it,' he said.

The following morning he surprised me. 'Jim, you can have Zulu Golf 3. They're going to scrap your Casspir and we'll get a new one. Tomorrow we'll have to deploy with three Casspirs.'

At last I was happy! I finally had a decent Casspir. Zulu Golf 3 had an open roof, so it wouldn't be so hot in the vehicle.

The original Casspirs had closed roofs with two hatches. A lot of guys simply cut the roofs open with an angle grinder, but that was a hell of a job because the Casspir was made of armoured steel. A few guys tried a quicker method. They used an oxyacetylene cutting torch. Cutting through the steel from the outside, a few of them forgot that the inside of the Casspir was covered with carpets, and boy did they make a mess when the heat from the cutting torch melted and burnt those carpets on the inside!

My old Casspir had to stand at the base for another two weeks and everyone asked about its owner. This became an embarrassment for me. Most people assumed that it had hit a big landmine, so I just went with the flow in order to avoid further embarrassment.

'Yes, one big motherfucker of a landmine,' I would say.

We deployed to Okongo on the Wednesday. Kallie came with us to keep a watchful eye on the lieutenant as it was his first week back in the bush.

Okongo was the furthest east that we generally operated from Oshakati. Further east of Okongo lay the Okavango area, where the Okavango people lived. Koevoet had a base at Rundu, Zulu 4, which was responsible for patrolling the Okavango. Further east of Okavango lay Botswana and the Caprivi.

Jackie, Kallie and I managed to persuade the lieutenant to come to the pub at Okongo. Jackie and I drank beer while the lieutenant and Kallie sipped their soft drinks. There we met a strange group of mercenaries led by a former French Foreign Legionnaire.

'Just look at my babies,' he boasted, gesturing towards the tough-looking men with him. 'These are the best soldiers in the world. Do you know how many wars we have fought in together?' he asked.

'How long have you been fighting here?' Kallie asked.

'Five months,' he said. 'We have a six-month contract, so we have one month left.'

'How many enemy have you guys killed in that time?' Jackie was stirring.

'None,' he admitted, 'we can't kill an enemy that we can't see. If we could find them, we would kill them.'

'We've had 19 kills in the last six months,' Jackie said, rubbing it in.

'I don't know how you guys do it,' the Frenchman said. 'I have great respect for you.' This mercenary was surely being decent.

I was surprised to learn that the army was employing mercenaries.

The following morning we headed east from Okongo and came across three guys from the army's famous 32 Battalion. To my surprise they were wearing camouflage uniforms while working internally. They were meant to wear them only when they operated externally.

They asked if they could ride with us as they had been in the bush for weeks now and were sick and tired of walking. One of them rode with me and I had the opportunity to talk to him.

After we had dropped them off, I decided that if that was the famous 32 Battalion, I didn't think much of them. All my passenger did was moan and complain about how shit it was to be in 32 Battalion.

A few days later and after a couple of fruitless follow-ups, we finally picked up the spoor of six insurgents and gave chase. The vegetation in the east was very dense and in some places the tall kiaat forests were almost impossible to penetrate with a Casspir. In the thick bush the enemy could be 20 metres ahead and we would not be able to see them. It also gave them good cover from the gunships.

The closest gunships were based at Eenhana, over 100 kilometres to the west, and it took them some time to reach us. By then they had only enough fuel left for a limited period of air cover for our follow-up.

The advantage we had in the east was that the population of Kwanyama, which was very cooperative and helpful, gave accurate and valuable information.

With the sun about to set, we realised that we were not going to win that round. Kallie was so frustrated that he stood on the roof of his Casspir and fired an RPG rocket in the direction of the six insurgents who had been slowly but surely gaining on us by anti-tracking.

It was a long haul from Okongo back to Oshakati. We set off early in the morning and soon came up behind the sapper team that was sweeping the road for landmines. It was winter now, the dry season. The last rain had fallen in February and it wouldn't rain again until November. A good rainy season had finally broken the drought, turned the dull grey landscape lush green and made the ground harder. Good mahangu crops and grazing had fattened both the people and the cattle. It was a good year for the locals. This suited SWAPO, but not us.

In 1981 SWAPO's tactics had been to infiltrate in groups towards the end of the heavy rains. They were trained to avoid the security forces and stay on the move. In the grip of a severe drought it was easy to track them down. Our tactics had been to chase them until they could no longer outrun us and then destroy them.

In 1982 their tactics seemed to change and they were trained to ambush us in bigger groups. Many of our groups were ambushed in that year, but the SWAPO ambushes simply made our work a lot easier. Instead of looking for the enemy, the enemy was looking for us. It became a lot less difficult to drive into their ambushes and destroy them. Their new tactics were simply not working. The Soviet advisors and Cuban instructors back at the training bases deep in Angola were surely scratching their heads to think of new tactics.

When we reached the sapper team on the road on our way back to Oshakati, Lieutenant Goosen must have remembered detonating the anti-tank landmine in the Odila River, as he did not want to drive further on the unswept part.

He moved off the road, having decided to bundu-bash next to it. The bush was dense and his plan was crazy, because the bundu-bashing was causing more wear and tear and damage to our Casspirs than a landmine would.

In the worst-case scenario the damage from a landmine would mean having to replace a differential. During the bundu-bashing brake pipes and air pipes broke off. The engines overheated and we moved slowly.

When I later told colleagues that Lieutenant Goosen had tried to bundu-bash from Okongo to Eenhana, they shook their heads and said that he must really have lost some of his brains when that RPG hit his head.

It was soon clear that other vehicles had done some bundu-bashing too. There were hundreds of vehicle tracks on both sides of the road, and it would have been easy for SWAPO to notice this. They might have planted landmines in the tracks next to the road.

Back at Oshakati, with Lieutenant Goosen back, Kallie decided to return to Zulu Sierra. I set about building a new bumper for my Casspir, because the original bumper was too weak for bundu-bashing. I cut a piece off an old railway line and mounted it in such a way that it could be detached. I did a magnificent job and the lieutenant commended me on it.

Lieutenant Goosen was now determined to develop a countermeasure to do something about the ambushes. He explored the possibility of mounting claymore mines on the Casspirs, which could be detonated from the inside in the event of hitting an ambush. We found the side of an old army Buffel and took it to the shooting range just out of town with a case of claymores.

The backblast of the claymores blew a hole right through the armoured steel. Mission impossible.

While back at Oshakati, we were summoned to the tree behind the ops room for what we thought would be another lecture from Brigadier Dreyer. He seemed happy and he surprised us.

'Boys, things are quiet at the moment, so I've decided that we're all going fishing.'

Fishing? I wondered where the fuck we could be going fishing, but the brigadier soon cleared that up. 'We're all going down to Mile 108 near Henties Bay,' he said, before informing us about the arrangements.

An advance party under the command of Captain Sakkie van der Merwe from Onamwandi was despatched to Mile 108 on the famous Skeleton Coast to set up a camp.

Lieutenant Goosen, Jackie, Wessie and I were tasked with driving three Blesboks filled with food and supplies down to the coast to join Captain Van der Merwe.

Jackie and I drove the Blesbok that carried all the alcohol. Thousands of rands' worth of booze was lying behind us as we drove along, hitting the occasional cow, donkey or goat that got in our way. A Casspir or Blesbok could hit a cow at 90 kilometres per hour without its occupants even feeling the impact, and we left a trail of dead cows, donkeys and goats behind us as we drove along. We managed to drink a dent into the load of booze by the time we were past the Etosha National Park. We hoped a kudu would cross the road so that we could kill it and take it with us.

After passing Tsumeb and then Otavi, we turned off the main highway at Otjiwarongo and headed for the coast. At Omaruru we stopped and decided to spend the night at an old railway depot. We could have continued but did not want to arrive at the camp in darkness. In any case, Jackie and I were so pissed by that point that we could hardly talk or walk, let alone drive the Blesbok.

The lieutenant was mad at us. He said we were being irresponsible and that we were stealing the liquor. Jackie pointed out that it was meant for us and that if we didn't drink it someone else would. Jackie eventually persuaded the lieutenant to drink a couple of soft drinks, and he became party to our crime.

Jackie started to tease the lieutenant, telling him that we deserved this because he had been lying in hospital while we had been going through hell. He kept telling the lieutenant how much he loved him.

The next morning we left the tar road at Usakos and took the dirt road through the Namib Desert to Henties Bay. For breakfast Jackie and I opened a case of beer.

It was very hot as we drove through the desert. We could see a thick grey mist ahead in the distance. It grew closer as we progressed. Suddenly we came to a T-junction, and in front of us was the sea. It was as if the sea wasn't supposed to be there, as if someone had just plonked it right in the middle of the desert.

We stopped at a shop in the little village of Henties Bay. Lieutenant Goosen and Jackie bought some fishing gear. They were disgusted with me because I was not interested in fishing – I had spent all my childhood weekends, public holidays and school holidays with my family at Umdloti, where my dad fished. That was enough fishing for a lifetime.

'I'll catch a bigger fish than all of you,' I promised.

'How are you going to do that without a fishing rod?' the lieutenant challenged me.

'Don't worry, I have a plan.'

It was late afternoon when we reached the campsite at Mile 108. Jackie and I drove straight onto the beach and nearly got stuck – this sand was different from that in Ovamboland and we had pumped the tyres hard for the long tar road.

Captain Van der Merwe came running out and crapped all over us, shouting, 'You're not allowed to drive on the beach with that Blesbok!' I couldn't hear everything he screamed, but I did hear, '… and the brigadier will be arriving shortly.'

'All he worries about is impressing the brigadier,' I said to Jackie. 'Fucking jam stealer. We impress the brigadier by shooting gooks.'

'Fuck him,' Jackie said.

Lieutenant Goosen was making a plan to get away from the camp as quickly and as far as possible. He could see what was coming: one big mess. The White Horse whisky was going to make us all very drunk and very stupid. And he didn't have time for the other officers.

I too could see what was coming. Jackie and I were the piss cats in the team. Wessie had made other friends and we didn't care about that. He irritated the shit out of us.

I felt sorry for the lieutenant and didn't want him to go off on his own, although he I knew that he liked to be alone. He was our group leader and our friend.

We were meant to share a Toyota Hiace 4×4 with Zulu Sierra, but they always hogged it. Kallie arrived at the camp and was happy to hand the Toyota to the lieutenant so that he could set up his camp. Kallie understood the situation and I appreciated his thoughtfulness.

The guys started to arrive in dribs and drabs. Oosie and Leon Lotz from Zulu Whisky arrived in a tan Mazda pick-up. They went screaming straight onto the beach and got stuck at the low-water mark. They had heard that a 2×4 pick-up could be driven on the beach, but they didn't know that the tyres had to be deflated first.

The tide was coming in and the pick-up was about to get swallowed by the ocean. Oosie panicked and shouted, 'Go fetch a 4×4, go get a Blesbok!'

I was standing next to the pick-up. 'Wait,' I said, 'stop panicking, let the sea take it, it's no big deal.'

'No, we can't let the sea take it.' Leon didn't like my idea. 'We have to save it.'

'Okay, let's pick it up and carry it,' I suggested. They looked at me as if I were mad.

'No, seriously, 10 of us can carry it if we work together,' I maintained. 'I can get some POWs and then we can lift it.' By now more guys had arrived from the campsite, like curious onlookers at an accident scene.

'Come guys, let's pick up this pick-up. All together now and we pick up the pick-up!'

The pick-up became light as many hands lifted it and simply carried it back to the camp – just in time to meet the brigadier. He was watching us with a big smile.

We put the pick-up down in front of him and Oosie said, 'It was Jim's idea.'

'No,' I objected, 'I didn't drive it into the sea.'

'No, sorry Jim. I mean it was your idea to carry it back here,' Oosie said. 'I never knew it would be possible to do that. You are quite clever.'

'No, intelligent,' I corrected him jokingly.

It was time to get out of there and go with Lieutenant Goosen to set up a little TB a few kilometres south of this camp, where we could get some peace and quiet. I persuaded Jackie to go with me.

Jackie and I were set up to have the best of both worlds. With the lieutenant we could have stillness and calm at his private TB, and at the main camp we could party. The problem was that the two were so far apart that we couldn't walk between them. We ended up catching lifts back and forth with guys who were passing up and down along the beach.

Early that evening it got so cold at the lieutenant's TB that Jackie and I grabbed a lift back to the main base. Soon things were getting out of hand there and fights were about to start, so just after midnight we decided to go and check on the lieutenant.

When we arrived, Lieutenant Goosen was looking for his fishing rod. 'I've just put it down here and now it's gone,' he told us, and we hoped that for once in his life he was also pissed. But then Jackie yelled, 'Look over there, there goes your fishing rod!'

The mist had cleared and under a full moon we could see the rod and reel bouncing over the sand dunes as it disappeared into the distance.

The lieutenant had caught a sea barbel and had not been able to get the hook out of its mouth. He had left the rod with the barbel still attached to the line and had walked back to the pick-up to find a pair of pliers with which to remove the hook. He hadn't seen a jackal grab the barbel and take off towards the distant mountains.

Jackie gave chase and ran after the jackal into the desert. Eventually the jackal dropped the barbel and Jackie triumphantly returned with the lieutenant's rod and reel.

'What would you do without me?' Jackie asked as he handed the lieutenant his rod and reel. 'It's a good thing that Jim and I came to check on you!'

The lieutenant had chosen the right spot. When we woke up the next morning, we found that he had set up his private TB at a tiny bay that was quite deep and teeming with fish. He had hit the jackpot.

It was still cold and soon Jackie and I got up and opened a bottle of Old Brown sherry to warm us up.

'No, you're supposed to heat it,' I said to Jackie. I stoked up the fire, poured some sherry into a mug and heated it over the fire.

'Give me the bottle,' Jackie demanded, and rolled the bottle in the hot fire. Suddenly it exploded as Jackie was bending over it. The flames singed his hair and face. He ran down to the sea and jumped in, head first. He came back shivering and very miserable. The lieutenant was not impressed.

Oosie and Leon came driving along and stopped to watch the lieutenant hauling out one fish after another. Jackie sat by himself at the fire, wrapped in a blanket and moaning.

'Jim, come and watch this,' Oosie said as he walked towards the sea, carrying something in his hand. He pulled the pin from an M26 hand grenade and tossed it into the sea. BOOM! It exploded with a fine spout of water.

I saw a huge steenbras flapping on the surface. The concussion from the explosion had burst its swim bladder and it flapped helplessly on the water.

I couldn't let a fish like that get away, and I dived after it into the cold water.

When I came out of the sea, cold and wet, I was holding the big fish in my arms. 'You see, I said I would catch the biggest fish,' I said triumphantly.

Oosie and Leon gave Jackie and me a lift back to the main camp, where we showered in hot water and got changed into dry clothes. Then we caught a lift back to Lieutenant Goosen's TB again and for the next few days helped to fill a 25-ton freezer truck we borrowed from the army with fish.

Jackie couldn't master the Scarborough reel he had bought in Henties Bay, but even with hand lines we were able to haul fish out of the sea.

Some of the guys didn't make it to Mile 108. They got stuck in the pub at Henties Bay for the whole week. They slept in the pub when the owner closed it at night and they drank in the pub when it opened at 10 in the morning. The owner didn't mind, because he made more money in that one week than he had made in a whole year.

Our fishing trip soon came to an end and it was time to get back to Oshakati to do what we did best.

11

A close shave

SWAPO had learnt to anti-track. They disguised their spoor by stepping on hard patches of ground, brushing over their spoor with branches and even going barefoot. We heard that for their entire training period in the bases in Angola, the SWAPO trainees had to anti-track, even when they went to the toilet. That improved their chances of survival when they infiltrated South West Africa.

Initially we were usually able to hunt down a group of SWAPO fighters and eliminate them soon after they had infiltrated, but the longer they survived, the greater their chances of further survival became. If they escaped their first contact with us, they gained experience and would do everything to avoid another contact. No matter how much training they received, nothing was worth more than experience. This applied to our side too.

A problem we had with hunting the enemy was that some of them, after infiltrating and usually after surviving their first contact with us, would decide that they no longer wanted to fight. They would bury their weapons, equipment and uniforms and go on the run, trying to stay alive. In these cases they would be hunted both by us and by SWAPO. SWAPO executed their deserters and often sent executioners to find and deal with their members who had absconded.

The Ovambo were a deeply religious nation. They had embraced Christianity long before, when the missionaries had arrived from Europe. SWAPO training included converting Ovambo trainees, a good number of whom had been abducted at gunpoint and forced to the training camps in Angola, from Christianity to atheism. Many captives and former SWAPO members who were now fighting for us explained the training process.

'We stand on parade in the training camps every day,' one former SWAPO member told us. 'The instructors come up to us and shout in our faces, "What are you thinking about? Your God? There is no God! Forget about your God and think about the total liberation of your country."'

SWAPO, it was said, lied to their recruits about the real situation in Namibia. The insurgents would come across the border with the idea that they were in control of the country and that they were going to help to defend it against us, the enemy. They would often stop at a local kraal or Cuca shop to ask for directions to Oshakati, where they were going to join their comrades to help them defend the town against us, the unwelcome invaders from the Pretoria regime.

As the insurgents gathered more information from locals, many of them seemed to form a clearer picture of what was really going on in the country. A local headman once told us, 'There were 10 of them. They came from the north and were heading south. They demanded food and water and asked for directions to Oshakati. They asked if I had seen the Koevoet, because they were going to destroy the Koevoet. I showed them down that pathway, where two days ago there was a contact. The bodies of seven of their comrades still lay there in the sun, rotting. They came back later and their attitude had changed. I could see they were worried. They spoke quietly among themselves. When they left I offered them a Bible, but they said that they did not need it as there is no God who will help them. One of them turned back and accepted the Bible. He hid it so that the others would not see.'

Often after a contact we would go through the enemy's weapons and equipment and find a brand-new Bible in one of their rucksacks. The Bibles were definitely not Soviet issue.

I am not trying to persuade you to believe that we were right and that they were wrong. My objective is purely to give you the opportunity to experience what I experienced. I'll leave it to you to decide for yourself what the rights, the wrongs and any moral justification of the conflict were.

We needed to do something to counteract the anti-tracking. As long as the enemy could keep a cool head and continue to anti-track, they would slowly gain ground and be able to stay ahead of us and stay alive, even if we were only 100 metres behind them.

One way to counteract SWAPO's anti-tracking would be to call in air support. The gunships could fly low overhead and either see the enemy and shoot them, or make them panic and run. We would fire mortars ahead in the general direction of the spoor. Voorsny was also an option, one that I was perfecting. As opposed to spoorsny – tracking – it meant that I would load my trackers into my Casspir, leapfrog a few kilometres ahead, find the spoor again and then call up the rear, thereby gaining ground on the enemy. Often while racing ahead to look for the spoor, I would get lucky and drive straight into the enemy.

The SWAPO insurgents needed nerves of steel. Imagine being alone in the bush with a bunch of Casspirs and a group of guys 200 metres behind you, hell-bent on killing you. Gunships are circling above you and, if they spot you, they will kill you immediately with their 20-mm cannons. Mortar bombs are exploding around you. Casspirs drive past you 50 metres to your left, but luckily they don't see you.

You are tired, hot and hungry. If you surrender, you will be tortured and killed anyway. Your only hope of survival is to stay calm and to keep anti-tracking to the best of your ability. Imagine having to keep this up for up to three days.

If you manage to survive this, you might consider a career change, but you also know that your former boss will come looking for you, and he is not going to accept your resignation.

Life for SWAPO was shit. Often their fighters found themselves in situations that they didn't want to be in, with no way out. These were the ones who had learnt to survive and they were the ones with whom we battled to catch up.

So it was time for Lieutenant Goosen to try to develop an anti-anti-tracking method, because they learnt to survive through anti-tracking and we needed to destroy them.

The lieutenant said he had a plan and was about to test it, but first there seemed to be some deviation. One morning he announced, 'We must go to the airbase at Ondangwa. Laura is coming on the flight from Waterkloof and I need to fetch her.'

'Laura?' Jackie and I said simultaneously and looked at him with surprise.

'Did that RPG and the landmine blow some of your shyness away?' Jackie teased.

'Hey, guys, the lieutenant's got a girlfriend and she's coming to visit,' Jackie announced.

We were baffled. We remembered how the blonde who had sold us our canvas boots had made the lieutenant blush. The army had a shop up the road past Sector 10 that sold civilian shoes and clothing. It was run by the army dentist's wife, a very beautiful blonde woman. It was at that shop that Lieutenant Goosen had found and bought his first pair of Israeli canvas combat boots. Those boots later became standard issue for Koevoet and the SAP.

Shortly after Lieutenant Goosen had discovered the boots, he took Jackie and me to the shop so that we could each buy ourselves a pair and, so we teased him afterwards, so that he could eye the beautiful blonde. While we were in the shop, she was also eyeing him keenly. I have never seen a man blush like the lieutenant did that day.

After we had left the shop, he nearly killed Jackie and me.

'But she's married!' he protested, trying to defend himself.

'So what?' I teased. 'The more rings the better the compression.'

'You were just looking,' Jackie chirped. 'Nothing wrong with that, and she was checking you out too.'

We found ourselves walking back to the base after Lieutenant Goosen kicked us out of the pick-up truck and drove off, still bright red.

The dentist was found dead a few weeks later. His wife, the beautiful blonde, found him lying on their bed, strangled with their telephone cord. The Oshakati police believed her story that he had committed suicide, but everyone took it with a pinch of salt. After all, we knew that she was having an affair. Thank God it wasn't with our lieutenant.

But now the lieutenant was expecting his girlfriend, Laura. All the way to the airbase, 40 kilometres away, Jackie and I pestered him for information about her. We couldn't believe that this shy, withdrawn introvert of whom we had grown so fond could have a girlfriend.

The C-130 had landed and most of the passengers had come through. Jackie and I stood back to give the lieutenant space to meet his girlfriend, but there was no sign of her. We were dying to see this – not only to meet her, but to see how he would treat a lady.

'I can't wait to see this,' Jackie whispered.

The lieutenant went to the counter and made an enquiry.

'Come, we must go to the back to meet her,' he called to Jackie and me.

He was looking at a crate and, as we came closer, we heard the whimpering of a puppy from inside the crate.

Laura was a Dobermann-cross-bloodhound and had been sent from the SAP's dog school in Pretoria. He was going to put some of his world-famous expertise in dog training to use to experiment with countering SWAPO's anti-tracking.

Koevoet was growing and a lot of new members were arriving. Okavi was getting full and noisy. It was becoming impossible to sleep at night, so Jackie and I put our names down to move into the SWA Police barracks where Lieutenant Goosen was staying. Soon we were granted a room and we moved there.

We deployed as usual that Wednesday. Laura was left with a babysitter, because she was still too young to come out with us.

We were driving along a pathway in single file in the Oshigambo area with Lieutenant Goosen in the lead. Suddenly he called a halt and told us all to switch off our engines. He then told us to start up again. After a few minutes he once more told us to switch off our engines.

He had our only long-distance B25 radio mounted in his Casspir. We were unaware of the conversation taking place between him and Captain Adams at Zulu 2.

The army had frozen an area to the north of us so that a group of reconnaissance soldiers could operate in the area dressed in fake SWAPO uniforms with SWAPO weapons and gear.

Zulu 2 was questioning our position. They thought that Lieutenant Goosen had given them the wrong coordinates and they were worried that we were in a frozen area with recces running around dressed up as SWAPO.

The recces contacted Zulu 2 and informed them that they could hear our Casspirs. That's why we had stopped and started, stopped and started. Now they were sure that it was us, 100 per cent sure.

The lieutenant turned off his small radio, the RSA53, while he was talking to Zulu 2 on his big radio. Then he informed us on his small radio of the situation and instructed us that, no matter what happened, we must under no circumstances open fire. If we shot anyone, we would be shooting our own guys. What he did not realise was that his radio was turned off when he issued the order. We did not receive it.

We proceed up the pathway and, 500 metres later, 'Contact, contact, contact!' We drive straight into six 'SWAPO' insurgents. Bennie, in our new Zulu Golf 4, opens fire. The lieutenant has turned his radio back on and shouts frantically for a ceasefire while he tries to explain the situation.

It's too late. Bennie's guys have floored one and killed him in a hail of automatic gunfire. I have one of them lined up in front of me. My plan is to flatten him with my Casspir because our LMG has jammed. When we realise that he's an army recce dressed as SWAPO, we try to catch him instead of killing him.

He runs past my Casspir while my Ovambos shout for him to stop. He disappears into the bush.

Jackie, who has also realised by this stage that the 'insurgents' are really army recces, stops his Casspir, jumps out and tries to stop one by tackling him, but the guy gets away.

We gather around the dead body of the recce that Bennie has just killed. Lieutenant Goosen now has to give Zulu 2 the news before the army does that we have shot and killed one of our own.

Captain Adams goes ballistic and for the next half an hour we stand around weighed down by this heavy burden, thinking about what we should do.

'Zulu Golf, Zulu Golf, Zulu 2,' they call us over the radio. 'That contact you've just had – the army knows nothing about it and the recces are fine. Turns out that they are much further to the north, so your coordinates must be correct,' they inform us.

Our lieutenant is happy again and we are relieved, but what a fuck up! We could have had six kills but we have only one.

'I tried to rugby-tackle one,' Jackie laughs. 'Imagine what he's going to tell them if he gets back to his base in Angola. In the middle of a contact a mad Koevoet guy jumped out of his Casspir and tried to catch me!' By now we are all laughing.

Jackie has a new story to tell. I wonder how this one is going to sound after a few drinks.

The next modification I made to my Casspir was to cut the front grill out and put it on hinges. The radiator and the fan sat behind the front grill. When we bundu-bashed, the front of the grill clogged up with leaves and debris, which caused the engines to overheat. Someone modified the grill in this way and soon everyone was copying it. Eventually the manufacturers sent their engineers to come and look at what we were doing to our Casspirs and slowly improvements were perfected at the factory.

I was cutting my front grill open while the lieutenant was building a cage for Laura in the back of his Casspir. We were working under the roof of the shed at the back of Okavi next to Daan du Toit's radio workshop. As we worked, I heard a familiar voice behind me.

'Hi, I'm Wally Boden and this is Sergeant Claasen.' I remembered Wally, a police dog handler from Durban. I turned round and he recognised me. I greeted him and the sergeant and asked Wally how things were in Durban.

In Durban the members of the dog squad considered themselves to be the main men, glory boys with big egos and self-images bigger than a Rottweiler, but here in Koevoet they soon realised that they were small fish in a big pond.

Koevoet was always short of manpower. It tried to attract guys from various police departments, and the latest attempt was to use dog handlers. They could serve for a two-month tour only, as their dogs had to be considered. Those dogs were of no use to us. They were mostly German shepherds, a breed that can't cope with the heat, so they had to stay caged up while the handlers were in the bush.

Now it was Wally and Sergeant Claasen's turn with Koevoet. 'They said we can come with you guys, with Zulu Golf. Do you know where Lieutenant Goosen is?'

I could see that something was troubling Wally. 'I was put in Zulu Sierra,' Wally told me, looking hurt, 'but when I met Piet Stassen he just looked at me and said, "We don't need amateurs; there's no place for fucking amateurs in my group."'

Just then Lieutenant Goosen joined us and I introduced them.

Wally was at the stage I was at a year before, during my three-month temporary stint in the operational area. At that time I was desperate for my first contact. He made me promise that he would not have to go home without having been in a contact.

I said that he was with the right group. We were more than two-thirds of the way through the year and we had had 20 kills so far. He would have four deployments with us and those would be the only opportunities for contact before he had to go back to Durban. I promised him that his dream would be fulfilled. And then I nearly failed him.

Wally and Boo Boo soon had their first trip with us. Boo Boo was Sergeant Claasen's nickname, but only behind his back. He was big and well built, with red hair and eyes that were too close together. Not a handsome guy. Not a clever guy.

As we left Okavi on our way to Elundu, Wally got into my Casspir and promptly made himself comfortable in the gunner's seat next to me. That was Lakulya's seat. He had been my gunner all along and I trusted him with my life.

'Wally, that's Lakulya's seat,' I said. 'He is my gunner and has been that all along.'

'It's okay, Sergeant Jimmy, he can sit there.' Lakulya saved Wally from being kicked to the back of our Casspir. Wally did not look too happy, but I knew Lakulya appreciated what I had just said.

So now Wally was my gunner, but I would have preferred Lakulya. I didn't know how Wally would shape in a contact or an ambush. I would also have preferred Lakulya's keen eyesight. I would rather have had an Ovambo I knew and trusted next to me than some glory boy dog handler from the city who had never seen action.

We were north-east of Oshigambo, moving through the bush looking for spoor and trying to squeeze information out of the locals.

We were bundu-bashing when suddenly there was a commotion in the back of our Casspir. Some of our Ovambos bailed out over the side. I thought that a snake had probably fallen from a tree into the Casspir. I stopped and climbed out of my seat to sort out the problem.

The Ovambos were all shouting, 'Bad luck, bad luck! We are going to have bad luck!' I realised that I had a riot on my hands.

'What is it, Lakulya?'

With terror in his eyes he pointed to an insect in the back of the Casspir.

'It's only a stick insect,' I said. 'Look, it's harmless.'

A stick insect's body and legs are just like thin brown sticks and it is very well camouflaged when sitting on a brown tree trunk or branch. It looks like a praying mantis – which is revered as a god by the Bushmen – and it belongs to the same family of insects. Although the Ovambo do not regard the praying mantis as a god, they don't fear the praying mantis. The stick insect, or *efingwe*, as the Ovambo call it, is another matter entirely.

The praying mantis has the most bizarre mating ritual. The female chooses to mate with the smaller male. She mounts him from the back and, after she has finished mating, she kills the male by biting him in the neck. Then she eats him.

I often wondered whether the stick insect mated in the same way as the praying mantis and why the Ovambo were so afraid of it, but this was one explanation they were not going to give me. They would not even talk about it.

As I picked up the stick insect, Lakulya jumped out, horrified. So I tossed the insect out of the Casspir, climbed back into the driver's seat and started up. One or two of our crew got back in, but the others wouldn't.

It took me 15 minutes to persuade them all to get back into the Casspir.

'Something bad is going to happen. That stick insect will bring bad luck to us,' they muttered, and started jabbering away in Oshivambo.

The other Casspirs have stopped and we eventually catch up with them.

Zulu Papa has just been ambushed ahead of us. Billy has been shot through the back and they need our help. We race to their assistance and soon we arrive at the scene of the ambush.

Billy has been casevaced with a bullet through his spine. He is paralysed from the waist down and, although we don't know it yet, will spend the rest of his life in a wheelchair.

No one wants to say it. No one wants to talk about it. But it seems that Billy has been hit in the back by friendly fire. He was inside his Casspir when shot, and the only way he could have been hit was from inside the vehicle. One of his own guys has accidentally shot him.

The enemy weapons must still be gathered. An RPG-7 is lying on the ground and I can see that the rocket is still in the tube. Luckily for Zulu Papa, the owner was killed before he could fire it. The rocket has been hit by a bullet and part of the head has been blown away.

Be careful, I want to warn Botes from Zulu Papa as he walks up to the RPG, picks it up and swings it over his shoulder. What an overconfident arrogant prick, I think. He takes his first step and BANG! Part of the head of the rocket explodes above his head and he falls to the ground instantly. Chris Luiters, standing nearby, catches a piece of the shrapnel in his chest and he too goes down.

Lieutenant Goosen has to call for another casevac.

With three of Zulu Papa's members out of action we have to help them back to Oshakati.

The Ovambos were right about the stick insect, but luckily the bad luck had not been meant for us. Not yet, anyway.

For the next few weeks in town Lieutenant Goosen tried to train Laura to track. He even made little leather shoes for her to protect her paws from the hot sand and the heat on the floor of the Casspir.

Laura was getting bigger and came on her first trip to the bush to see if she would be able to cope with the conditions in which we worked. It soon became clear that this would not be the life for her. The job was not fit for a dog. The extreme heat, the noise, the discomfort of her cage in the back of the Casspir, and the commotion and stress on a follow-up all took their toll on her. It would be better to leave the tracking and the anti-anti-tracking to the Ovambos.

Soon Laura's days fighting for Koevoet had to come to an end. The lieutenant had to send her back to the dog school in Pretoria for her to be retrained for some other purpose, used in a breeding programme or put down. Such is the way of man, who treats humans badly and animals even worse.

Laura's leaving indirectly led to Jackie and me being kicked out of the barracks and living in a bungalow at Okavi with Koos Valentine, a coloured man from Mossel Bay. He was Koevoet's only coloured member and was in Captain Joost Engelbrecht's group. Koos had a stutter that made it almost impossible to understand him.

It was mostly Jackie's fault that we were evicted from the SWA Police barracks, but I suppose I had a hand in it too.

On Laura's last night with us Jackie insisted that Lieutenant Goosen let her sleep with us in our room. Later the next day Jackie gave her back to the lieutenant and she was taken to the airbase at Ondangwa, from where she was sent home.

And that was when the caretaker at the barracks decided to inspect our room. He found it in a mess – Laura had pissed on our floor. The caretaker went to the brigadier with the story that Jackie and I lived like pigs and that we had pissed on our own floor.

The brigadier threatened to expel us and put us on a train home. He said we must go and live in the bush or live in a tent across from Okavi next to the communication tower, which was the tallest steel structure in the southern hemisphere.

There was no point in trying to explain to the brigadier that we had kept Laura in our room and she was the culprit. Standing on the brigadier's red carpet, I knew it was better just to take the brigadier's crap and face his wrath silently.

That is how Jackie and I became outcasts, sharing a room with Koos from Mossel Bay.

Jackie was getting out of hand while I was trying to reform. We were both falling apart and drinking far too much. We both had accounts with Lobo at the bar of the Guest House and nearly all of our wages was going towards paying our bar bill. Jackie one night brought another man's wife to our bungalow. He was totally trashed and he had sex with her right there on his bed in front of Koos and me. Koos was so shocked that he left the room. I pretended to sleep. Jackie thought it was very funny, but I was not impressed.

When Lieutenant Goosen found out about Jackie's little sexcapade with another man's wife, he nearly killed him.

Poor old Wally had only two more deployments to go and we were letting him down: still no contact.

We deployed to the east once again. Some groups preferred the west, while others favoured the east. Captain John Adams decided where each group would deploy to and we were always given a raw deal.

After a fruitless week – not for lack of trying – we arrived at Elundu. Zulu Whisky had left their diesel tanker at the army base there and asked if we could bring it back to Oshakati for them.

Lieutenant Goosen told Boo Boo to drive it, but he flatly refused. He had had enough. He was no longer coping and he wanted out. I could see that a confrontation was brewing between the lieutenant and Boo Boo, so I asked Wally to drive my Casspir. I jumped out and got into the tanker in order to solve the problem and restore peace. 'Blessed are the peacemakers: for they shall inherit the earth,' I said, misquoting the Good Book.

We drive along the long hard road to Eenhana and then head south for Ondangwa.

I'm behind the wheel of Zulu Whisky's diesel tanker; the other Casspirs are way ahead and far behind me. I'm on Chandelier Road, heading south. The tar road is about 10 kilometres away. Soon we'll reach it and turn right to the west. Another 40 kilometres and we're home. It's the end of a long week in the bush.

I ease back in the driver's seat, relaxing my grip on the steering wheel as I drive along at about 60 kilometres per hour.

I am imagining an hour under the shower, hot water streaming down on me as I get rid of a week's worth of dirt. I'm coated with sweat, dust, diesel, grease and black oil. I stink. I haven't shaved, washed, brushed my teeth or changed my clothes for a week. I can almost smell the soap and taste the steak and the whisky that I'll be having tonight at the Guest House.

A bright white flash bursts around me, instantly turning to yellow and orange as we're shot up into the air. Black smoke, dust and dirt engulf us as we come down again to a crashing halt.

Fucking landmine, I realise, as I check if Lakulya next to me is still alive. He's okay. As the black cloud settles, my ears are numb and blocked from the explosion, but I can hear machine gunfire coming from far behind.

An ambush? Fuck, we don't have a gun between us. We've hit a landmine, we're in the middle of an ambush and we don't have a single gun. No weapons, nothing. We're a sitting duck. We're fucked!

I debate whether we should stay or go, and decide that it would be better to stay where I am. I brace for the impact of the RPG that will come my way if this is an ambush.

Nothing happens. The Casspirs from behind pull up around me, but still I stay in the tanker, just to make sure it is safe when I do get out.

'Congratulations,' Jackie, Wally and Wessie say.

I've survived an anti-tank landmine explosion in a diesel tanker.

'What are you all congratulating me for?' I ask. 'I've fucked up Zulu Whisky's diesel tanker.' Lieutenant Goosen is the only one who seems to agree with me. He calls for a recovery vehicle and we are faced with a delay of a few hours while we wait for its arrival.

The crater that the landmine explosion has left in the road is deep enough for me to stand in without being able to see out of it, and the diesel tanker is pretty fucked. I find a big tree next to the road and sit with my back against it after checking for anti-personnel mines and booby traps. The base of the tree would have been a perfect place for the enemy to have planted a few of them.

I look at the scene in front of me. The tanker lies ahead of the huge crater in the middle of the road. I wish I had a camera.

Some of the Ovambos are playing in the crater. I'm dozing and my mind drifts away. Then I am suddenly alert. Some instinct brings me to my feet to look more closely at the Ovambos, who are tugging at a piece of cable protruding from the crater.

'What are they doing?' I ask David, who is standing next to the crater.

'They found that piece of electrical cable and want to take it home,' he says.

Suddenly something clicks in my mind and a warning bell rings as I see the dull yellow and red stripes of the cable. Cordtex – highly explosive detonating cord!

'Don't touch that!' I shout. 'Let go and get the fuck out of there!'

Luckily they take me seriously. They let go of the cable and clamber out of the crater.

The interest in the crater has changed. I shout, 'Who has an AK-47? Bring me an AK!'

Paulus arrives with an AK and hands it to me. I slide its thin cleaning rod out of its recess under the barrel.

I climb into the crater and with the AK's cleaning rod I start to scratch the soil away from the side of the crater where the Cordtex is buried. Slowly and very gently I work the soil away and dig deeper into the side of the crater around the Cordtex. To calm my nerves, I think of a double whisky at the Guest House.

'Hey, what are you doing, Jim?' Jackie shouts, and I realise that I have an audience standing behind me on the side of the crater.

'I would move back if I were you guys,' I say calmly, feeling my heart beating wildly. 'This is Cordtex and it's probably connected to something still buried here.'

'Here it is,' I murmur as I scratch open a big pack of blocks of TNT high explosives. I see them, 250- and 500-gram blocks, stacked and packed to form a booster for the landmine, which was connected to them by the Cordtex.

'Time to get the fuck out of here,' I say to myself and scramble up the side of the crater to safety.

About 15 minutes later a group of sappers arrives from the army base at Oshigambo down the road. They had heard the detonation when I hit the landmine and had decided to come and investigate. They are just in time to deal with my discovery, which they do by blowing up the TNT with some P4 plastic explosives.

'Jim, what if the TNT had exploded when you hit the landmine?' Jackie asks.

'Well it didn't, did it?'

'You would have been blown straight to heaven,' Jackie says.

'I don't believe in heaven,' I reply. 'The Cordtex didn't burn or ignite all the way to the TNT. It must have been old or defective.'

Now I need a cigarette.

I can't believe my ears when I hear Lieutenant Goosen tell

the recovery team that the diesel tanker must be left at the COIN garage at Ondangwa because we are going to fix it.

We arrive back at Oshakati and offload at our store.

Wally and Boo Boo have only one more chance of a contact, and that chance is one week away.

12

Ambush

Bravery is the will to survive when you know that you are about to die. Look Death in his eyes and challenge him. Say to him, 'No, you will not take me.'

It was a Friday night. Jackie and I arrived back at Okavi from the SWA Police barracks, where we had just eaten. A new pub and restaurant had been built in the north-eastern corner of Okavi. A kitchen and a mess had also been added to the eastern side of the base, so the guys no longer had to walk across to Onamwandi to eat.

The food in the new kitchen was prepared by SWAPO POWs from Onamwandi who had been trained to cook. This is why Jackie and I didn't eat there – we were worried that the POWs might put something in the food. And, indeed, a few years later they did one evening lace the food with rat poison. One of our guys was paralysed, one was blinded for life and one died. The official version was that the POWs responsible escaped after that. They were, in fact, taken out into the bush in Angola and executed.

There was a party going on at the new pub in the corner

of the base, a big party in honour of the gunship pilots. The brigadier had ordered it. It meant free drinks and food for all – food, we hoped, not prepared by the POWs.

The big guns were there and I was a little nervous as Jackie hauled me along. Arthur Walker was making a fool of himself, drinking Baileys out of a hollowed-out pineapple and hitting on Lieutenant Baker's wife, Linda. I wished that Lieutenant Baker were there to shove the pineapple up his arse. 'Ace in the air, arsehole on the ground,' I heard someone say about Arthur.

Jackie and I were in the middle of the crowd, making our way towards the bar counter, when we passed Captain Eugene de Kock and his best friend, Captain Adams. I moved ahead of Jackie. My instincts told me to keep away from them.

As Jackie passed Captain Adams, the captain grabbed Jackie's bum from behind and fondled it. Jackie swung around with raised fists. Just as he was about to hit Captain Adams, Captain De Kock intervened. I expected Jackie to back down, but instead I watched as he turned to Captain De Kock and prepared to attack him.

'You can fuck me up but I'll fight back and I'll hurt you,' he said to De Kock.

De Kock took a step back and hesitated. I could see fear in his eyes; I could see that he was afraid of Jackie. I couldn't believe it. The notorious captain with a reputation for being highly aggressive and violent had backed away from Jackie.

We never understood what bonded those two bosom buddies. To us it was a strange relationship, because some believed that Captain Adams was gay. Even after Captain De Kock had left Koevoet, though, he maintained that he didn't know anything about Captain Adams's sexual orientation.

A few weeks earlier, soon after we had arrived at Zulu 2 at

Eenhana, Tom Boom had approached us. He looked very bleak and troubled. He wanted to get a lift with us back to Oshakati because he said that he could not work with Captain Adams any longer. We asked him what the problem was and he told us that Captain Adams had proposed that he and Tom perform sexual acts and masturbate together.

Captain Adams later married a policewoman and had two sons.

I believe it's possible that Captain De Kock really did know nothing of Captain Adams's sexual orientation. A few years later I went to Club Med in Mauritius with a good friend, Anton, who was a colleague from Koevoet. At the time I didn't know he was gay. I wouldn't have minded had I known; perhaps we could have enjoyed our holiday even more – he could have stopped pretending to chase girls and left them all for me! He eventually came out of the closet and later died of AIDS. Perhaps people wondered about our relationship the way we wondered about Captain De Kock and Captain Adams. (Incidentally, it was while in Mauritius that I truly fell in love for the first time. I later married my first love. She is the finest woman in the world, but that is another story altogether.)

Jackie sat next to me at the bar and I ordered him a double rum and coke. He was angry, very angry, so I kept quiet and let him drink his anger away.

Jackie claimed that he was the illegitimate son of a country-and-western singer who had always been on the road and that that was where he'd got his singing talent from. This might have been true, but Jackie would never speak about his childhood. There was something deep in Jackie's past that hurt him and, as I sat next to him that evening at Okavi, I could feel his pain and anger.

It took me a long time to find out that Jackie had spent part of his childhood in an orphanage and that he had an older brother who was a priest.

Whatever his past was and however much it seemed to matter to him, it didn't matter to me. Jackie was a good person. Deep in his soul there was goodness, but he had picked up a lot of scars along the way.

What I liked most about Jackie was his fearlessness, his readiness to laugh in the face of death. The only thing I couldn't cope with was his singing. He was my friend and I knew that he would always stand by me, no matter what. If he had to, he would die for me. I don't think I would have done the same for him. I wasn't ready to die for anyone or anything back then.

It was time to deploy and it was Wally's last chance for some action. The enemy was scarce and I was hoping that they had not all been shot. We had not had a contact for a while now and we were getting frustrated.

We were about to leave Okavi and head for Okankolo and Epemba, where some SWAPO had managed to survive for some time now.

'Where is Boo Boo?' I asked Wally.

'He's not coming,' Wally replied. 'He says he's had enough.'

I informed Lieutenant Goosen and he gave the order to move out. I felt good and optimistic, but a little irritated because everyone else seemed so down.

A few days later we found a couple of easy spoor. It seemed too good to be true. We moved at great speed. From the spoor we determined that the guys couldn't be experienced terrs, but they couldn't be new ones either. There was no infiltration at the time and we were quite far south. They were in all likelihood inexperienced enemy. What we didn't know was that they were intentionally leading us into an ambush.

An ambush was always a possibility and didn't really matter to us. In fact, it made our work easier. If they ambushed us, there would be a lot of them together in one place and we would kill them.

An old trick in Koevoet was to poach someone else's spoor and cut in on their follow-up, as happened to us in the Tsintsabis area near Tsumeb. When picking up spoor and starting a follow-up, we would radio the information through to either Zulu or Zulu 2. The information would include our coordinates. Anyone listening would soon know exactly where we were and what we were doing.

This time Zulu Whisky was the poacher, but those guys had a new trick. Instead of cutting in in front of us, they claimed that we might be following the spoor they were tracking. It was their old trick in reverse: they were following us and intimating that we had stolen their spoor by cutting in in front of them. They were probably not able to overtake us to cut in ahead, so they came up from behind instead.

Lieutenant Goosen was not prepared to give up the spoor for them, but he did let them join us.

Zulu Whisky was Chris de Witt's group and was made up of SWA Police members. In my opinion, Chris didn't go to the bush to look for the enemy; he went to the bush to hunt animals and was reputed to have become one of the biggest animal poachers in the country. The only spoor his group seemed to look for were animal spoor. He got lucky on many of his hunts, as he often encountered SWAPO by chance. During the Tsumeb infiltration we came across him and his team loading a freshly slaughtered kudu onto their Blesbok.

Zulu Whisky normally operated in the west, where they had easy access to the Etosha National Park and an abundance of wildlife to poach. Someone told me how Chris once escaped the wardens of the Etosha National Park. He was on a poaching expedition and, having collected his trophies, he was chased by the wardens. They were gaining on him, so he dropped off two of his Ovambos, dressed in civilian clothes. When the wardens came across the Ovambos, they asked them if they had seen a Koevoet team come past. The two promptly sent the wardens in the wrong direction so that Chris could escape.

Zulu Whisky was the most undisciplined and dangerous group to work with. My chances of being killed by friendly fire suddenly increased tenfold when they caught up with us. Their attitude sucked.

Our follow-up had been going well. We were rapidly gaining on the enemy and it seemed like Wally's dream of a contact was about to come true.

'You bunch of fucking Zulu Golf cowards. You are too shit-scared to drive in front,' one of Zulu Whisky's guys shouted over the radio.

In the west it was always better to spread out and cover a large area. It was open, locals did not give information readily and it was difficult to track because of the hard terrain. There we usually bumped into the enemy by chance. But here in the east the thick bush took a toll on our Casspirs, so we normally kept them in two rows, single file, on either side of the trackers.

Whoever was shouting over the radio was pissing me off badly. I pumped the clutch, pushed the gear down, and floored the accelerator. Our Casspir surged forward past the follow-up, through a kraal complex, out the other side, over the fence of thorny acacia branches on the outer perimeter, into the bush and slap bang into an ambush.

Tack-a-tack-tack, they open fire with automatic rifles that sound very different when you are on the receiving end instead of giving it to them. Still pissed off by what some wanker said over the radio, I charge straight into the ambush. I see them in front of me and all I want to do is kill them. In my fury I don't realise that they are leading me into the ambush. They are the decoy. I change to second gear because of the soft sand and they open fire from the right.

Luckily Lakulya has a .30 Browning shoved out of a right gun porthole. The moment they fire their RPGs, he opens up, spraying bullets at them.

Wally has frozen. I've got two of them lined up in front of us for the kill, but he just sits looking.

'Shoot them, Wally,' I shout, spit flying from my mouth, 'shoot them!'

I want to swing a backhand at Wally to bring him out of his freeze, but then he opens up with the LMG as one of the insurgents turns and starts to run back past the left side of our Casspir, trying to avoid being run over.

I imagine that I hear the thud as one connects with the front of our Casspir and we drive straight over him.

The RPGs come flying and explode in front of us, above us and behind us. There are seven of them – each one misses us by a miracle.

One of the terrs runs up to the side of our Casspir with an F1 hand grenade in his right hand. The pin is pulled and he tries to climb up the Casspir to throw it in through the open roof, but Lakulya cuts him down with the Browning. BANG! We hear another explosion next to us, slightly softer this time. The hand grenade explodes in our enemy's hand as he dies. A piece of shrapnel punctures our left-rear tyre.

I have to change to first gear; I have to get us through this ambush and out the other side, taking as many enemy as possible with us on the way. Where are the other guys? Where are the lieutenant, Jackie, Wessie and Zulu Whisky? I am alone and soon we won't be able to keep on going – our tyre is almost totally flat.

The flat tyre forces us to stop. The firing has abated. I have driven us straight through the ambush. We are reasonably safe now and need to change the flat tyre, so we climb out of the vehicle.

Tommy is driving Zulu Golf 1. The army had at last agreed to treat our wounded, including our Ovambos, in 1 Military Hospital in Pretoria, so the injury that the phosphorus caused to his hand was eventually seen to. The hand is not 100 per cent, but Tommy can drive again. Now he takes off in a different direction, away from the ambush, and the lieutenant doesn't understand what is going through Tommy's mind as he does it.

Zulu Whisky has been left behind and catches up with us only when it is all over. Jackie is the only one who was anywhere near me during the ambush, but now, while we are changing the flat tyre, they all arrive back at the kill zone. After 45 minutes we too drive back there to join the others.

We establish that we took out six terrs in that ambush. We survived thanks largely to Lakulya, who kept the Browning firing towards our left flank, where the terrs were going to destroy us with their RPGs.

I cannot believe the jubilation at the scene of the ambush. The guys from Zulu Whisky are taking all the credit for the kills.

'Look here, they shot the radio antenna off Chris's Casspir,' one of the Zulu Whisky guys claims.

I take a look. No, if they shot it off, there would still be a piece left in the coil, I think. This antenna just came loose and fell out. But if these guys want to claim the glory, let them. I'm not going to get into an argument over who killed whom. At least Wally, our team and I know the truth. We are alive and six of the enemy are dead. Besides, the Ovambos talk among themselves and they will not lie about who shot whom.

There is no dignity in death. Six bodies are piled up in front of me, shot to shit. I can see that their bones are white, their blood is red and their brains are yellow. I've done this; I've helped to kill them.

It's a gruesome sight. Blood, bones, brains and limbs are bent the wrong way and bodies are broken by bullets. One terr has half a skull missing, blown away. This one's fingers are sticking out of his arm near his elbow. He's the one who tried to climb up my Casspir and throw a hand grenade into it. The grenade blew up his hand when we shot him down.

Look at this one. Wally shot him with the LMG. Look at these bullet holes. This one was shot in the back. Gaping holes through his stomach. There's a fucking tapeworm crawling out of a bullet hole in his stomach. It looks like something out of a science fiction movie.

Who drove over that one? Fuck, look what the wheel of a nine-ton Casspir can do! He's squashed flat, like a pancake.

We headed south-east to pick up the road to Ondangwa at Oshigambo. We stopped in a clearing while Lieutenant Goosen was communicating on the long-distance radio with Zulu Whisky. For some reason they needed to know where we were. We had run out of 1 000-foot rocket flares, so Jackie came up with a solution: we could shoot an illuminating mortar with our 60-mm patrol mortar, or 'patmor', as we called it.

'Hey, Jim, do you know how this thing works?' Jackie wanted to know as he climbed onto the roof of my Casspir and sat down next to me, looking at the white illuminating mortar.

'Give it to me,' I said. I twisted the fuze timer in the nose, set it to 10 seconds and attached two booster charges to the tail. 'You had better fire it from the ground,' I warned, but Jackie didn't listen. Instead he placed the base of the patmor on the cover of my open hatch and, before I could stop him, he dropped the illuminating mortar down the tube. It hit the firing pin at the bottom and went off up into the air, but at the same time the patmor bounced up, lifting Jackie off my Casspir with it. He fell onto the ground, where he landed upside down. After a while he got up, unhurt.

We made our way back to Oshakati. We now had 26 kills for the year and we had lost one member, Stiripo. We had two injuries, our lieutenant, and Tommy's hand. We were one point above the average of 25 kills to one for Koevoet, so statistically one of us was meant to die soon. But there are many ways to beat the odds – or for the odds to beat you.

And Wally would be returning to Durban shortly, telling everyone about his contact.

We were summoned to a meeting under the big tree behind the ops room. Brigadier Dreyer told us in his usual direct and confident way that an operation had been planned. We were going into Angola, and the plan was to move into the country from two points of entry and head north. This would be the first time that we were officially going into Angola to root out and destroy SWAPO at the source.

The army had agreed on certain terms and conditions, one of which was that they accompany us. As Koevoet's successes were now becoming well advertised and a major embarrassment to the army, they had to find out how we operated.

When the brigadier was speaking, the information about the planned operation had already started to leak to the enemy. They would know that we were coming; we would not have the element of surprise on our side.

Soon after the briefing, half of Koevoet assembled at Ohangwena while we were ready with the other half of Koevoet at Okongo. It was early morning and both groups began to head north.

Koevoet was invading Angola.

After about every 10 kilometres our groups headed east, one by one, while the groups who entered from Ohangwena did the same, some of them turning west. That way we would cover the entire vicinity of central southern Angola.

We advanced, ready for a fight. Zulu Golf was going to be the last group to swing to the west, which meant that we were going in the deepest, together with Zulu Mike. Zulu Mike, however, was on its own mission.

It was almost the end of the dry season. Part of the plan was to catch SWAPO just as they were waiting for the heavy rains to start so that they could begin to infiltrate to the south. Angola was very dry. We burnt the dry grass as we headed north, leaving huge veld fires behind us. We did this so that, during any follow-up later through the burnt veld, it would be impossible for SWAPO to anti-track, making it easy for us to chase them.

As southern Angola burnt, we headed north while SWAPO was retreating to the north. SWAPO's radio communications were intercepted. 'The situation is not normal,' one of them said. This became one of our favourite jokes.

The first sign of the enemy we found was a weapons cache consisting of a stack of B12 bombs, the type they would use to attack a major town or, more likely, an army base. The army made itself useful for the first time by blowing up the cache.

Koevoet had a reward system. As an incentive, groups were paid out a bounty of R800 for each enemy they killed, R1 000 for a captured enemy and various amounts for weapons recovered from the arms caches. The most valuable were landmines, at R1 500 apiece. The money was paid to the group from secret government funds. While the white members of Koevoet were paid high salaries and danger pay, the black members were paid a minimal amount only for the days they worked. So any reward money was distributed equally among those Ovambos who were present at the contact or when the weapons were recovered. I wondered what the pile of B12 bombs would have been worth and whether they were even listed as bounty. They went up in smoke with an earth-shattering bang.

On our first night in Angola we made a TB with Zulu Mike and the army, which had eventually caught up with us. They had assembled in teams similar to ours by using four Buffel armoured troop carriers and a Buffel supply truck. The army guys were almost all white South Africans. That was their first mistake: this was a black man's war.

I noticed that Zulu Mike's Blesbok was very overloaded. They told me that the more stuff they carried, the better. Stupid, I thought, because that Blesbok was so overloaded that it was going to break down. I didn't get on with the guys from Zulu Mike, so I left it to Jackie to mix with them.

Koevoet never wore rank while in the bush, for two reasons. The first was so that the enemy would not be able to target the senior members, and the second was simply that no one could be bothered to wear rank. Two army groups were next to us and it was obvious that they didn't understand how we operated.

We ignored the army guys until their commanding officer plucked up the courage to come and talk to us in an attempt to discuss tactics. He eventually found out that Lieutenant Goosen was the most senior of our members, and went to speak to him.

'We rely heavily on intelligence reports from HQ and then follow up on the information they give us. We don't quite follow how you guys operate,' he said to the lieutenant.

'We look for SWAPO spoor,' the lieutenant answered. 'We find them, we follow them and then we destroy them.'

'Oh, and what will happen if we have a contact together?' the captain wanted to know. He quickly went on to explain, 'We stop, de-bus and skirmish on the ground.'

'Then we will shoot you,' Jackie chirped, as the lieutenant said firmly, 'No, if we have a contact, stay in your vehicles and fight from your vehicle otherwise you could get yourselves killed.'

Fuck, I couldn't believe these guys were still using World War II tactics.

Next in the army captain's order of priorities was to sort out guard duties for the night. Our fires were about two metres high and later we were going to braai. Some of the guys were drinking beer.

'We don't stand guard at night,' our lieutenant explained to the army captain, who walked back to his little camp next to ours feeling somewhat confused.

The following morning we headed north and later in the day we left the army behind. Either they couldn't keep up with us or they didn't want to. Next we left Zulu Mike behind when their Blesbok broke down.

Xangongo was the last outpost. It once was a beautiful town, but it had been destroyed by the ravages of war and was now deserted. It seemed to have come to a sudden standstill; the people had simply vanished. It was a town like no other I had ever seen. The shops, hotels and other buildings had been built right up to the edges of the roads.

I had a strange feeling driving through the town. Suspended in time, it was like something out of a movie. We passed the football stadium and drove down the desolate main street. At the top of the street the road forked, and there we stopped at a Texaco petrol station, where a destroyed Soviet T-54 stood with its barrel pointing down the road.

The fuel tanks of the petrol station still had a lot of fuel in them. I wanted to take an M26 or a white phosphorus grenade and throw one into the fuel tank, just to see what would happen, but Jackie stopped me.

The main road led us out of town, and on the north-eastern side we stopped to look down over the Kunene River. The bridge across the river had been blown up by the army, so this was as far as we could advance.

We decided to make our way down to the river, but we had to go back halfway through the town in order to do so. The houses in the suburbs were also deserted. Locals had stripped the houses bare of all removable building material and used it to build shacks in the gardens, but by this stage the shacks were also standing empty. War had clearly been waged in this abandoned, devastated town.

We left the town and made our way down to the river. Still we had not seen a single soul, no form of life. It was eerie.

When we stopped on the southern bank of the river, some of the Ovambos went to wash and swim while some of us kept a vigilant lookout, especially to the north.

'Watch out for the crocodiles!' the lieutenant shouted and tossed an M26 into the river. It exploded and a waterspout shot into the air. Suddenly silvery, slimy things were flapping on the water's surface – fish, plenty of them.

'Hey, who's got more hand grenades?' Wessie shouted. I got one out of my chest webbing, pulled the pin, tossed it in and more fish came up.

Wessie got a case of M26s from the Blesbok and we went fishing. The Ovambos produced some hessian bags and filled about three of them with fish.

Although we finished the case of grenades, I hadn't had enough. I fetched a patmor from my Casspir and dropped a mortar bomb on the river, but on impact it exploded on the surface. When I tried another, the same thing happened again.

Then I fetched a case of claymores and was about to try them when the lieutenant stopped me. It was getting late and we were going to have to TB somewhere for the night.

We found a spot on the western side of the town that we felt would be safe. We had lots of fish, so the Ovambos made huge fires to cook on. It was a beautiful evening and soon darkness set in. Our spirits were high and we were making a lot of noise.

Suddenly someone in camouflage approached cautiously, with his hands in the air. He looked black, but as he came closer into the circle of firelight, I saw that he was white – his face had been blackened.

'Please guys,' he said as he lowered his hands, 'I am Captain Van der Merwe of 32 Battalion. You guys are crazy – you don't know what danger you're in. This is the last outpost. There are 30 of us holding this town and we could get revved at any moment. On the other side of the river FAPLA and the Cubans are just waiting to attack.'

'Cool,' Jackie chirped, 'then we'll have someone to fight with.'

Before Captain Van der Merwe left, he said, 'I recommend that you put those fires out. It'll be easy for them to home in on your fires from the other side.' Just as suddenly as he had come, he disappeared into the night, shaking his head.

'Put the fires out,' our lieutenant ordered. After a pause, he reflected, 'And maybe we should move to another location ...' We didn't feel like moving in the dark, though, so the fires burnt out and the Ovambos cooked over the glowing coals. We spent the night on the outskirts of Xangongo.

Morning came and it was time to head back to Okongo. We moved slowly, looking for any sign of SWAPO, but they seemed to have vanished. The situation in Angola was not normal.

We bumped into Zulu Mike on the way back, who said that they had picked up some spoor. The small group they were chasing had bombshelled and now they were on the trail of one of them. We joined the follow-up and found the insurgent. He was trapped on the recently burnt terrain, where trees were still smouldering. Unable to anti-track and outrun Zulu Mike and us, he was caught. He miraculously survived a hail of automatic gunfire without a scratch.

It was getting late and Zulu 2 was ordering all of our teams to get out of Angola. Zulu Mike left the captive with us and headed for Okongo. We wanted to interrogate him to see whether he could lead us to an arms cache.

It took little to persuade our cooperative prisoner to lead us to a kraal near the border, where he tried to remember where on the outskirts of the kraal complex the weapons were buried. After digging with his hands in a few places he came up with nothing except a freshly buried baby. The baby had been buried in an upright position and our captive had scraped some of its head off with his hand. The baby had most likely died of malaria, which was rife in Angola.

Our patience was running out. We were about to wake up our captive by torturing him when he came up with a huge jackpot. Landmines, RPG-7 rockets and boosters, Heat Stream and Pencil Stream rifle grenades, TNT explosives, Cordtex and detonators, F1 hand grenades, POMZ, Jumping Jack and Black Widow anti-personnel mines made up the bulk of the cache. Then Zulu 2 called us. Lieutenant Goosen informed them of our find, but they told him there was no money left in the secret funds for a reward.

'Are we going to load all of this onto the Blesbok?' Jackie asked the lieutenant.

'No, they won't pay out. So let's destroy everything. We don't want to transport this stuff as some of it might be unstable, and we don't want Wessie to get blown up, do we?'

We considered booby-trapping the cache and leaving it exactly as we'd found it so that SWAPO would get blown up when they returned and lifted it, but it was too big a find to risk that. It could just land up back in enemy hands as a result.

It would have been a good idea to keep everything and pretend to have found a cache at a later stage, when money was available again. I could see that our Ovambos were not happy, because the reward would have been for them. Lieutenant Goosen got Bennie on his side and after Bennie addressed the group they accepted the fact that this find would bring no financial reward. At times it was good to have Bennie as our black group leader – the big man with the squint was about 40 years old, twice the average age of our Ovambos.

'Let's fire off some of this stuff and show the Ovambos how it works,' the lieutenant said.

The Heat Stream and Pencil Stream were designed to be fired with a ballistic round from the barrel of an SKS carbine. The Pencil Stream, an anti-personnel rifle grenade that delivered shrapnel on impact, was long and thin and green in colour. The Heat Stream was designed in the same way as the RPG-7 missile, in that it also had a parabolic-shaped cone of copper–lead alloy in its nose with an explosive charge behind the cone. It would detonate on impact and penetrate almost anything. Although not as accurate as the RPG, at close quarters it was just as deadly and could easily knock out a Casspir.

We didn't have an SKS; our captive had been carrying an AK. Our Ovambos were still issued with the G3, which was an old Heckler & Koch assault rifle that South Africa had bought from the Portuguese when they withdrew from Angola.

The Heat Stream and the Pencil Stream both fitted perfectly over the barrel of the G3. Now all we had to do was improvise for a ballistic round, as we didn't have any. The AK round was 7.62 × 39-mm and the G3 fired the NATO 7.62 × 51-mm round. Both were the same diameter, but the G3 round was longer and more powerful.

I wiggled the head of a G3 round out of the casing and plugged the case with some toilet paper. Carefully I slid the round into the breach while keeping the barrel of the G3 slightly raised. I then slipped the Heat Stream over the barrel of the rifle and it was ready to fire. As a safety precaution I left the magazine off the rifle, as I didn't want to allow for the possibility of a live round flying into the back of the Heat Stream. That would have disastrous consequences.

'Right, who wants to fire it? I think it might work,' I said, smiling as I turned to my audience. I knew no one was going to volunteer and I would have to fire the bloody thing myself.

Paulus surprised me by stepping forward and taking it from me. Mr Know-It-All, Mr Ex-UNITA, was going to risk our modification.

He aimed at a huge tree and pulled the trigger. BANG! BOOM! The grenade hit the tree with a deafening explosion and we all ran to examine the damage. The slug that formed from the Heat Stream had gone right through the tree. It had penetrated a metre of wood.

It was time for fireworks, and we went wild with our new discovery.

It began to get late and soon it would be dark. We had to get moving if we wanted to make it to Okongo, or we would be sleeping in the bush.

The next problem was what to do with the rest of the cache. My plan was to dig a hole and pack everything carefully into the hole, place some white phosphorous grenades on top with a claymore as the cherry on the top, pour half a drum of diesel over the lot, run all the claymore cables as far from the cocktail as possible and then blow the whole lot up. It was a crude plan and it would have been effective, but the lieutenant wouldn't give me permission. He made us load everything that remained onto the Blesbok and we took it with us. Good luck, Wessie.

We had lost radio contact with Zulu 2, who kept calling us; we could receive them, but they could not receive us.

At Okongo the next morning we decided to wait for the army sapper teams to sweep the road. Later we drove to Eenhana with the road now reasonably safe. From Eenhana we would not be able to make it back to Oshakati before nightfall, so we set up a TB outside the army base against one of the sand walls.

All the other Koevoet teams were already back in Oshakati. Captain Adams and Tom Boom were still at Zulu 2 in the base behind us, but we did not know that. For a change Jackie and I decided not to head for the NCOs' pub in the base. Instead we settled down with the lieutenant, Wessie and our group.

Those were wonderful moments in the evenings out in the open, when the Ovambos would entertain us with their stories and we would tell them about life in the city. The Ovambos were friendly and outgoing by nature. They had a good sense of humour, but I always knew that there was a limit to their tolerance. As a team we had bonded – that is, all of us except Wessie, who could still irritate the shit out of some of us.

Lieutenant Goosen, Jackie and I were lying in a row in our sleeping bags. Wessie was sleeping next to his Blesbok. Suddenly old Potato Nose approached. He was drunk and looking for shit with Lieutenant Goosen.

An argument developed between the two of them. His problem was that we hadn't reported to him when we had arrived. He complained that the lieutenant never wanted to have anything to do with him.

The lieutenant was on his feet, but I couldn't believe his tolerance. It was 'Yes, Captain, no, Captain' all the time. Jackie or I would have smacked the captain long ago. That nose of his should have been turned into mashed potato.

'I'm going to fuck him up,' Jackie said quietly next to me. The lieutenant heard and warned Jackie to stay out of the fight.

Eventually the captain left, staggering off back to the base.

Jackie and I couldn't believe the way Lieutenant Goosen had behaved. There was a major difference between him and Jackie and me: he was a gentleman and we were hooligans.

'He's probably gone to masturbate with Tom,' I chirped as Potato Nose walked away. Jackie laughed.

Lieutenant Goosen was very upset, especially by the negative things the captain had said about our group, but no matter what people said about us and how they behaved towards us, the fact will always remain that soon we would be at the top of the scoreboard with the most kills of all the bravo teams.

13

Death has no mercy

Jackie and I didn't care much about the command structure of SWAPO. We were more interested in killing the enemy than capturing them. The valuable information they could provide meant nothing to us. For us our job was simple: find them and kill them.

After our largely unsuccessful first trip into Angola, we were now planning a second operation into the country. This time it was devised under a blanket of secrecy, so that when we went in again, the element of surprise was on our side and we could have a field day.

We went in at Namacunde and took the tarred road to the north. We drove through the town of Ondjiva, which was smaller than Xangongo but looked and felt the same: destroyed and desolate, there was not a living soul in sight. Again Zulu Golf was being sent the furthest north, all the way to Xangongo. From there we were going to head south-west and make our way back along the bank of the Kunene River. This time the army wasn't following us.

The army was learning and had established 101 Battalion in an attempt to copy Koevoet. It had woken up to the fact that the Casspir as a fighting vehicle was far superior to the Buffel, and they had started ordering Casspirs. The army also learnt that this was the Ovambos' war. In order to recruit Ovambos, it offered slightly higher wages than Koevoet. Soon a lot of our Ovambos began to leave us to join 101 Battalion. Koevoet put the Ovambos' wages up and a lot of them came back.

'Contact, contact, contact!'

Suddenly the radio waves come alive as several of our groups begin to engage SWAPO in various contacts in different places. All hell is breaking loose.

We make our way south-west along the south-eastern bank of the Kunene and then we turn south, away from the river. Our Ovambos spot three spoor that are heading south and we start a follow-up. After about an hour we are in hot pursuit. We are heading down a long open plain with heavy bush on our right.

Too late, the insurgents realise that we have caught up with them. They have no chance of escape. As we move towards them, they run for cover in the thick bush to the right and open fire at us in a feeble attempt to defend themselves.

Our Casspirs turn and chase them. Lieutenant Goosen and the trackers are caught in the open on the ground. I stop to pick them up. With the lieutenant and the trackers safely in the back of my Casspir, I race towards the bush, hoping to get lucky. Everyone has opened fire and bullets are flying everywhere.

I see one of them, 30 metres ahead, standing behind a big dead tree. Lakulya aims and pulls the trigger of the LMG. It jams. Twenty metres now, and Lakulya cocks and tries to fire. It jams again. Ten metres now, and it jams again. Fucking thing won't fire. There's only one thing left to do.

WHAM!

The front of my Casspir connects with the tree. The railway-line bumper smashes the tree and flattens it, squashing the terr, killing him instantly. The top of the tree snaps off and comes tumbling down into the back of my Casspir on top of the lieutenant and the trackers. It's old, dry and light, and they manage to stop its fall and push it out over the side as I go over the trunk and the terr with my nine-ton steel pony.

The shooting subsides and eventually stops. It's time to drag the dead out of the bush, do a body count, collect the weapons and radio all the information through to Zulu 2.

When we have done so, we leave the dead lying in the sun out in the open and make our way further south.

We stopped at an old settlement, where a few farm houses and some buildings stood stripped and bare, silent testimony to the time of Portuguese colonial rule.

We were lazing around, eating and drinking while we listened to the action over Lieutenant Goosen's long-distance radio. It was time to report our position, but with so much going on, the lieutenant delayed reporting it.

Piet Stassen, who was in command of Zulu Sierra, was destroying SWAPO's naval forces. We laughed at the name – the ocean was 500 kilometres away, but if SWAPO had a navy, it had just been sunk. Zulu Sierra had killed SWAPO's navy commander, radio operator, political commissar and all of their men except their second in command and the few who escaped. Zulu Sierra had also captured their radio.

Throughout southern Angola SWAPO was falling as Koevoet hunted its fighters down and destroyed them with no losses or casualties on our side.

Lieutenant Goosen finally finished his report to Zulu 2, then said to us, 'Guys, we need to get the hell out of here. We're in the middle of a minefield. According to our position, the army says they planted a minefield here a while ago.'

The problem with mines and minefields was that often the people who planted them got killed or forgot where they had placed them. The same applied to weapons caches that SWAPO planted. Often they were killed after stashing their weapons. Today there are probably still tons of weapons hidden in Angola and Namibia.

In single file, driving carefully in each other's tracks, Lieutenant Goosen led us away from that place without incident. We left Angola and headed for Oshakati. We now had 29 kills and one insurgent captured for the year so far.

It would take SWAPO a while to regroup and recover from the blow we had just delivered.

Lieutenant Goosen came out of the office at Okavi as Jackie and I were walking in. He had some news for us.

From time to time supplies had to be fetched from Pretoria. The Albatrosses were driven down, left for a week, serviced, loaded with supplies and equipment, and then driven back. It took a week to service and load them. During that week the drivers had time to do whatever they pleased.

The lieutenant had just fought hard for Jackie and me to have a chance to drive to Pretoria to fetch the supplies and equipment. It was most unlike him to do something like that. I did not really want to drive to Pretoria, but I accepted – I did not want to hurt his feelings. What he actually should have done was to apply for my promotion. I was long overdue for promotion, but I was not going to ask. I felt it was something that he and the office should do without any prompting from me.

We drove south in a convoy of four. The Albatrosses were slow and our maximum speed was 70 kilometres per hour. I would have been able to read a book while driving down that long open and deserted road. Jackie and I each drove an Albatross, Lieutenant Baker drove another, and Percy and Slit, a nasty character with no respect or manners, shared the driving of the fourth.

Jackie and I had taken good advice and had checked our vehicles' tyre pressure before we left, but at Okahandja Percy and Slit's Albatross had a blowout that delayed us for a few hours. It was one hell of a job to change the tyre and get the damaged one replaced in town.

Lieutenant Baker suggested that we find somewhere to sleep as it was getting dark.

'No, not a fuck. We are not sleeping over,' Slit said. 'We're going to drive through the night until we get to Pretoria.'

Jackie and I were shocked. We had never heard a junior speak to an officer the way Slit spoke to Lieutenant Baker.

The lieutenant gave in and Percy offered to drive my Albatross while I drove the lieutenant's, with him resting next to me. We drove through the night and reached Pretoria the next day. I drove in front while the lieutenant directed me to the place where we would leave the vehicles.

Jackie phoned his brother, who arrived with Jackie's VW Golf to fetch us.

'Have you ever been to Durban?' I asked Jackie, suggesting, 'Let's shoot down there tomorrow.' He thought it was a very good idea.

'Can I come too?' Percy asked. 'We can go via Vryheid and visit my folks.'

'Okay, let's stay at COIN HQ at the college tonight and go to Durban tomorrow,' Jackie said.

That night we had to visit an old lady Jackie knew. He wouldn't explain much, but he told us not to call him Jackie in front of her because she hated the name. We were to call him Magiel. Then the truth came out: Jackie's real name was Magiel. He had grown up in an orphanage and at some stage in his life he and his brother had been placed in the foster care of this kind old lady. All his adult life Jackie had been trying to bury the memory of his childhood.

We set off for Durban via Vryheid and arrived at Percy's home in time for dinner – and then Jackie freaked. Percy's Afrikaner folks were very fond and proud of their son and Jackie/Magiel just couldn't handle the warmth, kindness and affection that Percy's mother showed her son.

Jackie suddenly decided that we would leave Percy with his family and that only he and I would go to Durban. Fortunately I now knew how to handle the situation when we met my family.

My sister was still stationed at security headquarters in Durban and she came for dinner. She told us that a second attempt was being made to recruit mercenaries to try to topple the government of the Seychelles.

The first attempt had been made in 1980. Led by the notorious Mike Hoare, a mercenary who had worked in the Belgian Congo in the 1960s, the group consisted for the most part of former Rhodesian soldiers, but included one American.

They landed at the airport in the Seychelles and were caught with the AK-47s in their hand luggage. A fight broke out and they ran for an aircraft on the runway, which they hijacked. It was their only hope of escape. Only the American put up a fight on the tarmac and was wounded during a skirmish.

When the plane landed in Durban they were all promptly arrested. It was all a bit of a farce. The South Africans had been monitoring the operation, which they had sanctioned, but were now forced to put on a show. So the hijackers were detained, charged and brought to court. I had never heard of such a ludicrous plan in my life. Twenty mercenaries with 20 AK-47s and one 35-round magazine each planned to overthrow the government of the Seychelles after going through customs at the airport with their weapons!

I was working at the Durban law courts when they were brought to trial. Mike Hoare received a stiff jail sentence, but the others got off lightly and were soon out of prison. The case against the American was withdrawn as he was wounded and under the influence of morphine at the time of the hijacking.

An advance party of three was meant to have done the reconnaissance work in the Seychelles. They managed to escape. When the Seychelles authorities found the chalet where they had been staying, they cleaned out enough empty booze bottles to fill a truck.

My sister knew the person at security headquarters who was monitoring the second attempt.

'Tell them we will do it,' I said.

'Yes, we'll do it,' Jackie echoed.

'As long as we call the shots and do it our way,' I added brazenly. 'I'm not prepared to go along with someone else's plan. We'll do it, but we'll only do it our way.'

'Okay,' she said, 'I'll speak to them.'

The next day my mother offered to do our laundry. This made Jackie very agitated. He refused the offer and we had to go and look for a laundromat so that he could get his clothes washed and ironed. That afternoon we started to drink, and by the time we got home we were totally trashed.

Our plan to overthrow the government of the Seychelles

came to a sudden halt when my mother greeted us, saying, 'Lieutenant Baker phoned. He said you and Jackie must get to Waterkloof airbase by tomorrow morning. There is a major infiltration and you need to get back to Oshakati. Your flight leaves at 8 a.m.'

'Fuck the Seychelles,' Jackie and I agreed, and we left immediately.

We drove through the night and on our way to Waterkloof we got stuck in Pretoria's morning traffic.

We arrived at Waterkloof at 8.20 a.m. and burst into the commanding officer's office, explaining the urgency of the situation. He was not interested in our plight and was adamant that there was nothing he could do, as the plane had already taken off.

A female ground-crew member came into the office and told us that the plane was still on the runway waiting for us and that we should follow her.

I was still terribly hung over from the afternoon before and nearly ran into one of the C-130's propellers as I tried to board the plane. It took off and we were on our way.

When we arrived in Oshakati, we discovered that our group had already deployed without us to Okongo. Jackie and I looked at each other, wondering what to do.

All hell had broken loose. SWAPO had launched a major invasion from Angola into Ovamboland and there was fighting going on all over the place.

We were standing in the ops room at Okavi when Captain Winter walked in. 'The brigadier is not here, but he phoned and told me to put both of you on the first plane back to Waterkloof. So pack your things and I'm going to take the two of you straight to the airport,' he said with a sarcastic grin.

'What is this about?' I asked Jackie. 'What did we do to get fired?'

'I don't think they are firing us. He would have said so,' he replied. 'I think it's about that Seychelles thing – I think they want us to go, but they can't say as much. I don't know, but we need to get to Lieutenant Goosen.'

'How on earth are we going to get there?'

'I saw my Casspir outside. They must have deployed with just three. Let's take my Casspir and go and join up with our group.'

Jackie and I sneaked out of the base, unseen by the captain waiting to take us to the airbase at Ondangwa. We found Jackie's Casspir outside and had to break the lock off our storeroom door to get his LMG and some ammo. Soon we left for Okongo.

It was one of the most stupid and dangerous things the two of us had ever done together. We drove through the operational area from Oshakati to Okongo during a major infiltration in one Casspir without a long-distance radio and only an LMG. I still did not have a rifle at that stage and I hadn't been able to get one out of Uncle Bill at the stores at Ongwediva.

We thought of stopping at Zulu 2 at Eenhana, but decided to take a chance as Captain Adams might catch us, so we ran for Okongo, hoping that we could still make it before dark, if we made it at all. Just as it was growing dark, we drove up the road to the army base at Okongo and found our group.

It took Lieutenant Goosen 15 minutes to calm down after he saw us and realised what we had done. Our only excuse was to say that we hadn't wanted to get fired. Eventually he said he was glad that we were there.

Early the following morning we woke as a sapper team left to sweep the road towards Elundu. Poor bastards, I thought, as

I watched them go past. Zulu Mike was just about to leave as Jackie and I were refuelling Jackie's Casspir.

DOOM, DOOM, CLACK, CLACK, CLACK!

The explosions rock the air as we hear the AK automatic gunfire. Then we hear some retaliation from R4s just down the road.

The sapper team has just walked into an ambush. Zulu Mike goes screaming off ahead of us and is on the spoor in a flash. We follow close on their heels and join in. The follow-up goes so fast that within 30 minutes SWAPO tries to stand and fight, with disastrous consequences for them.

'Contact, contact, contact!'

We go in hard and fast and with such savagery that within two minutes seven enemy are cut to pieces by our retaliation.

I see one of Zulu Mike's Casspirs stop next to a bush and open fire at two insurgents hiding in it. My LMG has jammed, but there is hardly time to use it. As Zulu Mike's Casspir opens fire, I go racing over the two with my Casspir, not knowing who killed them, but it doesn't matter. Now they are properly dead.

It's over, the contact is over, and we have destroyed a SWAPO special-force ambush team.

'They want the bodies. We need to take the bodies to Okongo,' someone says after calling in the contact over the radio.

Zulu Mike doesn't want to go back to Okongo, so they leave us to the grizzly task of securing the dead on our spare wheels and bumpers to drive them back to Okongo.

We pulled up at the little trauma unit in the base, where two army doctors were on duty. They were obviously fresh out of medical school and were now doing their national service. They weren't accustomed to death and I could see that they were horrified as we cut the dead down and dumped them in a row. It was a gruesome scene and the condition of the bodies was horrific.

'Are you sure these are SWAPO fighters?' one of the doctors asked.

'They look like innocent civilians,' the other added, horrified.

'Yes, we're sure,' I replied.

'How do you know?' One of the doctors wanted to start an argument.

'Because they were shooting at us. First they ambushed your sapper teams, then they tried to ambush us, so we killed them,' I said.

'But they don't have any weapons – I'm sure they're civilians.'

'Their weapons are all loaded in our Casspirs and on the Blesbok. Their bodies have been stripped. They wear civilian clothes under their uniforms and this is how they look now. This is not how they looked when we killed them,' I tried to explain to the two liberal doctors.

I saw that I wasn't going to get anywhere with these two and decided to leave them with the dead and find a beer.

The infiltration was over soon after it had started. Koevoet acted swiftly, hunting down and destroying the insurgents.

We now had 36 kills for the year and had captured one. We were at the top of the scoreboard for the bravo teams – but it was not to be for long. We had about two weeks of glory before some other team beat us for that year.

It seemed that Jackie and I had been forgiven for whatever it was that they had wanted to put us on a plane home for. As a precaution we avoided Captain Winter for as long as possible.

Nothing was heard again of the second coup attempt in the Seychelles that my sister had said was being planned. Years later, in 1987, the British police uncovered a plot to overthrow the Seychelles government and to kidnap ANC leaders in Britain. Four people were arrested in connection with a conspiracy against the ANC leaders, but the charges were dropped for lack of evidence.

It was quiet during Christmas and New Year and all the Koevoet groups were able to celebrate at two of the biggest parties I had ever seen, thanks to Brigadier Hannes Dreyer. He saw to it that we were well looked after.

Then it was January 1983. A year of my life had passed with Koevoet. The heavy rains had come and it was time for SWAPO to infiltrate again. We had hurt SWAPO badly with our operations in Angola and with their last infiltration, but they would still throw what they had left at us.

I risked missing some action by taking time off to go home to Durban. My brother Neil was getting married and I wanted to be at his wedding.

Not long before that, my parents had had a bad experience. It must be hard for the parents of any son who goes off to fight in some stupid conflict, and it must be much harder if that son gets killed. It was the job of the police chaplain to inform the parents if that happened.

In Durban the chaplain was an Afrikaans dominee and he drove a big black Chevy. One day that big black Chevy turned into our driveway while my mother was in the kitchen. It was the dominee and my sister …

In Afrikaans the words 'moor' and 'moer' have various meanings. To 'moor' someone can be to murder him or to mistreat him, to fuck him up. 'Moer' is a derogatory word for 'mother', but it can also be used to refer to ground coffee or a nut, as in nut and bolt. It is often used figuratively. To be 'the moer in' is to be pissed off and ready for a fight. 'Jou moer' means 'fuck you'. To 'strip your moer' is to lose your temper. To 'moer' someone is to hit him hard.

I stripped my moer, was the moer in and wanted to moer and moor someone: the person who told my family and friends that I had been shot.

Amid panic and the shock at the news of my untimely death, my sister, who was still stationed at security police HQ, kept a cool head and contacted my HQ in Oshakati. She spoke to Captain Gene de Kock, who assured her that I was fine and at that moment was out in the bush chasing SWAPO around.

So, to my family, that visit to Durban for Neil's wedding was very special, because shortly before that they had thought they would never see me again.

The day after the wedding I drove my dad's pick-up truck up Northway. I was flying out the following morning. My brother was now married and I had been chasing girls as if they were SWAPO. I'd had three close contacts with three different girls in one day. As I passed the Bell Inn at the top of the road I decided to stop and have a drink.

I looked down to avoid the late-afternoon sun hurting my eyes and saw a pair of perfect feet in high-heeled sandals. Mesmerised, my eyes travelled upwards along the beautiful calves and a body to die for, in a dress that complemented the body.

She turned and looked at me.

'Hello, Arn.'

How did such a beautiful girl know my name? Then our eyes met. I recognised her immediately and I felt as if an RPG had hit me in the chest.

'Hello, Nicky.' It was Nicky Westhof, the first girl with whom I had almost fallen in love, but who had dumped me when I lied to her about the suburb where we lived. I had just left it there, but with great regret.

'I got married,' she said.

'Oh.' I tried to speak.

'He got killed,' she said.

'That's good.' Fuck, what did I say? What did she say? What do I say to someone who carries the burden of pain and sorrow after losing a husband and is now standing in front of me, looking into my eyes?

She smiled and said, 'I married a helicopter pilot. He was shot down over Angola last year and died.'

I had a flashback to my world at the Border. Friendly fire? I couldn't put it all together at that moment, but I knew something.

Two Puma helicopters were shot down over Angola in 1982. One was on 5 January. Captain Robinson, Lieutenant Earp and Sergeant Dalgleish died. The other was on 9 August. Captain John Twaddle, Lieutenant Chris Peterson, Sergeant Grobbies Grobler and nine parabats all died when their Puma was shot down. A few years earlier another Puma helicopter had been shot down by friendly fire. The SAAF admitted to that one.

Years after I had left Koevoet I ran a fishing charter company out of Plettenberg Bay and I got talking to a client who had fought in the Border War. He told me that he was the person who had shot down one of our own Pumas. He said he had been given the order to fire.

My eyes met Nicky's again.

'Yes, I've been fighting up there for a year now,' I said.

'I know. I work at Doctor Bailey's rooms around the corner

on Umhlanga Rocks Drive. Your mother comes in sometimes. I've just finished work and I'm waiting for my mother to fetch me. Don't you live around here?'

'Yes, just around the corner.' Sore point, I thought, after that lie a lifetime ago.

I didn't know what to say or do. I could hardly speak, but something was telling me to do something, to say something. I could tell by the way she was looking at me, into my eyes, that our souls were connecting, and I was overcome by a feeling so strong that I didn't understand it.

A car pulled up.

'I must go; it's my mom.'

I couldn't move and I didn't even open the door for her. She looked back at me and smiled at me one last time. Then she got into the car. Something deep inside me shouted, 'Do something, do something!' but the car drove off, taking her out of my life for ever.

For the next 27 years I often thought of her and hoped that she had found love, life and happiness. Recently I traced her niece on Facebook. Nicky remarried and had three children. Finally I could let it go. I also had to let go of the story about Pumas being shot down.

While carrying out research for my story, I learnt that an African-American special force, consisting of Stinger anti-aircraft-missile teams, was working and fighting with UNITA in Angola in the eighties. I received a warning that the CIA was not happy with my investigation and I was advised not to open a can of worms.

I discovered many strange truths during my research. The history books do not always convey the full truth. There is a former Koevoet member who carries a great burden of guilt for having shot one of our own. He didn't. The blame was placed on him and he was sent home in disgrace, as he was expendable.

I have not revealed in this book all the truths that I discovered, out of respect for the people who were involved in certain incidents and their families. The fact is that many of our members who died or were wounded were killed or wounded by friendly fire, as happens in most wars or conflicts. That is all that I shall say about the matter for now.

14

Closing the book

The Kavango area lies east of Ovamboland, and east of the Kavango lies Botswana. North of the Kavango is south-eastern Angola. Koevoet had a small base at Rundu in the Kavango, but there was little activity in this area.

It was difficult for SWAPO to infiltrate the Kavango from Angola because UNITA held most of south-eastern Angola. Our bravo teams were going on an operation to the Kavango area as things were very quiet in Ovamboland – we had killed most of the infiltrators.

The road east from Okongo could have taken us there, but it had not been used by anyone in many years. It was never swept for landmines and had not been repaired for a long time. So instead we took the long main road south-east to Oshivelo and then headed due east to Tsintsabis, where we stopped at the army base for the night.

The next morning we headed north-east and entered the Kavango through a gate in a fence separating the Kavango from Namibia to the south. The gate was locked and we were stuck. Zulu Tango caught up with us and solved the problem by shooting the lock to pieces.

Zulu Tango passed us and went ahead, but we later caught up with them. They had caught an elephant calf, which they had boxed in with their Casspirs after separating it from its mother. The herd stood nearby and was very agitated, but not prepared to charge.

'Call Hannes and ask him if he wants another elephant,' Kallie Calitz shouted.

'No, he wants to get rid of Ollie and Momphie – they are becoming alcoholics!' someone said loudly. 'The guys won't listen and give them too much beer. He's going to send them to a game park near Sun City.'

'Let it go back to its mother,' Lieutenant Goosen said. 'We don't need another elephant. The poor thing is terrified and its mother is very upset.'

They moved one of the Casspirs and the calf ran back to its mother. The herd moved off quickly, disappearing into the bush. Fortunately Chris de Witt was not there – he probably would have shot some of that herd for ivory.

We gradually worked our way north-east towards Rundu. After two days we hadn't found any sign of SWAPO. The area was almost uninhabited and still very wild. We were bored.

We came to the conclusion that this operation was a waste of time. We needed to break the monotony of driving for hours without finding spoor, so Lieutenant Goosen gave us permission to do a bit of hunting for the pot if we came across something decent.

Suddenly we drove into a herd of eland and all hell broke loose. Bennie, who was in charge of Zulu Golf 4, went charging at the herd while his guys opened fire. Some of them were firing on automatic. Lieutenant Goosen gave chase to try to stop them, so Jackie, Wessie and I followed. The lieutenant screamed at them over the radio to stop, but they ignored him. It looked just like a contact.

They wounded a big bull, but left it and went after the herd. The bull came to a halt and stood alone in the middle of the veld. I caught up with it and stopped about 10 metres away from it. It didn't move. I took an R1 from one of my Ovambos and with a single bullet through the eland's head I put it down.

Wessie pulled up next to me and we loaded it onto the Blesbok. We caught up with the rest of our group and finally prevented Bennie from trying to slaughter the entire herd. They had managed to kill one more eland, which we also loaded onto the Blesbok. We now had enough fresh meat to feed an army.

That was the end of our hunting trip. The lieutenant put a ban on any more hunting after the way Bennie and his guys had behaved.

We stopped on the bank of the Kavango River for the night. Zulu Tango was also there and they had also been hunting – they had a kudu. It was time to feast.

The Ovambos made huge fires and began cutting up the animals. The river looked inviting, but someone warned of its many crocodiles. We threw a couple of hand grenades into the water and some of us went swimming before the Ovambos began to wash in the river water.

By parking our vehicles in one big circle, we made a TB with Zulu Tango. At 10 p.m. we went to check on how the braai was coming on, only to find that our Ovambos, together with those of Zulu Tango, had done the impossible. About 90 of them had devoured two eland and a kudu. There was nothing left for us. They were stuffing the last of the bones with a bit of meat on them into some big pots. With their mouths full of meat they turned around and said that a cow would have been much better.

Further up the river Zulu Whisky had a fight with a group of UNITA soldiers who were camped on the other side. We didn't know what UNITA was doing on the other side of the river in Botswana. It was typical of Zulu Whisky to taunt the UNITA soldiers until they opened fire and things turned ugly.

That night I made a new friend. I was lying on top of my sleeping bag when I heard a voice next to me.

'Irish Barnard. Would you like a dop?' he said. Irish was Zulu Tango's group leader. 'I've got a bottle of Bells. If you want some, get a cup or something to drink out of.'

'What about Kallie and Koen?'

'Fuck them,' he said. 'They don't drink.'

'I don't have anything to drink out of – do you mind if I drink out of the bottle?' I asked.

'No, go ahead.' He handed me the bottle, I took it and I drank about a quarter of the whisky in one go before handing it back to him.

'That's quite good,' I said, turning over and pretending that I was going to sleep.

'My fuck, but you can drink!' he exclaimed. 'You drink like a pig.'

That's how I met my friend Irish. Over the next years he became my fat friend Irish and later the best man at my wedding.

We visited Rundu the next day and then decided to pack up and head back to Oshakati. The Tsumeb area was under threat. A group of PLAN fighters had infiltrated and made it all the way down there undetected. This was just like the big infiltration of the previous year, but this time it was a much smaller group. It seemed that SWAPO was running short on human resources.

Our alpha teams were the first to deploy and our bravo teams followed. By the time we reached Tsumeb, the fight was almost over. One of the most remarkable events during this infiltration was that an Angolan MiG-23 pilot had defected and landed near Tsumeb.

Some farm labourers got up early one morning to find that a Soviet-made MiG-23 had landed on one of the farm roads. The labourers ran to call the farmer, who arrived at the scene in his pick-up truck. He promptly arrested the pilot and took him to the Tsumeb police station.

The SADF issued a statement to avoid embarrassment. They claimed that they had been monitoring the MiG the whole time and were aware of the pilot's intention to defect. Like hell they were!

We needed to find new ways to fight SWAPO and take the conflict to a different level. SWAPO was using new tactics and weapons while we continued to fight in the same old way.

Frans Conradie was one of the masterminds who had developed Koevoet tactics years ago and he was looking for new tactics and strategies. In order to find a way forward a new group was formed. It was called Zulu X-ray and was the brainchild of Frans Conradie and Piet Stassen. They selected the best from the existing teams. Captain Joost Engelbrecht was put in command of Zulu X-ray to keep an eye on Frans and Piet, who had the habit of doing things in quite an unorthodox way, even by Koevoet standards.

The white members of Zulu X-ray were Captain Engelbrecht, Lieutenant Conradie, Warrant Officer Stassen, Sergeant Kallie Calitz, Koen Marais, Little Frans and Takkies. The majority of the 20 Ovambos came from Zulu Foxtrot and Zulu Sierra, but some came from other teams. They even stole one of our best trackers, whom Kallie had seen in action in the short time he was with us.

Once the group was formed, they went off for special training at a secret location. Koevoet now had its own special force, or our recces, as some called them.

With the Tsumeb infiltration coming to an end, we were at the base that had once again been set up at the airfield. Koevoet had bought a farm near Tsumeb as more POWs needed rehabilitation and the farm at Oshakati was not big enough. We all knew where the profits from the farms were going: into the pockets of the jam stealers, the officers who pushed pens and often stole the glory after contacts. Actually the farms were quite a racket. Rather than rehabilitating the POWs by teaching them farmwork, they were just used as cheap labour, paid from secret government funds, while the profits were scored by the jam stealers.

A Ford F350 was parked next to the tents at the airfield. I looked at all the new fancy equipment packed in the back and wondered why I still didn't have as much as a rifle.

'Hey, don't you try to steal our stuff!' Kallie joked.

Jackie joined in. 'Where did you get all this fancy gear?' he asked. 'Are you guys the main men now?'

'Yes, so watch out,' Kallie said.

'So, tell me Kallie, how many kills have you guys got?' Jackie taunted him. 'They must put Zulu X-ray on the ops board and we can put a nice big zero next to it.'

'Fuck off, Jackie,' Kallie replied. 'The less you know, the better it will be for everyone.'

Later, over a couple of beers, we were talking to Little Frans. He was pulling out of Zulu X-ray because of a problem with his knees. He was super-fit, as Zulu X-ray required, but his knees were giving in. That meant there was an opening in Zulu X-ray. I was interested, but decided to keep it to myself.

With the second Tsumeb infiltration over and most of the insurgents dead or running for Angola, it was time to leave for Oshakati.

We stopped at Otjikoto Lake. I never understood why it was called a lake. I would have called it a sinkhole, but it wasn't a sinkhole either. It was a hole of about 300 metres in diameter. It had water in it. The water level was about 50 metres down.

Beneath what was visible lay a wonder of nature. Scientists had put dye into the water and later found traces of the same dye in underground waterways in Botswana. That meant the water of this 'lake' was connected by underground waterways to Botswana and other regions.

Old German cannon had been discovered in Otjikoto Lake. They had been dumped there by the Germans almost 100 years earlier during the frontier wars between the German colonial rulers and the Ovambo people. Fort Namutoni lay about 10 kilometres north of Otjikoto Lake. It had been built in 1903 by the Germans on the frontier, but now it served as accommodation in the northern camp of the Etosha National Park. At some stage the Ovambo had forced the Germans to retreat in a hurry during the frontier wars. Unable to get away fast enough, they had dumped their heavy cannon into the lake in order to escape.

We watched from the side of the lake as scuba-divers attached cables to the cannon below so that they could be hoisted up and recovered. A scuba-diver had been killed during this operation a few days earlier; it was dangerous work in the murky, muddy waters below.

The old cannon had lain buried in the fine silt and mud. Deprived of oxygen, they were in almost the same condition as when they had been dumped.

Later, after we had been back at Oshakati for a while, Lieutenant Goosen still had not applied for my promotion and I was starting to get pissed off. The only other way to get promoted was to study law and write exams, which meant that I would be taking a lot of time off to study and wouldn't be able to work so much. But if they didn't want to do the paperwork, fuck them. I was going to study.

I received all my books, which I'd ordered through the police, and sat down at a table in our bungalow at Okavi. I started to study. With all the noise of drunken parties, country music and boeremusiek, it was difficult.

'Hey, Gentleman Jim!' It was Kallie Calitz. I didn't know why he was always calling me Gentleman Jim.

'I've been looking for you. I need to speak to you. I've been talking to Frans Conradie and we want you to join Zulu X-ray.'

'Why me? What would you want me in Zulu X-ray for?'

'Don't ask questions. Little Frans has dropped out and we need to replace him. Are you interested?'

I decided on the spur of the moment.

'Yes,' I said. 'But what do I say to Lieutenant Goosen and Jackie?'

'Don't worry, I'll speak to Frans Conradie – he'll deal with Goosen. So it's more or less definite then.'

'No, Kallie,' I said. 'It's something I have to do myself. I'll take care of it.'

'Okay, but Frans will also speak to him,' Kallie said. 'Why are you sitting here? What are you doing?'

'I'm studying. They haven't promoted me, so I'm going to promote myself.'

'You can't study here with all this noise,' he said. 'Come and stay with us; we share a house in town and Takkies has moved out. I'll speak to Irish and John Tate, but I'm sure you can move in tomorrow.'

I was still thinking about what Kallie had said, and what I had just done was still sinking in, when Jackie and Wessie came into the bungalow, carrying a steel trunk. They were excited.

'Look, Jim, look what we've found at the railway depot. It's got your name on it,' Jackie said.

It was the steel trunk that had been issued to me in the police college after training. When I'd been transferred to Koevoet more than a year and a half earlier, the one thing that headquarters in Durban had done for me was to send my trunk to Oshakati by rail. The railway line ended at Tsumeb and I didn't realise that the trunk had been brought by truck to the depot in Oshakati – I didn't even know there was a depot in Oshakati. I had completely forgotten about my trunk.

'Come, let's open it. It's locked. Where's the key?' Jackie was more excited than me.

'The key is long gone,' I said.

Jackie fetched an R1 and broke the lock open. Excitedly he opened the trunk – and there, lying on top of camouflage uniforms, was my FN assault rifle, which had been issued to me after college.

It had found me after a year and a half. At last, I had my own rifle!

'Jackie, I must tell you something …'

No matter what Jackie and Wessie's reaction would be, I had made up my mind. I knew what Lieutenant Goosen was going to say: that I must do what I want to do.

I was going to close the book on Zulu Golf and open a new one.

On the wings of a white angel

On the wings of a white angel, I rode into hell, slayed the devil's demons
and pissed on his head. When I was finished I rode
back out.
They made me a hero and called me a legend, but I was just doing my
best; to live through the chaos and survive like the rest.
Now the devil and his demons creep through my soul and into my head
as they carry me to bed.
So from hero and legend, now they say 'he's not right in the head.'
Damn them all and fuck the rest! On the wings of a white angel,
I rode into hell.
Their bones are plain white; their brains are dull yellow and their blood,
it's … bright red. As a tapeworm crawls out of a bullet hole in his
stomach I realise, my fuck, they're all dead because
I've slain the devil's demons again.
On the wings of a white angel, I rode into hell.
He had me lined up with his RPG-7, point blank. My 20-mm cannon
and .30 Browning had both jammed so I reached down for my R5,
knowing I was dead. When I looked up, I had been spared. He had
lost the nerve and stood in surrender, with hands in the air and
weapon at his feet.
Slay the demons.
With fear in his eyes he had lost the will to fight. Don't worry, my friend,
your bones will be pure white, your brains dull yellow and your
blood bright red because soon you will be quite dead.
I rode into hell and pissed on his head.
Fuck them all and damn the rest!

Glossary

1 Military Hospital: military hospital in Pretoria

AK/AK-47: Avtomat Kalashnikova Obrazets, Russian-designed 7.62-mm assault rifle, based on German-designed World War II Stg 44 – first assault rifle to fire shortened (7.62-mm) cartridge and capable of single-shot or automatic fire (Stg 44: Sturmgewehr – assault rifle)
AKM: modified version of AK-47
Albatross: 25-ton supply truck
Alouette: French-designed, single-engined light transport helicopter, mainly used for reconnaissance, fire support and search-and-rescue
ANC: African National Congress
Armscor: Armaments Corporation of South Africa Ltd, government-owned industry responsible for building and obtaining armaments, founded in 1976

B25 radio: SSB (single-sideband) long-distance radio
Bakelite: composite similar to hard plastic
bakkie: small pick-up truck
ballistic round: ammunition with no projectile, used to propel rifle grenade from barrel of rifle

Black Widows: type of anti-personnel mine
Blesbok: supply truck based on the Casspir
Boer: Afrikaner or farmer
boeremusiek: literally 'farmer's music'; traditional Afrikaans music played on concertina, guitar and/or piano accordion
boeretannie: literally 'Afrikaans auntie'; Afrikaans woman, typically a middle-aged
boerewors: traditional South African sausage
bombshell: sudden dispersal of (enemy) troops under fire or while being chased
boom: cannabis; literally 'tree'
boot: trunk of motor vehicle
Border, the: South West Africa's northern border with Angola and Zambia
bosbefok: aggressive, angry; mentally deranged, refers to the mental state of people who have spent extended periods in operations in the bush; literally 'bush mad'
Bosbok: Italian-made single-engined light aircraft used in a spotter/reconnaissance role
braai: cook meat over a fire, barbecue
bring and braai: slang term for a barbecue where the host supplies the fire and the guests bring their own meat and drink
buddy master: title given to the member in charge of the Ovambo special constables
Buffel: Armscor-produced mine-protected armoured personnel carrier (APC, 4×4) introduced in 1978; literally 'buffalo'
bully beef: corned beef
bundu-bash: to drive through dense bush crushing the bush and trees with the vehicle.
bust: caught out, to tell on a person

C-130: American-designed four-engined heavy transport aircraft, also known as the Hercules

casevac: casualty evacuation

Casspir: mine-protected counter-insurgency infantry combat vehicle (ICV, 4×4), acronym of CSIR and SAP. Used mainly by Koevoet and 101 Battalion

check out: look

CIA: Central Intelligence Agency

claymore: anti-personnel mine that directs shrapnel at a predetermined area, detonated electronically or by time fuze

COIN: counter-insurgency

com-ops: combined operations, referring to operations mounted by various branches of the armed forces

contact: meeting and exchange of fire with the enemy

Cordtex: detonation cord, highly explosive and fast-burning

CSIR: Council for Scientific and Industrial Research

Cuca shop: small makeshift commodities shop named after local Portuguese–Angolan beer

cut line: area cleared of bush in a straight line demarcating the Angolan/South West African border, cleared of vegetation in terms of 1962 agreement between South Africa and Portugal

dik babbelas: heavily hung over

dominee: minister

Doom: South African brand of insecticide

dop: drink (alcoholic)

Durban poison: sought-after variety of marijuana grown in KwaZulu-Natal and distributed across South Africa

Dutchmen: derogatory term for Afrikaners

F1: anti-personnel fragmentation defensive grenade based on the French F1 grenade, containing a 60-gram explosive charge

FAPLA: Forças Armadas Populares de Libertação de Angola (People's Armed Forces for the Liberation of Angola)

FN: Fabrique Nationale, 7.62-mm assault rifle; R1 in South Africa

FNLA: Frente Nacional de Libertação de Angola (National Front for the Liberation of Angola)

FRELIMO: Frente de Libertação de Moçambique (Front for the Liberation of Mozambique)

G3: German-designed Heckler and Koch 7.62-mm assault rifle manufactured under licence in Portugal

G5: British-designed Armscor-developed 155-mm gun/howitzer introduced in 1979, with a maximum firing range of 48 kilometres

G-force: gravity force

gook: enemy, terrorist

gunship: Alouette III helicopter with floor-mounted 20-mm machine guns; see also 'Alouette'

halfjack: flat bottle of alcoholic spirit, contains half of a 750-ml bottle

Harvard trainer: popular training aircraft originating in the United States, featuring heavy-duty construction, roll bars and landing gear

Heat Stream: rifle grenade fired from SKS, works on the same principle as the RPG

Hippo: petrol-engined forerunner of the Casspir, based on the Bedford truck

HQ: headquarters

jam stealer: office worker who takes credit for others' glory

Jumping Jacks: type of anti-personnel mine

kaffir: extremely derogatory term for black Africans

kak: shit

Khoi: Khoisan, collective name for the Khoikhoi and San peoples of southern Africa, also denotes the language family of the Khoikhoi and San people

kiaat tree: deciduous, slightly flat-crowned tree with a high canopy, growing predominantly in warm, frost-free areas of southern Africa, also known as the wild teak or bloodwood tree

Koevoet: South African Police COIN unit established in 1979. Units based in Oshakati (HQ), Opuwa and Rundu; literally 'crowbar', as in 'prying loose' of SWAPO insurgents from thick bush

kraal: rural collection of huts made from branches and woven grass, enclosed by either a log or a thorn-bush palisade, occupied by the local population

LMG: light machine gun

mahangu: pearl millet; grain sorghum or millet beer

matric: final year of high school

MiG/MiG-23: Mikoyan-Gurevich Russian-designed fighter-bomber and interceptor jet aircraft

Mirage: French-designed Atlas Aircraft Corporation–enhanced fighter jet or fighter-bomber, received in 1963

MK: Umkhonto we Sizwe (the Spear of the Nation), ANC's military wing

moer: anger; beat up, hit

moffie: homosexual

MPLA: Movimento Popular da Libertação de Angola (People's Movement for the Liberation of Angola)

mugu: idiot

NATO: North Atlantic Treaty Organisation

NCO: non-commissioned officer

Olifant: British-designed Armscor-produced main battle tank with a crew of four, introduced in 1981; literally 'elephant'

Oom Willie se Pad: Uncle Willie's Road, linking military bases from Okongo to Etali.

ops: operations
ops room: operations room
oshilulu: Oshivambo for evil spirit
Ovambo: largest ethnic group in South West Africa, constituting over 50 per cent of the population

PAC: Pan Africanist Congress
Paddapoot: literally 'frog paw', denotes a webbed hand
parabat: paratrooper
patmor: patrol mortar
PB: plaaslike bevolking (local population)
Pencil Stream: rifle grenade fired from an SKS with a ballistic round, delivers shrapnel on impact
pissed: drunk; angry
PLAN: People's Liberation Army of Namibia, SWAPO's military wing, founded in 1966
POMZ: Russian-made stake-mounted anti-personnel fragmentation mine with a small explosive charge inside a hollow cylindrical cast-iron fragmentation sleeve. On top is a weather cap that covers a standardised fuze well
POW: prisoner of war
pronto: radio operator
Puma: French-built twin-engined transport helicopter

R1: 7.62-mm NATO assault rifle based on Belgian 1964 FN-FAL (manufactured by Fabrique Nationale: Fusil Automatique Legere – Light Automatic Rifle), Armscor-produced
R4: 5.56-mm assault rifle based on Israeli Galil, replaced R1 from 1978 onwards, Armscor-produced and modified
R5: compact version of the R4, with shortened barrel
Ratel: armoured standard infantry combat vehicle (ICV, 6×6) introduced in 1976 and Armscor-designed. Named after the African honey badger, which is known for its viciousness

rat pack: ration pack
recce: a member of the Reconnaisance Unit
RENAMO: Resistência Nacional Moçambicana (Mozambican National Resistance)
RPD: Soviet light machine gun
RPG: Russian-designed recoilless shoulder-mounted rocket-propelled grenade launcher used as anti-tank weapon
RPG-7: modified and renamed rocket-propelled grenade launcher
RSA: Republic of South Africa
RSA53: short-distance FM radio

SAAF: South African Air Force
Sabre jet: high-performance fighter aircraft with swept-back wing and 11.2-metre wingspan. Originating in the United States, it was the most-produced Western jet fighter, with a total production of 9 860 units (all variations)
SADF: South African Defence Force (pre-1994)
SAP: South African Police (pre-1994)
sapper: military engineer
Saracen armoured car: armoured personnel carrier with small turret on roof that carries a Browning .30 machine gun. A .303 Bren gun can be mounted on anti-aircraft ring-mount accessed through roof hatch
section: basic unit of 10 to 12 members
shebeen: illegal township pub without liquor licence
shirumbu: white person in Oshivambo
shona: large, open pan that is arid in the dry season but fills with water in the rainy season
SKS: Soviet carbine
Slidex: encoding system for radio messages
soutpiel: derogatory term for English-speaking South African, who has one foot in South Africa and the other in England with his penis dangling in the ocean; literally 'salty penis'

Soviet bloc: former communist states of Eastern and Central Europe, including countries of the Warsaw Pact, the Soviet Union and, later, Cuba
spaza: informal local convenience shop, often run from home
spoor: signs left by a person or animal, including tracks, trail or droppings
spoorsny: tracking
SSB: single-sideband modulation, type of long-distance radio transmission
stirring: deliberately causing trouble
SWAPO: South West African People's Organisation

T-54: Russian battle tank
TB: temporary base
terr: terrorist
Tokarev: 7.62-mm pistol
tokoloshe: evil demon in Zulu and Xhosa folklore
TR28: long-distance radio
Typhoon forces: SWAPO units specialising in deep penetration

UN: United Nations
Unimog: 4×4 troop-carrier manufactured by Mercedes-Benz
UNITA: Uniáo Nacional para a Independência Total de Angola (National Union for the Total Independence of Angola)
US: United States

veld: field, grassland
volaron: oral painkiller, no longer available
voorsny: to cut ahead

Walther P38: 9-mm pistol
webbing: canvas or nylon body kit

white phosphorus: incendiary agent commonly found in hand grenades, mortar and artillery rounds, and smoke bombs

ZANU: Zimbabwe African National Union

ZANU-PF: Zimbabwe African National Union-Patriotic Front, far-left party that was the ruling government in Zimbabwe since independence in 1980, led by Robert Mugabe. ZANU-PF lost sole control of parliament for the first time in party history in 2008

ZAPU: Zimbabwe African People's Union

Zulu Golf: Call sign for Koevoet team taken from the phonetic alphabet, along with Zulu Foxtrot, Zulu Oscar, Zulu Sierra, Zulu Whisky and others